REPLAYING MARC ANTHONY

GLOBAL LATIN/O AMERICAS
Frederick Luis Aldama and Lourdes Torres, Series Editors

REPLAYING MARC ANTHONY

SONIC, POLITICAL, AND CULTURAL RESONANCES

Frances R. Aparicio

THE OHIO STATE UNIVERSITY PRESS
COLUMBUS

Copyright © 2025 by Frances R. Aparicio.
All rights reserved.
Published by The Ohio State University Press.

Library of Congress Cataloging-in-Publication Data
Names: Aparicio, Frances R. author
Title: Replaying Marc Anthony : sonic, political, and cultural resonances / Frances R.
   Aparicio.
Other titles: Global Latin/o Americas
Description: Columbus : The Ohio State University Press, [2025] | Series: Global Latin/o
   Americas | Includes bibliographical references and index. | Summary: "Through a close
   analysis of five songs, examines the cultural, aesthetic, and political contributions of
   Nuyorican singer Marc Anthony to Latinx popular music, Latinx communities, and
   Global South solidarities, arguing that Anthony shapes social spaces through his sounds
   and grounds his repertoire within the sonic traditions of the Americas and the Global
   South"—Provided by publisher.
Identifiers: LCCN 2025019040 | ISBN 9780814215951 hardback | ISBN 0814215955 hardback
   | ISBN 9780814284322 ebook | ISBN 0814284329 ebook
Subjects: LCSH: Anthony, Marc—Criticism and interpretation | Anthony, Marc. Preciosa |
   Anthony, Marc. Hasta que te conocí | Anthony, Marc. I need to know | Anthony, Marc.
   Aguanile | Anthony, Marc. Vivir mi vida | Latin pop (Music)—History and criticism |
   Masculinity in music | Popular music—Social aspects—United States | Popular music—
   Political aspects—United States
Classification: LCC ML420.A7337 A83 2025 | DDC 782.42164092—dc23/eng/20250527
LC record available at https://lccn.loc.gov/2025019040

Other identifiers: ISBN 9780814259573 (paperback) | ISBN 081425957X (paperback)

Cover design by Ashley Muehlbauer
Text composition by Stuart Rodriguez
Type set in Minion Pro

*To his fans
and critical listeners*

CONTENTS

List of Illustrations		viii
INTRODUCTION	The Singer as Listener	1
CHAPTER 1	"Preciosa" (1998): Diasporican Subjectivities and the Sounds of Itinerancy	25
CHAPTER 2	"Hasta Que Te Conocí" (1993): Latinidad as Suffering	61
CHAPTER 3	"I Need to Know" (1999): Singing in English and the Sonic Struggles for Americanness	91
CHAPTER 4	"Aguanile" (2007): Critical Listening, Mourning, and Decolonial Healing	120
CHAPTER 5	"Vivir Mi Vida" (2013): Toward a Critical Salsa Romántica and a Global South Brownness	136
CODA	Listening as Struggle	153
Acknowledgments		157
References		159
Index		171

ILLUSTRATIONS

FIGURE 1.1	Rafael Hernández professional portrait	39
FIGURE 1.2	The fermata in musical notation	56
FIGURE 3.1	Meme featuring Marc Anthony	95
FIGURE 4.1	Héctor Lavoe souvenirs in San Juan	126
FIGURE 4.2	Paro Nacional, San Juan, Puerto Rico, 2019	135
FIGURE 5.1	Cheb Khaled	141
FIGURE 5.2	Marc Anthony veiled	144
FIGURE 5.3	Ramón Sierra Reverón and Victoria Sierra Guzmán in Granada, Spain	146

INTRODUCTION

The Singer as Listener

"Killing Me Softly with His Song," a hit that despite its initial uneven critical reviews has reached impressive degrees of popularity since its 1973 recording by the late Roberta Flack, is a landmark song that textualizes the power of music on listeners. After the 1996 Fugees version with Lauryn Hill, listeners and fans consider it a classic of its times, as we still sing and whisper its lyrics, which, infused with the sounds and rhythms of the blues, powerfully resonate with the process of critical listening, a term that I have defined as "an analytical process through which the listener grapples with, and acknowledges the potential meanings of the songs in his/her social and personal life and also structurally, thus acquiring a new and empowering awareness of life and social identities" (Aparicio 2021a). Critical listening allows listeners to engage with music and a singer beyond the limitations of pop and capital.[1] In brief, music's metaphoric potential to softly kill its listeners, fans, and audiences reveals how songs and popular music in general can amaze and stun listeners and thus facilitate the affective and emotional acknowledgments and recognitions that are required to reclaim our humanity in the journeys of our lives. As the lyrics "singing my life with his words" suggest, popular songs perform our presence

---

1. Scholarship on "listening" as a hermeneutic and critical concept has increased in the last ten years and by now almost constitutes its own methodology. The interventions of Jennifer Lynn Stoever, Roshanak Khesti, Dolores Inés Casillas, Brandon LaBelle, and Dylan Robinson, among many others, have been critical to my own thinking about "critical listening."

in the world. If music "is a way of communicating that somehow, by evoking without referring, has extraordinary power to help people find their deepest selves, bring them together, and feel connected to what feels most important" (Baym 2018, 31) and it "helps us cope with difficulty" (39), then popular songs cannot be studied exclusively as an aesthetic or sonic text but only more fully within their relational and affective dynamics with listeners. "Killing Me Softly," moreover, powerfully performs the double role of *the singer as listener,* for in fact the singer assumes the persona of a listener who reflects on how the song "mirrors" her life. When the singer sings "Telling my whole life with his words, / Killing me softly with his song," she reaffirms the emotional impact of music on her inner, affective self. When the singer-listener states that "I felt all flushed with fever," the meaning of "killing" with music is clearly articulated, as her body is unable to function normally. For a moment, time stops for the singer-listener as the song continues to trigger a deep acknowledgment of her "dark despairs." "Killing Me Softly" articulates the role of individual songs and their performances in allowing us to acknowledge the difficult emotional labor that is central to our human experience.

I thus open this book around the significance of songs, as I aim to unsettle commonsense notions about popular music and about Marc Anthony as a Latin pop singer. Despite the impressive critical scholarship that has examined the functions of popular music in the Western world, lingering public perceptions tend to trivialize the serious value of Latino pop songs in our lives because of their formulaic or repetitive nature or because of how popular songs are produced and circulated by the industry.[2] Despite the fact that popular singers in salsa, hip-hop, and reggaetón today are having a profound impact on their listeners' awareness of social and political issues—and here I highlight Bad Bunny as the epitome of this power—many scholars still tend to bracket these voices as secondary to more serious and established music, whether it is classical music, opera, or even folklore music from around the world. The commercialized structures of Latino pop music and the celebrity status of many of its interpreters somehow diminish the authenticity of pop songs in the eyes of many scholars. For instance, I was told by a colleague that Marc Anthony cannot be listened to as a political singer given his celebrity

---

2. Contesting the disavowals of popular music by Theodor Adorno (1941), the foundational scholarship of Richard Middleton (*Studying Popular Music,* 1990); George Lipsitz (*Dangerous Crossroads,* 1994); Juan Flores (*Salsa Rising,* 2016); and Deborah Pacini Hernández (*Bachata,* 1995; and *Oye Como Va!,* 2009) as well as the more recent publications of Alexandra T. Vázquez (*The Florida Room,* 2022); Raquel Z. Rivera, Wayne Marshall, and Deborah Pacini Hernández (*Reggaeton,* 2009); Petra Rivera-Rideau (*Remixing Reggaetón,* 2015); Licia Fiol-Matta (*The Great Woman Singer,* 2017); and Marisol Negrón (*Made in NuyoRico,* 2024) have made significant contributions to acknowledging the social, racial, and cultural power of Latinx popular music.

status and his financial wealth, thus foreclosing any possible approach to understanding the social, cultural, and political meanings behind his repertoire. For many, then, Latino pop music continues to be deemed mere entertainment, void of powerful meanings for its audiences.

In this book, I exhort readers to "replay" and critically listen to Marc Anthony's songs not exclusively as texts but with an approach that recognizes and legitimates the even more serious work of sonic aesthetics, intimate listening, musical genealogies, and cultural resonance. Entertainment journalists write that Marc Anthony's key musical formula is "infusing slow, romantic ballads with the fast-driving energy of salsa" (Lopetegui 1996). These statements tend to reify el Marc's repertoire as a formulaic salsa romántica, which it is not; they dangerously elide the very sophisticated and dynamic arrangements that have made his music resonate with such a vast and heterogeneous community of listeners. Initially curious as to Marc Anthony's immense impact on his community of listeners, fans, and followers, and the public love that he receives from his adoring fans, I embarked on this research to understand more fully the power of some of his songs on us, the Latinx community in the US and in the hemispheric Americas. Despite the general perception against him for inserting salsa music into pop arrangements, the fact is that his selection of songs and his talent in curating his repertoire have truly resonated with the historical and political moments that have affected Latinx communities, both in the United States as well as throughout Latin America. This book, then, repositions Marc Anthony as a listener himself, a singer who has listened to a rich, heterogeneous archive of musical traditions, from boleros to salsa, from R&B to hip-hop, from rock to Algerian raï music, and who integrates and proposes a dialogue with these otherwise disparate sounds in his arrangements. Approaching Marc Anthony not exclusively as a singer but as a "listener" reimagines him as a public figure who acknowledges the sonic artistry and craft of others, finds inspiration in them, and thus positions himself within the longer genealogies of US, Puerto Rican, Latin American, and Algerian musics, engaging in sonic and musical dialogues and exchanges through his creative arrangements and performances. Ultimately, my purpose in the reflections that follow is to share my personal critical listenings about how five of his songs have strongly resonated with me and with so many of his listeners and fans. When songs "resonate," "they are connected to audiences' socially situated conditions or to broader cultural themes and narratives that they recognize" (McDonnell, Bail, and Tavory 2017, 3). Resonance also involves the possibility of "revising people's desires and imagining of what is possible" (McDonnell, Bail, and Tavory 2017, 4). I also examine how the songs have circulated and accrued a history of their own as cultural texts and how they have become canonical among US Latinx communities, hemispherically throughout Latin America and globally as well. I hope that these personal, critical reflections about his songs may help to explain Marc Anthony's status as a musical phenomenon, a superstar, yet one whose status as a celebrity does not preclude his songs from functioning as serious sonic labor, that is, as social spaces shaped through his sounds, which produce the intimacy of listening that blends the book across autohistory, musical analysis, and aesthetic political critique.

•

Marc Anthony's exceptional status as a singer, arranger, entrepreneur, actor, and philanthropist means that he "possesses the quality of attracting attention" (Furedi 2010, 493), given his brilliantly textured and moving voice, his vast musical repertoire, and his charisma and sex appeal on stage. According to Leila Cobo, the Latin music journalist for *Billboard*, the Nuyorican singer is "one of the highest-grossing touring acts in the Latin world" (2021b). If, as Cobo writes, "within ten years, the 'Nuyorican' kid from the Bronx who had begun his career freestyling in English had evolved into one of the most versatile and commercially successful artists," then Marc Anthony could easily be constructed as the embodiment of the American Dream and of neoliberal success. For example, in 2019, twenty-four shows brought him $25.4 million in profits. Having been recognized for numerous and important awards, including three Grammy Awards and six Latin Grammy Awards, and having been included in the *Guinness Book of World Records* for being the "one of the best selling salsa artists of all time"[3] (Rocher 2016), Marc Anthony may undoubtedly be one of the most successful Puerto Rican artists ever. As the King of Latin Trap and Spotify's most streamed artist, Bad Bunny's rapid ascendance in the music industry in reggaetón and "urban music" has outsized this level of popularity, yet Marc Anthony has retained his impressive level of success within the tropical category.[4] Marc Anthony is referred to as "the King

---

3. Sofia Rocher writes that in 2016 Marc Anthony received the Guinness World Record for "most year-end best-selling albums in the tropical albums' chart by a solo artist" for three albums: *Desde un Principio: From the Beginning*; *Libre*; and *3.0* in 2000, 2002, and 2013, respectively. He shares this recognition with two other tropical singers, Romeo Santos and Eddie Santiago.

4. According to ChartMasters.org, Bad Bunny has sold an equivalent of 44,589,000 albums in his six-year career. In 2016 he was working as a bagger in Vega Baja, and by 2020 he had become Spotify's most streamed artist in the world. However, Marc Anthony's prominence resides in the tropical category, which is equated with mostly salsa music. Tropical includes all the Afro-Caribbean musical genres, bachata, merengue, salsa, bomba and plena, calypso, and others.

of Salsa" (Quiñonez 2011; Harrington 2002b). Ricky Martin has called him "a force" (Cobo 2021b). Henry Cárdenas, a producer and philanthropist, has stated, "There's no one like him in the Latin market" (Cobo 2021b). Journalists have described his voice as "transfixing vocals" (Caramanica 2008). This celebratory language, well justified and earned, reaffirms his prominence as a star.

Yet celebrities are also commodities, products of the media and the cultural industry. As Martha González has discussed, the superstar status is the direct product of the music industry, its profit-making values, and the ways in which the "market systems accept and proliferate any message or artifact so long as it is a thriving commodity" (M. González 2020, 2). Indeed, capitalism "isolates the products from the roots of their inception" (2). El Marc's music, then, deeply embedded within the capitalist tenets of the industry, promoted by Sony Music for many years, inherently decontextualizes and separates him from the long musical genealogies, histories, exchanges, and sonic dialogues that have made it possible for him to be a singer, interpreter, and arranger in the first place. This superstar status may partly explain why such an exceptionally talented vocalist and performer has not been written about in scholarly articles or books. Why are his musical, cultural, and performative contributions to Boricua, Latinx, American, Latin American, and global communities been ignored and dismissed by academics at a time when there is a growing body of scholarship devoted to taking pop music seriously? Is Marc Anthony so "big" in the entertainment world that no scholar feels up to the task of analyzing his musical contributions? Or is it that his celebrity status has distanced him from his Puerto Rican community? This book is the first academic attempt to begin a scholarly conversation about Marc Anthony, to whom I will refer here and there as "el Marc," and to his cultural sonic legacy.[5]

This book is an invitation to relisten and replay five of Marc Anthony's most canonical songs and their power to engage us affectively as well as culturally, socially, and politically. My selection of "Preciosa," "Hasta Que Te Conocí," "I Need to Know," "Aguanile," and "Vivir Mi Vida," each of which structures a chapter in this book, was informed by my own personal intuitions as a listener of el Marc. If, as Heather Leigh writes, "music somehow remains intangible. We can try to explain and to rationalize it but we're seduced back

---

5. This moniker is my contestatory gesture that reclaims him as one of us, as familia, as hermano, as Boricua, and as Latino. If we refer to many celebrities by their first names—Jennifer, Ben, Britney, Madonna, Beyoncé, Gaga—as a language that "offers the promise of a relation of intimacy," I deploy this "affectation of familiarity" (Furedi 2010, 494) and call Marc Anthony "el Marc" throughout the book as my rhetorical strategy for returning him, as global celebrity, to the everyday lives of our communities. Referring to him by his first name only and adding the definitive article "el" allows me to rewrite his exceptional status, unraveling him from his celebrity status and returning him to us, his fans and critical listeners.

by the song. Music catches you. You can't explain it, you have to experience it" (2022, 3), my own ideas about how each of these songs express and offer us more than what we can ever write or analyze seem valid. I first heard about Marc Anthony in the late 1990s when he performed in Detroit, and I soon began to follow him as a salsa singer. While I missed the Detroit concert, since I moved to Chicago in 2000, I have attended almost every single concert he has held for the last twenty years. I also play his CDs at home or in the car while driving and have been following his musical career throughout the first quarter of the twenty-first century. I had the honor of meeting him in a Maestro Cares Foundation fundraiser in Chicago in September 2013, where he agreed to pose for a photo with me in a very cordial manner.

•

While entertainment journalism has focused much on his personal life, marriages, and children, I was long fascinated by the affective power of his repertoire on us, his listeners. My early intuitions about his music were inspired by the general ways in which he was able to sing to multiple identities simultaneously. How could he move so easily and smoothly between the Puerto Rican diasporic self in "Preciosa," to a hemispheric Latinidad in "Hasta Que Te Conocí," to the solidarity with the Global South / Algerian in "Vivir Mi Vida"? My selection of these five songs was informed by these initial questions as well as by the communal power behind their canonical status.

My final selection gradually unfolded as I reflected on el Marc's talent for hailing diverse identities and geocultural spaces through his musical curation. It piqued my interest that, outside of the more traditional love songs ("Y Hubo Alguien," "You Sang to Me," "Contra la Corriente," "¿Y Cómo Es Él?"), el Marc had interpreted songs that became canonical as public performances of a diverse array of various subjectivities, including Nuyorican, MexiRican, Latino, US American, and the anticolonial brownness of the Global South. While a diverse repertoire is usually explained as a strategy for expanding audiences, it can also be a tool for producing sonic communities, that is, interpretive communities that share specific musical histories and traditions as well as cultural experiences. These five songs possess their own stories as musical productions and performative iterations, revealing rich routes and histories mediated by their sounds and rhythms. Indeed, each of these songs marks a pivotal moment in Marc Anthony's musical career; thus, my critical analysis of each song not only reveals a rich array of identities, cultural themes and politics, musical genealogies, debates, sonic aesthetics, performative styles, and listening communities but also unearths the largely unacknowledged sonic and musical traditions that locate these songs within specific moments in el Marc's musical journey. I situate each song within a critical cultural and communal framework that grounds and locates it in powerful experiences and pivotal moments that have affected our Latinx communities, thus offering us social, cultural, and political meanings.

If "Hasta Que Te Conocí" ushered el Marc into his brilliant decision to sing salsa and love ballads in Spanish in 1993, "Preciosa" was the song that allowed him entry into the musical communities in Puerto Rico while textualizing his own personal reclaiming of his Nuyorican hybridity and subjectivity. "I Need to Know," his assumed crossover hit in 1999, surfaced el Marc's own vexed relationship with his American citizenship and identity and his constructed otherness within the country of his birth, a racialization inherent in the media narratives about him as a "crossover" during the Latin boom of the late 1990s. "Aguanile" was the major song in the 2006 biopic *El Cantante* (Ichaso 2007), where el Marc performed as Héctor Lavoe, the Ponce-born salsa singer who pioneered, along with Willie Colón, the early styles of salsa dura in New York, and who became a cultural hero to Boricua listeners both on the island and in the diaspora. Performing "Aguanile" in the film and in later concerts as his opening song relocated el Marc within the Fania years of salsa in New York, most notably during the early 1970s, a salsa dura style that is not usually associated with his repertoire of love ballads, and, most significantly, inserted him within a Caribbean Blackness that Nuyorican salsa music articulated so powerfully. Finally, "Vivir Mi Vida" (2013) marked el Marc's return to recording and producing music following his separation from Jennifer Lopez. This song extends Marc Anthony's musical geographies and connects him to the North African and Algerian musical traditions, thus redefining his global status less within the logics of neoliberalism and closer to an alternative politics of a Global South brownness.[6]

---

6. I want to thank Jorge Coronado for suggesting this phrase to me during a presentation at Northwestern University. The "brownness" here differs from the queer affective "brownness" that José Esteban Muñoz so lucidly outlined in his "Feeling Brown" and highlights the solidarity and alliances between subordinated communities across the Atlantic and within the Global South. Afro-Latinx scholars have denounced the term *brown* as an anti-Black discourse that privileges mestizaje as a whitening tool and that erases Blackness among us. I deploy *brown* here differently, mostly as a marker for anticolonial subjectivities across the Global South that foster a community of resistance and political awareness, yet am keenly aware of the long history of racialization of Black Moroccans and of slavery in that country, lucidly examined by Chouki El Hamel (2013).

These five songs inspired me to reflect critically on issues of race, gender, language, and identities that have been central to Latinx scholarly epistemologies about US Latinidades. I have traced the social meanings of these songs as they have circulated locally, transnationally, and globally. Moreover, I have critically listened to them as sites of resistance through which Marc Anthony engages a Latinx cultural politics that unearths our collective affects, pain, suffering, and displacements, and our joys and pleasures, that is, as a sonic community. By identifying not only the social and communal meanings that emanate from these sonic texts but also the ways el Marc produces social spaces and a sociality through his performances, concerts, musical arrangements, and musical repertoires, I argue that despite the category of "pop Latinx singer" that has been imposed on him and that undermines and trivializes his contributions to Latinx and Latin American culture, el Marc's musical impact is the result of a profoundly serious sonic labor that fosters and produces community among his listening audiences and fans. Lin Manuel Miranda, a long-term fan of Marc Anthony, has celebrated the ways in which el Marc's songs have framed his own life events, including meeting his spouse and his own wedding, as soundtracks that framed his memories of these special moments (2024). Like Miranda, many listeners share this powerful association between el Marc's repertoire and their own life stories. This power is evident in the numerous comments by fans on social media who admire, love, and desire him but, most significantly, identify with his vast repertoire of songs. His concert audiences sing his lyrics by heart and, even if this is not unique to Marc Anthony, it does reveal the intensity of his fans' and listeners' engagement with his repertoire. Moreover, this collective sonic expression transforms what Thomas Turino would categorize as "presentational performance," a concert event, into a "participatory" one, thus blurring the boundaries between these two modes of music making (Turino 2008, 26). I propose that Marc's concerts, then, are not exclusively staged performances to be enjoyed by a paying audience as entertainment exclusively, but intersubjective spaces where singer and listener engage affectively through sounds and songs. Given the predominance of love ballads in his musical works, it is not surprising that female, queer, and some male listeners easily memorize these lyrics as a way of grappling with their intimate romantic relationships and with their life struggles. His local (New York), national (Latinx and non-Latinx fans), hemispheric (Latin America), and global (Europe) followers have made Marc Anthony a global phenomenon and a highly popular celebrity. Yet this vast fanhood also brings up questions about how the category of "popular music" has undermined and trivialized the social and communal meanings of his songs as well as elided the politics of affect that moves his listeners.

Listening Intimacies

This is a book about Marc Anthony but was created without his direct input. It emanates mostly from my own personal process of significations, of giving meaning to his songs and of researching the cultural resonance of his repertoire. After years of repeated requests for an interview with him, which failed, I realized that my contributions resided in the innovative ways in which I sutured the songs themselves to the longer musical genealogies that made them possible as well as to the historical and political moments that seemed to emerge as I studied and identified the story of each song. There is a vast archive of entertainment journalism documenting Marc Anthony's musical career, concerts, and discography, so my decision was not to reproduce what has already been documented about his work, information that is easily accessible on the internet, although I still engage key articles or journalists. Unlike the tabloids, I am not interested in his personal and social life, marriages, children, or financial status. Rather, I want to examine these selected songs as his sonic legacy, powerful texts that we associate with him and that he has canonized, as multiple sites from which I can situate el Marc within the longer genealogies of Puerto Rican, Mexican, Latin American, and Algerian musics as well as analyze the cultural resonances for his listeners at historical moments in the Americas. Having been inspired by the songs themselves, I rehearsed each of them on my piano; I studied their musical structures, phrasings, and dynamics; I listened to Marc Anthony's recordings; and I analyzed, observed, and attended his concerts in Chicago for twenty years and watched key performances of these songs on YouTube.

Each of these five songs holds a most intimate meaning for me as a critical listener, as each resonates with specific experiences in my life as a Diasporican and Latina feminist scholar. "Preciosa," the song that organizes the first chapter on "Diasporican Subjectivities and the Sounds of Itinerancy," inspired me to reflect on the displacements that structured the life of its composer, Rafael Hernández; of Marc Anthony's parents, who migrated from the island to New York; and on my own displacements that marked my life as a young Puerto Rican woman who left home and the island in 1974 to attend college in the United States. What in my case was a sign of social privilege, this educational migration not only strengthened my appreciation for the island as home, ironically a repressive, Catholic home that I was desperately trying to flee from, but also situated me in social networks that introduced me to Mexican American and Chicanx families and communities, to the realities of their long-colonized and precarious lives and, most significantly, to the forms of empowerment that their political activism and conciencia offered me.

The second chapter, "'Hasta Que Te Conocí' (1993): Latinidad as Suffering," was thus conceptualized and inspired by my own personal incursions into the MexiRican families that I formed throughout my adult life as well as by the struggles around gender that have informed my personal journeys.[7] Listening to "Hasta Que Te Conocí," written by the late queer Mexican divo Juan Gabriel, constitutes a text that speaks of Latinidad as suffering. This song inspired me to reflect on my own gradual transformation into a US Latina and my MexiRican social networks and family lives.

The third chapter listens to "I Need to Know," the canonical song that transformed el Marc into a crossover success. I replay and relisten to this hit as a sonic text that integrates the multiracial sonic traditions that constitute "American" music, as it also challenges dominant versions of America as exclusively white. The song returned me to my 1970s college years at Indiana University, where I began to listen to and appreciate the heterogeneous styles of US rock 'n' roll that I had enjoyed on the island but had rejected as imperial music. The affective excess and pain of Janis Joplin's blues, the singing guitar of Carlos Santana, "Color My World" by Chicago, the Moody Blues, and Grace Slick and Jefferson Airplane were but some of the bands that populated the soundtrack of my college years. Writing about the sonic dialogues between mainstream rock and "I Need to Know" led me to rethink the social meanings that classic rock had for me as I transformed myself in the United States from a good Catholic Puerto Rican girl to a feminist intellectual Latina.

Marc Anthony's stellar performance of "Aguanile" in the biopic film *El Cantante* caught my attention as a performance that is singularly demanding of its vocality. Returning to Héctor Lavoe in the fourth chapter, "Aguanile" was a means of critically examining Puerto Rican masculinity, race, and Blackness through Amina Gautier's short story of the same name. The sonoroliterary reading of this story in my chapter, with the abuelo as a major character in the narrative, likewise led me to reflect on my new family role as an abuela, an emerging stage that has triggered my own recollections of my maternal grandmother, Victoria, and of how I and my sisters, her three nietas, perceived her as an elderly woman.

Finally, writing in chapter 5 about "Vivir Mi Vida," its celebratory, loud, and dynamic textures meant for dancing, reconnected me to the diasporic and global Puerto Rican poet Victor Hernández Cruz and his poetic incursions into the North African presence, legacy, and ethnic heritage among

---

7. *MexiRican* refers to those families and individuals who are both of Mexican and Puerto Rican ethnic heritages. My book *Negotiating Latinidad* (2019) analyzes the national negotiations that Chicago intra-Latinx individuals confront as they navigate their multiple communities.

Boricuas. The song continues to inspire us to gain a more complicated self-understanding as Boricuas who are also global entities in and throughout the world, as the long-held Arab presence among Puerto Ricans and Latin Americans remains hidden and rendered invisible by dominant institutions, school curricula, and cultural paradigms. That my Spanish and southern European heritage also includes North African heritage was a discovery that resulted from a long journey into my family history and that coincided with the writing of this book. This new knowledge has revitalized in me an affirmation of our rich heritages that tend to be reified and reduced under the official tripartite paradigm of Puerto Ricans as exclusively Spanish, Taíno, and African, whereby the "African" needs to be expanded to the North African, Arab, and Muslim communities in the imagined ancestries of our lives. "Vivir Mi Vida" allowed me to rethink not only how the song is a resistant response to post-9/11 cultural politics but also how popular songs and musical experiences and events, the acts that Small (1998, 9) describes as "musicking," enact collective subjectivities and solidarities across geographical distances.[8]

These affective and mnemonic journeys as a critical listener of these five songs are not unique, as I share these experiences of identification with thousands of other ardent fans of el Marc. These songs structure the chapters in this book because they live and continue to impact us as critical texts and sonic experiences that resonate with our most intimate lives and that can only produce meanings through the act of listening. As Nancy K. Baym explains in *Playing to the Crowd: Musicians, Audiences, and the Intimate Work of Connection*, intimacy between the artist and their audience "became a public and moral good" with the rise of capitalism, secularism, and urbanization. In today's global context, where most musicians are part of a "gig economy" made possible through the internet and social media platforms (Baym 2018, 7–11), intimacy has been commodified in terms of the new ways in which fans and listeners expect their idols to be available as friends and family through fan groups, Twitter, and Facebook pages, as their private and individual lives become open texts for the consumption of fans. Yet within this utilitarian and profit-making framework, there is still a need for "intimacy" with the artists on the part of fans. This desire is "best viewed as part of a larger historical quest for community and for a world in which all needs for intimacy and affiliation

---

8. Small defines "musicking" as follows: "To music is to take part, in any capacity, in a musical performance, whether by performing, by listening, by rehearsing or practicing, by providing material for performance (what is called composing), or by dancing" (1998, 9). Small's original approach to understanding musical performances as social events, as human encounters, and as action has been central to later studies about music concerts from the methodologies of performance studies and cultural studies.

are satisfied" (Parks 1981, quoted in Baym 2018, 21). Following Baym's argument, I would add that intimacy can also be considered as a gesture of resistance, as it offers Latinx audiences a sense of collectivity and community, an experience of wholeness that racial capitalism has fractured through multiple forms of dispossession. As fleeting as a two-hour Marc Anthony concert may be, these instances of community strengthen our long-colonized selves and offer us a sense of belonging, a breath of hope and restored humanity.

Musical Genealogies and Relationalities

This book also documents and examines the musical exchanges and dialogues that have informed el Marc's own musical repertoire and that anchor him within larger sonic genealogies. Contrary to the discourses of exceptionalism about singers and celebrities promulgated by the music industry, and to the profit-making structures that separate and segment songs from their own histories and listening communities, my reflections and interpretations of these five songs reveal that el Marc's musical repertoire, his performative identities, and his aesthetics cannot be separated from key musicians who were central to his own music-making. Again, the trope of the "singer as listener" leads us to a more profound understanding of el Marc's relationality to composers and songwriters. Like many other music celebrities, Marc Anthony himself is not a composer but a singer, interpreter, and arranger. The fact that my selected five songs could all be considered "cover" songs reveals the mutual exchanges between el Marc and the music world. If "cover" songs constitute a "new performance or recording by a musician other than the original performer,"[9] the existence of these cover songs in Marc Anthony's repertoire suggests, once more, intense, ongoing dialogues and exchanges with both composers and other interpreters. Yet singing a "cover" song should not diminish the authorial agency of el Marc in rewriting the original songs, whether this means recreating them into new salsa arrangements for younger generations or inflecting the original texts with additional musical content. Contesting the critiques against el Marc for not authoring his own songs, I argue that these rewritings or adaptations evince the sonic relationalities that frame the Nuyorican singer's work with respect to Puerto Rico, to the United States, to the hemispheric Americas, and to the Global South.

---

9. Wikipedia, s.v. "cover version," last modified June 20, 2024, https://en.wikipedia.org/wiki/Cover_version.

If "Preciosa" cannot be understood without recognizing the centrality of migration and displacement in the life of its composer, Afro–Puerto Rican Rafael Hernández, el Marc cannot be understood without acknowledging this historical antecedent in the Nuyorican musician's world. Thus, the melodies, sounds, and rhythms of "Preciosa" can be listened to as the "sounds of itinerancy" proposed by Brandon LaBelle (2020) that connect Rafael Hernández with Marc Anthony within the longer histories of Puerto Rican migrations to New York and that publicly inscribe the social displacements of Diasporicans and of Black Puerto Rican musicians.

Likewise, in chapter 2, where I discuss Marc Anthony's pivotal selection of the late Mexican queer divo Juan Gabriel's hit "Hasta Que Te Conocí," a Mexican song that initiated el Marc's own journey into the world of singing salsa love songs in Spanish, I identified el Marc's own doubling with Marco Antonio Muñiz, the Mexican ballad singer after whom el Marc was named. This onomastic homage, born from his Puerto Rican parents' love for Mexican music, embodies the long history of musical exchanges between Mexico and Puerto Rico (at times via New York) and thus constitutes a sonic Latinidad that may explain why el Marc was so profoundly touched by Juan Gabriel's song in the first place. "Hasta Que Te Conocí," a song about suffering in and through love, suggests the relationship between Latinidad, suffering, gender, and sexuality, as both Juan Gabriel and Marc Anthony have performed this song throughout Latin America.

Marc Anthony's association with Héctor Lavoe, established mostly since the film *El Cantante*, is another dyad or coupling that paves the way for situating el Marc within the longer genealogies of Nuyorican salsa during the 1960s and 1970s. While too young to have participated in those early musical productions with Fania, and despite other salseros' attacks on him for not being a "real" salsa singer (which I discuss in chapter 5), Marc Anthony, as a Nuyorican, continues to honor this musical and political legacy in his own original way. In fact, he and La India were the two young salsa singers who represented the emergence of "salsa for the high-tops generation" by the mid-1990s, a music that rejected the salsa romántica of the 1980s, which "had no edge" (Sergio George, quoted in McLane 1996), and recharged itself for the younger generations by incorporating Black sonic traditions like rhythm and blues, hip-hop, and Jamaican dancehall (McLane 1996). In fact, this revitalization of salsa, embodied by Marc Anthony in his collaborative arrangements with Nuyorican musical producer, pianist, and arranger Sergio George, has made possible the long survival and continuity of this salsa sonic tradition for the younger generations as well as hemispherically and globally.

Finally, "Vivir Mi Vida" exemplifies the global relationalities of el Marc with Algerian French raï singer Cheb Khaled, whose own "C'est la Vie" serves as the subtext and original song that inspired the salsa arrangements of "Vivir Mi Vida." These key figures in my analyses of Marc Anthony's musical hits reveal the hidden histories of inspirations, exchanges, and genealogies that give meaning to el Marc's repertoire, informing our critical listenings and, most significantly, producing moments of resistance among his audiences.

Critical Listening to El Marc

Let me clarify that my critical listening of el Marc's five selected songs does not constitute a return to traditional methods of literary close textual readings. After decades of impressive and brilliant interventions into Latinx and Latin American popular music by other scholars, it is possible for me to now select songs as major sites of analysis given the inter-, multi-, and transdisciplinary theoretical and scholarly tools that so many academics have offered us from a variety of fields and disciplines. It is possible to read these songs not only as sonic texts that circulate across interpretive communities but as sites for unveiling these unacknowledged musical genealogies that help us understand the critical role that el Marc plays in the lives of so many of his listeners. The rich and sophisticated concepts from sound studies brilliantly trace how race and racism travel through sounds and their social constructions via critical concepts such as Stoever's "the listening ear," Khesti's "modernity's ear," and Casillas's "sounds of belonging" (Stoever 2016; Casillas 2014; Khesti 2015). They also include the revisions of "American" musical history, through which Latinx music is central to our multiracial imaginings of "American music," as in the traveling exhibit *American Sabor* (Berríos-Miranda, Dudley, and Habell-Pallán 2018), and the social and cultural meanings of the national and transnational circulation of musical genres, such as the Dominican bachata, Puerto Rican reggaetón, Mexican musics, and Colombian popular musics like the cumbia (Aguilar 2020; Cepeda 2001, 2010, 2017, 2022; Chávez 2017; Madrid 2008, 2018; Pacini Hernández 1995, 2010; Rivera-Rideau 2015). Furthermore, feminist and queer readings of popular singers and performers in diasporic Mexican, Dominican, and Puerto Rican communities (Alvarado 2012; Dávila Ellis 2020; Fiol-Matta 2017; Vargas 2012) reclaim the gender, social, and cultural meanings of queer and feminist singers, otherwise rendered inaudible by masculinist writings; the performance studies methods center on the racial, gendered, and social meanings of the moving body on stage (Alvarado 2012; La Fountain-Stokes 2009; Rivera-Servera 2012); and other lucid interventions integrate the political power of sounds to interracial social spaces and geographic places (Dorr 2007, 2018; Johnson 2013, 2017). I will refer to these scholars and their original analyses of numerous popular singers, interpreters, and performers throughout the book, for they have allowed me to reengage popular music not only as a scholar "synthesizing a diverse range of musical output, tracking themes through a body of work" but also through my own personal critical readings, "making aesthetic, political, and biographical associations" (Baym 2018, 39), thus performing my own "listening intimacies."

We need more interventions that complicate our understandings about how popular songs engage in cultural and political work, without the explicitly rigid categories that describe certain songs or genres as "political," such as Rubén Blades and Willie Colón's "Siembra," Marvin Gaye's "What's Going On?" (1971), Public Enemy's "Fight the Power" (1989), the music of Rage Against the Machine, and dismiss others—such as Latin American boleros and romantic ballads—as not. Martha González (2020), the renowned singer, musician, and performer from the group Quetzal, reflects critically on the ways that for her, "music could be a liberatory process, a deliberate act of love, and a source of empowerment for self and community" (1), pointing toward the communal alternative to music-making that Quetzal has proposed in composing and arranging their musical performances through "participatory, process-based community art practices" (3). This alternative music represents a contestatory form of music-making that elides how the capitalist market system extracts and appropriates communal arts, turning them into products and commodities for profit-making (M. González 2020, 2). Within the context of salsa as inserted within the music industry, owned, managed, and circulated by Fania Records among other record labels, however, critic Andrés Espinosa Agurto (2022) defined "salsa consciente" as

> an educational tool of conscientization that not only develops its aesthetics as grounded in entertaining dance music but also engages the listeners, largely from a lyrical perspective, and asks them to conscientize themselves in regard to history, colonialism, imperialism, communal strife, politics, discrimination, racism, etc., as well as engaging them in questioning and facing the current situations. (xxii)

This element of interpellation and hailing proposed by Althusser (Espinoza Agurto 2002, xxii) is critical to these very specific definitions of politics in popular music. Espinosa Agurto exclusively locates this concientización in the songs of Rubén Blades and Tite Curet Alonso, a selection informed by a very specific definition of politics as only overtly didactic content.

In this book, I grapple with how what we usually dismiss as pop music—music that is apolitical, superficial, formulaic, and for the "unthinking masses"—engages in a "relational labor" that could also be politically meaningful if we think of the concept of "politics" in wider ways. Brandon LaBelle's discussion on the communal power of sounds lucidly highlights the major function of sounds and listening in the process of producing relationalities and in constituting what he calls "an acoustics of social becoming" (2020, 2). He writes: "sound and listening [are] underscored as an expansive relational means affording dialogical exchange, the plays of recognition and the affective processes intrinsic to finding place, as well as escape routes and new social formations beyond the strictly verbal and visible" (2). Following LaBelle, if "sound works to unsettle and exceed arenas of visibility by relating us to the unseen, the non-represented or the not-yet-apparent," then "sound may carry those that struggle by way of reverberant intensities, the vibrations as well as the echoes that pass over or around structures of dominance" (2).

Marc Anthony himself has publicly commented on the anxiety-provoking business of making music as an "invisible" activity that associates sounds with the production of feelings and that unsettles the capitalist profit-making goal and the idea of selling a tangible product: "I've always said that: Music is about moving air. It's invisible—it's in the air, and then it's gone. That's quite a business to be in; it'll scare the shit out of you if you think about it too much. You're playing to 50,000 people, and what you've got to offer them is invisible. You've gotta make 50,000 people feel something" (Rosen 2013).

These words lucidly express Marc Anthony's investment in music and sounds as an affective practice, however framed by industry and profit-making. He highlights the tensions between the invisibility of sounds and music and the expectations of a paying audience in exchange for a material, physical product or commodity. Instead, he concludes that what he can offer as a singer is the experience of "feel[ing] something." Although mediated by capitalism, his songs intentionally create an affective experience.

I am interested here in how the sounds and sonic arrangements—lyrics, melodies, and rhythms—allow for the identification and resonance of listeners and fans. How do these songs trigger emotional states and affective scapes, that is, spaces and contexts that create feelings, that allow us to heal from the precarity of our colonized lives? How is el Marc deploying sounds, rhythms, melodies, and lyrics to create a space for collectivity and community? In contrast to scholars like Espinosa Agurto who locate concientización exclusively in a limited repertoire, I argue that the notion of "politics" in popular music needs to be attentive to the social and affective dimensions of musicking. Rather than delimit politics to a more overt didacticism through interpellation, I am more interested in how el Marc's love ballads and salsa arrangements may serve as sites of resistance through affect. Rather than argue for music as a decolonial tool, which Afro-Caribbean and Latinx music have historically exemplified, here I am more interested in grappling with the relations between sound, affect, resonance, and resistance. To claim that Marc Anthony's songs are decolonial may be counterintuitive to our established political notions of decoloniality as a historical and material process of liberation and reclaiming of land.[10] How can an artist of Marc Anthony's popularity and stature be considered decolonial? His magnitude, his high record sales, and his celebrity status constrain his agency and intentionality in engaging in progressive politics. Yet his stage presence and repertoire reveal purposeful political interventions. His megaconcerts are far from a decolonial politics that we associate with revolutionary reclaimings of the land, the culture, the language. Yet if we think about the role of the arts and of music in contesting the repressive forces of imperial governments since colonial times in the Caribbean, for instance, there is a long history of drumming, singing, dancing, and performing that have gestured resistance and survival against dominant institutions. The drumming in Afro-Cuban popular and sacred musics, the dancing of Puerto Rican bomba, the Trinidadian calypso, are among numerous examples of how music, rhythm, body, and voice become sites of resistance and reaffirmation. Voice and song among the colonized and enslaved in the Caribbean plantation economy cannot be fully understood without recognizing how singing, speaking, and dancing were practices of resistance as reaffirmations of our humanity, our identity, and our right to survive and live. The afterlives of these creative performances of resistance and reaffirmation remain alive and well in the minds of el Marc's Latinx listeners and fans. As racial minorities are fully aware, the creative arts—acts of writing one's story, song and music, and the power of visual images—are all instances of performing our presence in the world by refusing the captivity of institutional domination. Considered in this light, a selection of el Marc's music may be considered decolonial within this larger historical arc. Even Bad Bunny, whose

---

10. I want to acknowledge recent scholarly debates around the use of the term *decolonial* and its function as a metaphor. Eve Tuck and K. Wayne Yang's essay "Decolonization Is Not a Metaphor" (2012) stands as a lucid denouncement and critique of the ways in which decolonization has been diluted and deployed as symbol or metaphor, particularly in education studies. Yet numerous scholars in postcolonial studies, Caribbean studies, race studies, and ethnic studies continue to deploy the term in such metaphorical ways, yet always alluding to the imperial histories of land occupation, settler colonialism, and the ensuing displacements of Indigenous, Brown and Black communities. In the case of Marc Anthony, the concept of "decolonial" is central to my analysis of "Preciosa" given the centrality of the island of Puerto Rico as land, while I use it less so in the rest of the book.

song lyrics embody strong anticolonial politics, is located within the capitalist frameworks of the music industry.

This book stands as an acknowledgment of el Marc for the seriously nuanced political work that he engages in through his singing. Licia Fiol-Matta's (2017) concept of "the thinking voice" in her analysis of Puerto Rican singer Lucecita Benítez and how her songs articulated her "left-leaning politics" (14) is a lucid intervention that adds to Baym's and LaBelle's contributions in this reflection about pop music and politics. As Fiol-Matta explains, "Pure pop is not readily associated with thought, although female stars often evoke feelings precisely because they only come to being as creatures of thought," that is, through their public lives only made possible through intelligence and intent. The "thinking voice" is thus defined as a "voice [that] carries with it the history of struggles, the reality of duress, and the relative triumph of endurance" (14). In her discussion of Lucecita as a thinking voice, Fiol-Matta defines the singer's impact on the listener through Jean-Luc Nancy's concept of "resonance," that is, a resonance "orienting the listener toward the intangible sense of hearing through her multifold performances across decades of Puerto Rican and Latin American life" (173). For Fiol-Matta, the thinking voice "cannot be marshaled at will or silenced when inconvenient. Its aim is not to dazzle or enthrall, although it may do so" (173).

These descriptions attempt to reclaim the intelligence and thought-provoking nature behind a singer's voice, whether this "resonance" is ultimately found in the content of the song, in its performative styles and aesthetics, or in the texture of a powerful voice. Most significantly, I approach "the thinking voice" as a decolonial gesture that restores meaning, seriousness, and profundity to the musical labor of female singers in Puerto Rico, as Fiol-Matta writes. It can be applied to the original and creative ways that Marc Anthony's songs articulate meaningful and profound sonic instances for his listeners. For instance, when el Marc sings "Preciosa," the song produces particular emotions of love for the island, a nostalgia for the home country among Diasporicans that could evoke memories of particular histories of displacements and struggles against settler colonialist practices throughout the history of the island. Rethinking politics through affect, aesthetics, and sounds allows us scholars to acknowledge the serious transformational labor that popular singers enact, while critiquing the very circumscribed frameworks for politics that continue to limit our understanding of the power of "pure pop" (Fiol-Matta 2017, 14).

In this book, I refer to the voices of listeners and fans, including myself, who have been inspired by el Marc's songs to reflect on their own intimacies, relationships, and life experiences. I deploy the concept of "critical listening," defined in the opening page, as a tool for teasing out the messy attachments that el Marc's listeners experience through his music. Latinx listeners engage with his songs in ways that are more sophisticated and complex than what traditional dominant discourses about pop music have allowed. For example, a Cuban immigrant woman who has lived in northern Italy for the last thirty years showed me two lines from "Vivir Mi Vida"—"Voy a vivir el momento / Para entender el destino"—tattooed onto her left upper chest area. With other song lyrics of Marc Anthony's tattooed on her back, which have transformed the invisible sounds into tangible and legible letters on her body as text, she has been an ardent fan of el Marc for decades, and she bonded with me as we talked about the power of his songs in our lives during a brief and unplanned encounter.

The impact of his music can be seen in his Latin American fans, who continuously send warm greetings to el Marc on Facebook fan groups, expressing their love, cariño, and desire for him. They call him "mi flaco adorado" [my lovely skinny man], "the King of Salsa," "talented," and "with an amazing voice." They tell him "te adoro" and "te amo." These small examples of the intense admiration and loyalty of Marc Anthony's fans are partly a construction of the musical industry per se, as fan clubs have become institutional spaces for increasing the capital value of popular celebrities and singers today. Yet the erotics of desire and the informal conversations around el Marc's sexiness sent on social media by female fans, open to the commodification of intimacy, also reveal themselves as a space for communication between the singer and the fans. As Baym writes, "the new demand for intimacy can also be traced in part to the relational affordances of social media, which favor a norm of 'personal authenticity and connection'" (174).

Yet Marc Anthony's own performances onstage, even in megaconcerts with thousands of listeners, are also opportunities for him to engage personally with his fans and audiences. He does so through the flirtatious blinking of an eye, throwing kisses, or speaking to us with cariño, love, and gratitude. Even when we know that these gestures are performative details, as Alexandra Vázquez (2013) has proposed, we, as his fans and listeners, take pleasure in feeling that we are the objects of these corporeal and affective intimacies, as he maintains an aura of humility, humanity, and relatability. I have heard Marc's fans comment that he "se entrega a su público" [gives of himself to his audience], and despite the arena-sized venues, that sense of love, generosity, familiarity, and intimacy offers an affective texture of belonging and community. A Mexican Polish female friend from Chicago who doesn't understand Spanish has shared with me the very "special feeling" she has experienced during el Marc's concerts. She finds these events "collective experiences," "togetherness with other strangers around you," and characterized by "a communal energy" absent in other musical events. Listening to el Marc at the Allstate Arena outside Chicago every winter for the last ten years has become for her a way to reconnect with her own Mexican Latinx heritage and celebrate her long friendships with Puerto Ricans. Returning to the Cuban woman in Italy, the act of inscribing el Marc's lyrics onto her skin, making these words a permanent part of her body and flesh, constitutes a powerful instantiation and metaphor for acknowledging the multiple meanings and the affective power that his songs have represented for so many of his avid listeners. As one of those long-term listeners and fans, I share in this book my own personal, scholarly, and critical reflections to document my claims.

The first chapter examines how el Marc has performed "Preciosa" since 1998 and documents his central role in cementing the song's longevity and intergenerational pertinence as a sonic text that has become a "national anthem" for islanders and Diasporicans. Penned in 1937 by Afro-Boricua composer and musician Rafael Hernández, "Preciosa" expresses the pain of geographical and cultural displacements. Thus, it is a most meaningful song for those Puerto Ricans who reside outside the island, which is now over 60 percent of the entire Puerto Rican population. I propose understanding el Marc's dynamic and powerful performances of "Preciosa" in the larger context of Hernández's own migrations during his adult years and suggest that both figures serve as the beginning and the pinnacle of an arc of Boricua music-making from and in New York. My discussion about the shifts in the ways Puerto Ricans from the island have constructed Diasporicans—and vice versa—allows for a more nuanced cultural mapping that can inform our analysis of the social meanings of this song, a song that like many other patriotic songs about Puerto Rico was composed in exile. Framing el Marc as a "listener" of "Preciosa" in my reading of the Banco Popular de Puerto Rico's video *Romance del Cumbanchero* (1998), I suggest that his Nuyorican version, transformed by the montuno and soneo section added to the traditional bolero melody, is one of el Marc's most poignant contributions to the growing legitimacy and valorization of Nuyorican and Diasporican subjectivities outside the island as well as to the rhythms and sounds of a Boricua Blackness included in the montuno section. These aesthetic details allow for a reflection about Rafael Hernández's contradictory relationship with Blackness, as is clear from a reading of the lyrics of "Preciosa."

By documenting the rich transformations that the original song has undergone, I contribute to a critical listening that encompasses its heterogeneous iterations, its sonic migrations, throughout time and space. The fact that el

Marc has performed "Preciosa" during times of crisis for the island, such as after Hurricane María in 2017, and at concerts in predominantly Puerto Rican communities—such as New York, Orlando, and San Juan—reveals the strategic selection of a song that has allowed the Nuyorican singer to express his love for his heritage country, Puerto Rico, as well as reaffirm his pride in his Nuyorican identity. His performances signal the brilliant ways that el Marc has deployed this sonic text as a tool for political activism and healing. His presence on the stage when he sings "Preciosa" invites his listeners to remember the long history of extreme precarity and the imperial extractive policies that have injured the land and its peoples. If decoloniality implies reclaiming our land, then "Preciosa" is decidedly decolonial given the strong evocations it produces among Puerto Ricans and Diasporicans regarding the island's long colonial history of occupation.

"Hasta Que Te Conocí"—best known as one of the most popular songs of Juan Gabriel, Mexico's late queer divo and one of the most beloved singers of his time—is the critical object in the second chapter. I frame my listening of the song through the analytics of Latinidad as suffering and through José Esteban Muñoz's (2020) critical concept of "brown" as "excessive affect," a proposal that moves Latinidad away from identity politics and frames it within affect, race, and sexuality. I first reclaim the sites of MexiRican musical exchanges and the sonic genealogies in which I locate Marc Anthony and through which I discuss his initial and unplanned attraction to this love song. Focusing on the theme of suffering as the result of a cruel love relationship, the song has been performed by numerous singers, interpreters, and musicians throughout Latin America, and it has been rewritten and transformed into a rich variety of musical genres and performative styles, from Peruvian salsa and Dominican merengues to piano solos and arrangements for youth bands.

Chapter 2 also discusses gender and sexuality through an analysis of the performative bodies and movements of Juan Gabriel and Marc Anthony in their respective stagings of the song in the Viña del Mar Festival in Chile in 2002 and 2009. In dialogue with Alejandro Madrid's engaging article (2018) about Juan Gabriel's queer sexuality—a "secreto a voces"—I read the Mexican singer's body movements as queering dominant masculinities through excessive affect, while Marc Anthony's own performances, which include vocal and facial excesses, move his body as what I refer to as "untouched masculinity." As a conclusion to the chapter and to the section that traces the hemispheric circulation of the song as an urtext, I also discuss Willie Colón's own performance of "Hasta Que Te Conocí" as part of his competition with and enmity against el Marc as well as his own complicated and contradictory gender discourses around gay love.[11] Closing the chapter with Willie Colón allows me to highlight the underlying debates, competitions, enmities, and contradictions between two cisgendered male salsa singers of different generations within the spaces of sonic Latinidades.

Chapter 3 focuses on "I Need to Know" and proposes an alternative, multiracial reading of this English-language song that catapulted Marc Anthony into the Latin music boom's marketing discourses in 1999 and early 2000. I first discuss the concept of "Americanness" and engage with the central role of English in the legal processes through which United States courts define an immigrant's worthiness of accessing legal residency, citizenship, and being embraced as an "American." Despite having been born in New York, el Marc has been egregiously excluded from the larger Anglo and white American national imaginary due to his Puerto Rican ethnic heritage. This lingering "foreignness" shared by numerous Latinx individuals continues to racialize el Marc as a cultural Other outside the United States dominant imaginary. After discussing the strong critiques against the journalistic and music industry's narratives about the Latin music boom, I offer my alternative listening of "I Need to Know" as a song that integrates in its instrumentation, arrangements, and musical video production a rich, diverse combination of multiracial sonic traditions in the United States, most notably R&B, freestyle, rock, boogaloo, and salsa. If Marc Anthony's song shares the same title with Tom Petty's 1978 rock hit, "I Need to Know," I argue that, rather than a sonic document that signals assimilation and crossover, this song relocates el Marc within the larger genealogies of US rock, naturalized as Anglo and white, and allows for a reclaiming of Black and Brown rhythms in rock through his Latinx urban version of the song.

Chapter 4, dedicated to "Aguanile," replays, relistens to, and relocates this song within the context of Puerto Rico post–Hurricane María in 2017. If this song reclaims the powerful singing of Héctor Lavoe and inserts Marc Anthony within the early years of salsa in New York, as an homage to his musical antecedents visualized in the biopic film *El Cantante*, it also needs to be understood within the context of Blackness in the Diasporican community. Specifically, we must understand the song within the context of searching for home via a return to Africa. Reading Amina Gautier's short story "Aguanile," about an Afro–Puerto Rican transnational family and their intergenerational traumas and dynamics, which is structured around the phone calls between the granddaughter and her grandfather, who frequently talk about the deaths

---

11. This is particularly salient in light of Colón's major hit, "El Gran Varón" (1989), which first acknowledged sonically and lyrically the AIDS crisis in the Latinx gay communities, a meaningful intervention that has been undermined by the pioneering salsero's more recent right-wing politics and Trump-affiliated political stances.

of major salsa singers, introduces the theme of grieving and mourning late loved ones through processes such as listening to "Aguanile." The act of listening to this song, experienced by the nieta narrator, inspired me to frame this chapter around the ways the sounds of Blackness, located within the search for one's origins in Africa, allow Afro- and all Puerto Ricans to engage in the pain and sorrows of collective mourning after Hurricane María, an expansion of Latinidad as suffering through the presence of Afro–Puerto Ricans amid precarity. If "Aguanile" has shifted meanings through its migrations and circulations into mainstream spaces, including but not limited to its staging by Marc Anthony and Jennifer Lopez in the 2011 finale of *American Idol*, Gautier's story grounds the song as a metaphor for sonic memories that acknowledge our grief. My intervention into "Aguanile" constitutes a reverse temporality, as I move from 2017, the year of Hurricane María, to 2007, when Marc Anthony interpreted the song in the film as Héctor Lavoe. The trilogy of water, home, and mourning constitutes the tools for collective healing and remembrance, and for finding our sense of home and belonging amid environmental catastrophes and crises.

The final chapter examines el Marc's outstanding dance song, "Vivir Mi Vida," released in 2013 after his long hiatus from musical productions. I frame this chapter by analyzing the concept of love not only in the internal debates around salsa and salsa romántica, with which Marc Anthony has been associated, but also as one of the emotions associated with his fans and critical listeners. Most significantly, my critical approach to "Vivir Mi Vida" engages Cheb Khaled's "C'est la Vie," an Algerian French song that celebrates the multicultural and multiracial North African diasporas in Europe and served as a subtext for el Marc's salsa song. Integrating the meanings of the sounds with the images of a veiled Marc in the CD insert, I argue that this song unfolds the longer genealogies of a Global South brownness embodied in the Arab, Boricua, and Latinx figures of young Brown men who were marked as potential criminals and terrorists after 9/11. Unearthing selected sites for theorizing the Arab-Boricua couplings—Frantz Fanon and the Algerian independence movement in 1970s Puerto Rican New York; Christopher Rivera's concept of the "brown threat"; Victor Hernández Cruz and his Moroccan life and poetry, informed by Marisel Moreno's scholarly analysis of Cruz; and my personal reclaiming of the North African ancestry in my family[12]—allows us

---

12. See Sonia Manzano (2012) on the influence of Franz Fanon among 1970s Nuyorican youth, Christopher Rivera's article (2014) on the targeting of Brown and Arab young men after the 9/11 attack in New York City, Victor Hernández Cruz's poetic collections that include reflections on the North African and Muslim geocultural influences on Puerto Ricans (2011), and Marisel Moreno's (2015) lucid exploration of Arab cultures and subjectivities in Hernández Cruz's poetry.

to acknowledge the song's political meanings and to recognize the mutual interactions and collaborations between Arab and Boricua-Latinx musicians and artists. My discussion of the notorious photo of el Marc covering his face with a veil unfolds a problematic history of intercultural tensions between Western Europe and North Africa, mediated by women's use of the hijab. By proposing this "Global South brownness" through which the song articulates a politics of solidarity with North African and Algerian diasporic singers and communities, "Vivir Mi Vida" exemplifies not only the "sonic palimpsests" that allow multiply located sounds to coexist,[13] but also what Sara Ahmed (2004) defines as "affectionate solidarity"[14] in her analysis of the politics of "love." I conclude this last chapter with a discussion of Ahmed's proposals as an alternative discourse from which to understand the power of el Marc's songs and love ballads on his local, hemispheric, and global audiences. Indeed, el Marc's powerful, serious sonic labor is what this book aims to acknowledge.

---

13. The term "sonic palimpsests" is derived from J. Martin Daughtry's concept of "acoustic palimpsests" in his important article "Acoustic Palimpsests and the Politics of Listening" (2014).

14. Sara Ahmed (2004) proposes this term, "affectionate solidarity," as a feminist and queer alternative to the mainstream values that associate multicultural love for the nation with a presumed unity or acceptance of immigrants.

CHAPTER 1

"Preciosa" (1998)

Diasporican Subjectivities and the Sounds of Itinerancy

My Music Is My Flag, Ruth Glasser's monumental book about the history of Puerto Rican musicians and their communities in New York City during the interwar years, 1917–40, is an apt point of entry into Marc Anthony's iconic song "Preciosa." Glasser's title eloquently equates sonic traditions with national pride and love for one's home country. She says it was inspired "as a sort of riff off something Afro-Cuban musician Mario Bauzá complained to [me] about—how Puerto Ricans 'wrap themselves in their flag'—and the use of the flag as a kind of metonym for Puerto Rican political/cultural identity in songs and other cultural expressions."[1] The metaphoric equivalence of the sounds of the nation with the visual iconicity of the Puerto Rican flag keenly encapsulates the performative textures of national pride, nationalism, and love for the patria [home country] that so many twentieth-century Puerto Rican popular songs express. Songs such as "Preciosa," "Soñando con Puerto Rico," "Lamento Borincano," "En Mi Viejo San Juan," "Verde Luz," and more recently, Bad Bunny's "El Apagón" have triggered strong emotions among Boricua listeners, wherever they may be, that express their love for the island. Songs, their lyrics, rhythms, and performances, and the acts of musical listening and reception together constitute public and private sites for exploring the

---

1. Ruth Glasser, personal communication, April 28, 2020.

critical role of doing music, or musicking,[2] as an expression of love for the nation. "Preciosa," composed by Rafael Hernández in Mexico in 1937, after all, is a classic song of nostalgia and love for Puerto Rico that has become an unofficial national anthem for all Puerto Ricans. Like "En Mi Viejo San Juan," composed by Noel Estrada at the request of his brother, who was stationed in Panama during World War II, "Preciosa" has established itself as "a soundtrack for the heartache that people old and young felt over this somber reality [of displacement]" (Florido 2019).

As displacements fueled by economic migrations, political changes, and environmental catastrophes have continuously marked the colonial politics and social lives of the Caribbean archipelago, the sense of longing and nostalgia for the home country once abandoned becomes a strong fuel and motivation for composing songs of love to la patria. As music historians, scholars, and musicians themselves have highlighted, "Puerto Rico is the only Latin American country whose popular music was mainly created on foreign soil" (Jorge Javariz, quoted in Glasser 1995, 90). Ironically, Puerto Rican popular songs became even more Puerto Rican when composed abroad. Indeed, the histories of displacement underlying the creation of Puerto Rican music and about Puerto Rico reveal the many decades of cultural exile that permeated these musicians' psyches, a longing for the lost homeland that songs can evoke. As Fatima Bhutto writes, "when I hear certain songs, certain music, I am sure that in all the archipelagos of grief, there is a large swath of land reserved for lost homelands" (2022, 19).

As Alejandro Chalí Hernández, Rafael Hernández's son, shared, "No hay lugar en el mundo que le haya cantado más a la patria que en Puerto Rico" [There is no place in the world that has sang its love for the home country more than in Puerto Rico].[3] The reference to "Puerto Rico" may also include "cuando se está fuera de la patria," that is, when nostalgia and a desire for belonging reign. Marc Anthony himself identifies with the displaced and itinerant subjectivity of the Puerto Rican musician: "Las canciones sobre Puerto Rico todas fueron escritas fuera de Puerto Rico y yo me identifico con eso" [All songs about Puerto Rico were written outside of the island and I identify

---

2. Christopher Small, in *Musicking: The Meanings of Performing and Listening* (1998), proposes "music" as a verb, an act: "To music is to take part, in any capacity, in a musical performance, whether by performing, by listening, by rehearsing or practicing, by providing material for performance (what is called composing), or by dancing" (9). By highlighting music as a social event, a "human encounter" (10), and an action, Small unsettles the dominant and elite notions of music as "expertise" (8).

3. Alejandro "Chalí" Hernández made this comment during my personal interview and conversation we held in February 2020 at the Sala Museo Rafael Hernández, Interamerican University, San Juan Campus.

with that] (Banco Popular de Puerto Rico 1998). Therefore, migratory circuits, displacements, and the growing presence of Puerto Ricans in New York City as early as the 1920s and 1930s—in many ways the consequences of the political colonial conditions of the island in the aftermath of the 1917 Jones Act[4] and the fact that New York was becoming a center for a growing musical industry that began to cater to this growing Latinx community—framed a most important foundational moment for the (re)production and performance of Puerto Rican music. As ethnomusicologists have reminded us, "New York City played an important role in the creation not only of US Latino culture but of Latin American culture generally" (Berríos-Miranda, Dudley, and Habell-Pallán 2018, 75). In New York, as Omar Ruiz Vega argues, "Puerto Rican musicians encountered a vibrant music scene that gave them the necessary means—strong recording and radio industries, vast networks of nightclubs, theater and social clubs—to employ and further develop their musical skills" (2020, 21), resources that were not available in Puerto Rico at the time. Given his frequent travels and multiple residencies, Rafael Hernández may be one of the most iconic Puerto Rican musicians in terms of his itinerary: "Rafael Hernández moved to New York after World War I, worked briefly at a theater in Cuba, and settled in Mexico City in the 1930s" (Berríos-Miranda, Dudley, and Habell-Pallán 2018, 29). "Preciosa," as so many of his other compositions, emerged out of the pain of colonial displacement and exemplifies what Brandon LaBelle has described as "sound . . . always moving away from a source; it abandons origin, it longs and is perennially leaving" (2020, 127).

Marc Anthony, who was born in 1968 in New York City to Puerto Rican migrant parents, is today the most iconic singer and interpreter who (literally) wraps himself in the Puerto Rican flag, as he ritualistically performs in his concerts. Whenever he sings "Preciosa"—and numerous videos on YouTube attest to this—he picks up a Puerto Rican flag from his listeners, opens it up, covers his shoulders with it, sings while carrying the flag, and usually places it over the microphone while he moves around the stage singing. The omnipresent and much-anticipated presence of the Puerto Rican flag in Marc Anthony's concerts visually signifies the centrality of nationalism and national pride and love for the island of Puerto Rico, but, most importantly, it constitutes his performative affirmation of a puertorriqueñidad, a collective sense

---

4. Signed by President Woodrow Wilson, the Jones-Shafroth Act of 1917 gave Puerto Ricans US statutory citizenship, a legal status that allowed them to migrate easily to New York City without a passport. The Jones Act, however, also required that any cargo sailing between two US ports would be transported by US ships and mercantile marines, a requirement that has severely limited Puerto Rican trading with other countries in the world and that has secured Puerto Rico as a market for US corporations. This act has also significantly increased retail prices for Puerto Ricans on the island and has severely limited food sovereignty there.

of Puerto Rican identity, one that is complicated and multivalent and that unsettles the centralist geographical territoriality of the island as the site for Boricua authenticity.

Imbued with the political meanings of a long history of repression, the Puerto Rican flag is Marc Anthony's aesthetic gesture and prop that aims to complicate his Nuyorican identity in constant relationality to Puerto Rico the island. As many scholars have noted, the public use of the Puerto Rican flag was censored by the US government, during the 1950s and earlier, as a threat given its status as an index for Puerto Rican nationalism (Ruiz 2019, 189). In this context, Marc Anthony's purposeful deployment of the flag onstage hails past revolutionaries such as nationalist leader Blanca Canales, who hoisted the flag in the Jayuya uprising in 1950 and declared Puerto Rico a republic, and many others who risked their lives to express their love for their nation in the past. In this context, the flag continues to be deployed onstage as an object that signals resistance and political consciousness. This strong legacy was most evident in Jennifer Lopez's Super Bowl halftime show in 2020, when she wrapped herself in a large shawl with the US flag on one side and the Puerto Rican flag on the other, revealing the Nuyorican diva's nascent political conscientization about US racism.[5]

In this chapter, I engage the various interpretive iterations of "Preciosa," composed by Rafael Hernández and performed by Marc Anthony and others. Following Christopher Small, I "ask the wider and more interesting question," informed by the concept of musicking: "What does it mean when this performance [of this work] takes place at this time and this place, with these participants?" (1998, 10). I also propose a critical genealogy that connects Rafael Hernández to Marc Anthony within the historical arc of Puerto Rican music-making in and from New York. This genealogy suggests that the transnational connections between Puerto Rico the island and New York City are not always linear topographically or chronologically, as a back-and-forth or the vaivén that has been proposed by social science scholars like Jorge Duany (2002), but that these identities are simultaneously relational and intertwined as they are symbolically and discursively performed and reclaimed by islanders, by Nuyoricans, and by other Latinx voices. For example, when we think of Willie Colón and Héctor Lavoe's collaborations during the early years of salsa music in New York as a pair of musicians rooted in the urban Boricua spaces of New York, despite Lavoe's birth and formative years on the island and his migrant positionality, we situate salsa as Nuyorican, an ascription that

---

5. In the 2022 documentary *Halftime*, Jennifer Lopez reflects on her own growing political awareness as a singer and producer, which led to the specific choices of the children in cages and the flags for her performance in the 2020 Super Bowl.

is historically correct but that simultaneously overshadows the major contributions of numerous Puerto Rican island musicians to salsa, such as Papo Lucca, Héctor Lavoe, Ismael Rivera, and other figures that belonged to the Fania All-Stars, the iconic ensemble for salsa music that illustrates the "interrelationship between New York's and Puerto Rico's Latin music scenes" (Ruiz Vega 2020, 37), one of collaboration and coparticipation. Indeed, what makes salsa Nuyorican is not necessarily the singers' or musicians' home countries but the countercultural texture that only a Latinx New York could offer them and that made salsa possible during the 1970s.

Aware of the risk of erasing Rafael Hernández's island-based positionality, which is not my intention, I propose that we think of Rafael Hernández and Marc Anthony as two Diasporican subjects whose musical compositions and performances are situated within the experiences of itinerancy and displacement (for Hernández, his real-life travels, and for Marc Anthony, an imposed displacement from birth as a second-generation Nuyorican). In this light, "Preciosa," Hernández's musical compositions, and Marc Anthony's vocal interpretations constitute *sounds of itinerancy* (LaBelle 2020, 113), highlighting the "fleeting and punctuated event of sound" as "one of transience and transition; an itinerant and migratory sensorial matter, sound is both a thing of the past and a signal of the future; it points us toward what has happened—for every sound is an index of an event that, by the time we hear it, has already transpired—while equally pulling us forward by echoing beyond, toward a distance over there. The articulated presence of any sound, at one and the same moment, is to be found in its disappearance and its becoming" (95).

Following the itinerant textures of sounds and their politics of temporality as proposed by LaBelle, the colonial displaced subjectivities of the Caribbean and of Puerto Rico, in our case, suggest that popular music, whether composed by Rafael Hernández or performed by Marc Anthony, constitutes an evanescent colonial site that allows us as listeners to move between the past, the present, and the future, between origins and destination, and that allows us as Diasporicans to root ourselves in the in-betweenness of colonial temporalities, multiple residencies, and spatial displacements.[6] Fueled by a long history of imperial control, racial capitalism, and neoliberalism, the migrant positionality, as LaBelle reflects, is the "voice . . . [that] forces into the spaces

---

6. Scholarship about the role of sounds in frameworks of migration and displacement is vast. See Aparicio and Jáquez (2003), Casillas (2014), and Chávez (2017), among others. Alex E. Chávez (2017) defines "sounds of crossing," which is also the title of his book on the huapango arribeño and the transnational lives of the music, the musicians, and their families. He claims that "sound claims space physically and culturally in ways that rebuke politically motivated nationalist and segregationist epistemologies" (20), thus highlighting the circulation of sounds that transcend political borders and racial boundaries.

of national culture a sound of displacement, a rhythmed orality: this voice that I may not understand fully, that speaks to me from a beyond suddenly so clear, and that percusses the file of meaning. This broken tongue. The migrant voice is one that carries this doubling within it" (2020, 113).

As my analysis will reveal, Marc Anthony's iterative performances of "Preciosa" resituate the diaspora, the Nuyorican subjectivity, as the primary space from which to sing (to) the nation. The resituating and reaffirmation of the Diasporican and Nuyorican subjectivities are marked by the addition of a coda, what I will later call the Nuyorican montuno, to the original bolero penned by Rafael Hernández. It is in this transition from the bolero to the salsa-based montuno where Marc Anthony sonically reaffirms his Diasporican identity, thus leaving a profound imprint on the canonical status of "Preciosa" and extending the immortality of Rafael Hernández by revitalizing—that is, doubling—the composer's canonical song. Moreover, Marc Anthony subtly performs a Boricua Blackness that has been historically deleted in the dominant narratives about Rafael Hernández as Afro–Puerto Rican. El Marc reclaims this Blackness precisely through his Nuyorican sounds, as I will argue later. He achieves all of this while simultaneously reclaiming the legitimacy of the Nuyorican subjectivity as fully embedded within puertorriqueñidad and, as a decolonial gesture, destabilizing the traditional construct of the Puerto Rican nation. Marc's iterative performances of "Preciosa" have, across the last couple of decades, unsettled the binary discursive frameworks that have structured the social constructions of Nuyoricans and Diasporicans as in opposition to the island, thus provocatively suggesting that his musical performances and songs need to be listened to critically, as sites for a decolonial imaginary.

Nuyorican, Diasporican, Ricanness

The relationship between the island population and Puerto Ricans outside of the national territory has long been fraught with hierarchical power dynamics and by antagonisms. Informed by dominant narratives that always already defined those in the diaspora and in New York, the oldest diasporic community since the 1920s, as never Puerto Rican enough, as not pure members of the nation, as not fully Puerto Rican, these exclusions from national belonging have been made possible by the imposition of social constructs regarding authenticity and purity—measured in one's fluency in Spanish, years living outside the island, and other cultural practices such as cooking, music, and dance. Ultimately, after decades of a continuing and increasing migration from the island to the United States, these exclusions are beginning to shift.

If the Nuyorican subject has been, historically, an abject identity for those residing on the island, by 2020 Puerto Ricans were redefined as a "pueblo diaspórico" [diasporic people] (Ayala 2020). The term *Diasporican* was coined as early as 1993 by Nuyorican spoken-word poet Mariposa Fernández in her poem "Ode to the Diasporican," as it acknowledges the larger diasporas that have become home to many Puerto Ricans, even outside of New York.[7] The fact that Orlando, Florida, now has the largest Puerto Rican community outside of the island, and that there are Puerto Rican families living in Alaska, Oregon, and California, in addition to the more established East Coast and Midwest communities, makes the term *Diasporican* much more relevant than *Nuyorican* by decentering New York as the primary destination for all Boricuas. After decades of Rican activists and academics advocating for the public recognition of other settled communities outside of New York, the concept of the Diasporican has expanded to refer to all Puerto Ricans who reside outside of the island.

Shifting data reveal the changing demographics of both the island and the diaspora, as they also signal a markedly evident transformation of attitudes toward those displaced Puerto Ricans. César Ayala (2020) succinctly summarizes these changes, noting that by 2018 two-thirds of Puerto Ricans lived outside the island, while only one-third still resided in the national territory. The hegemony long held by island residents over defining puertorriqueñidad has decreased significantly, as 64 percent of Puerto Ricans now live in the continental United States. This increased migration has been fueled by a violent colonial history of labor contracts and economic pulls (Operation Bootstrap is just one example of a governmental program that prioritized industrialization over agriculture in the name of American progress yet displaced hundreds of farmers), by natural disasters such as hurricanes that have triggered the relocations of environmental refugees, and by political changes such as the revoking of Section 936, which destroyed the long-term presence of manufacturing on the island. What is more, la Deuda, the financial crisis that has led to draconian austerity measures for island residents, has continued to grow as many more middle-class and professional Puerto Ricans have departed for the United States. At a time when the financial crisis has destroyed numerous businesses and communities on the island after Hurricanes Irma and María in 2017 and with the COVID-19 pandemic in 2020, Puerto Ricans feel they have no choice but to escape the precarious conditions on the island and to survive

---

7. While "Ode to the Diasporican" was first performed in 1993, it appeared published in June 1994 in a special centerfold of *New York Newsday* edited by Pedro Pietri commemorating the Puerto Rican Day Parade. See Fernández (n.d.) for the poem and Pérez Rosario (2014) for additional information on Fernández.

somewhere else. The strategic colonial occupation of the island by the Anglo elite and millionaires, facilitated by Act 22, which allows them tax-free real estate, is accompanied by the bleeding of Puerto Rican professionals, middle-class families, and the working class into Florida, Texas, and other states. In contrast to the last four decades of the twentieth century, it may not be far-fetched to assume that by now, all Puerto Ricans on the island are related to, or affiliated with, families and individuals in the diaspora.

Since the large return migration of New York Puerto Ricans to the island in the 1970s, the formerly negative attitudes that long pathologized Nuyoricans beginning with their displacements in the 1940s have begun to subside, although there are still lingering and problematic constructs regarding the Nuyorican identity as stereotypical. If, as Jorge Duany (2002) documents, Nuyoricans were earlier defined as residing outside the national territory (28) and as "hybrid, dangerous and contaminated outsiders" (29), today the growing Puerto Rican diaspora has strengthened their political power and played a major role in advocating for their conationals on the island. They have protested the Puerto Rico Oversight, Management, and Economic Stability Act (PROMESA) of 2016 and denounced the creation of the fiscal control board that now governs Puerto Rican government financial decisions. They also created impressive networks of support right after Hurricane María and donated major funding for recovery efforts on the island, not to mention the earlier mobilizations for the demilitarization of the island of Vieques in the early 2000s, and the eventual liberation of the Puerto Rican political prisoners, among other forms of mobilizations. In 2021 US Puerto Rican Congresspeople Nydia Velázquez, Alexandria Ocasio-Cortes, and others introduced a self-determination bill to Congress that would allow residents of the island to determine their own political status. When eminent figures such as island-based Puerto Rican visual artist Antonio Martorell have commented that the diaspora and the island have bonded in unprecedented ways since Hurricane María, it suggests that those negative discourses and exclusions are beginning to change.[8]

The fact that the diaspora is demographically larger than the island population, a fact documented since 2006, leads us to question the established notions of the nation as bound by territoriality.[9] As César Ayala (2020) shares,

---

8. Antonio Martorell, personal conversation with author, July 2018.

9. See Jorge Duany's "'May God Take Me to Orlando'" (2020). This article traces the data of Puerto Ricans migrating to the three major regions of Florida where they have settled. It also documents the more privileged socioeconomic status of these migrants, which contrast with the working-class and working-poor families in earlier migration flows that settled in New York, Chicago, and Philadelphia.

questions such as the following are currently relevant for all Puerto Rican peoples: "¿Qué significa que dos terceras partes de los boricuas vivan fuera de la Isla?" [What does it mean that two-thirds of Boricuas live outside the island?]; "¿Qué impacto tiene sobre la Isla, y sus opciones de estatus político, el hecho demográfico de una mayoría Boricua en los cincuenta estados?" [What impact does this demographic fact—of a majority of Boricuas living in the fifty states—have over the island and on its options for a political status?]; and, finally, "¿Persistirá en Estados Unidos la identidad puertorriqueña?" [Will the Puerto Rican identity persist in the United States?]. These questions are critical for our continued understanding of the impact of migrations on our national identity. Yet they also tend to limit us to a discourse that presumes a unitary and homogeneous Puerto Rican identity and prioritizes the island over the displaced communities. Instead, I argue for the need to rethink the possibility of a plural mode of Puerto Rican identities marked by skin color, social class, gender politics and sexualities, regional locations, and generational identities. If Ayala seems more preoccupied with the impact of Diasporican communities on the island's political status, thus framing the PR diaspora as marginal to, yet at the service of, the island, here I would argue that the process of acknowledging the Diasporican subject allows us not only to question and unmoor the notions of nation as bound by territoriality but also to acknowledge the political power and cultural authorship that the diaspora has increasingly enacted. Since Lisa Sánchez-González (2001) argued in *Boricua Literature* that Nuyorican literature and the arts should not be defined as derivative of island cultures, we are still grappling in many ways with the validity and legitimacy accorded (or not) to the Nuyorican and Diasporican communities and to their social, cultural, artistic, and political agency and power.

Indisputably, the arts, literature, and popular music have played a major role in reaffirming, validating, and inscribing Nuyorican and other Diasporican identities in the public sphere. By now, fifty years since the Nuyorican Poets Café in the Lower East Side was founded in 1973, the artistic agency of Nuyoricans in the sphere of poetry and theater has finally begun to be legitimized as a new aesthetic (Algarín and Piñero 1975). The late Tato Laviera unearthed in his canonical poem "nuyorican" (2003) the political projects and goals behind the forced migration of its working poor families, but he also denounced the measures of authenticity that marked those outside the island as not fully Puerto Rican given their cultural hybridity, their use of English and Spanglish, and their subordinated social status. Poet Mariposa echoes Laviera's celebration and reaffirmation of the Nuyorican when she writes in her "Ode to the Diasporican" that "being Boricua is a state of mind / a state of heart / a state of soul" (Fernández, n.d.), rewriting the geography-based hierarchy as affect and thus undermining its legal and political boundaries.

The fact that social-class differences and classism have long informed the abjection of Nuyorican subjects by middle-class and professional island sectors continues to be pertinent. Let us recall Rosario Ferré (1991), the late renowned feminist writer from the island who described the loss of Spanish among US Puerto Rican working-class families as "cultural suicide," a harsh judgment that exposed the upper-class attitudes of islanders against the working-poor families forced to leave and that ironically blamed colonized and racialized families for the processes of dispossession initiated by US social institutions. Contesting these dominant discourses against Nuyoricans, salsa music, born in the streets of el Bronx in the late 1960s and early 1970s, constitutes another central artistic practice that has afforded national, hemispheric, and global visibility to the New York Puerto Rican experience while also reaffirming the translocal Caribbeanness of its musical flows. Since the pioneering and foundational recordings of Willie Colón and Héctor Lavoe, the sounds of salsa have denounced the racial, economic, cultural, and social forms of subordination that Nuyoricans have faced since their early years in New York. As a musical tradition steeped in working-poor, Afro-Caribbean male social experiences, this rich sonic tradition has been responsible for reclaiming the historical presence and the cultural authority of the Nuyorican community in a global context. Thus, literature, popular music, and the visual and performative arts have all served as foundational discourses and symbolic practices that have transformed the Nuyorican subject from its original abjection to one endowed with cultural, social, political, and artistic agency.

Boricua performance studies scholar Sandra Ruiz has proposed the critical concept of "Ricanness" as a term that pays less attention to geographical location, residence, or place of birth and instead centers its critical power on the conditions of resilience that all Puerto Ricans have developed as colonial subjects. For Ruiz, "Ricanness is animated by acts of political and aesthetic endurance," constituted by "those moments of staying power in the face of cultural, personal, and national subjection" (2019, 10). At a historical moment where both Diasporicans and island Puerto Ricans have faced "displacement, relocation and dispossession" (9) after Hurricanes Irma and María in 2017; the ongoing seismic activity in the southwestern region of the island, which has left numerous families sleeping on the streets; and the more recent COVID-19 pandemic, which has taken the lives of many Latinx and Diasporican essential workers and their families, Ruiz's concept of Ricanness suggests that our national imaginary should be less rooted in territories and geographies and more in the potential of aesthetics within political gestures and actions that reveal our long and consistently contested struggles against colonial violence.

As a second-generation, New York–born Puerto Rican singer, Marc Anthony's performances, repertoire, arrangements, and voice assume cultural, social, racial, and national meanings within this longer discursive history about the Nuyorican. The powerful meanings and the strong affective energy that Marc Anthony's performances of "Preciosa" carry for his listeners demand such historicizing and position Marc Anthony as a central voice in the reclaiming of Nuyorican and the legitimizing of Diasporican subjectivities within the larger Puerto Rican national imaginaries.

El Jibarito and the Nuyorican (Rafael and El Marc)

When I asked Alejandro Chalí Hernández, Rafael Hernández's youngest son, about the possibility of considering his father as part of a foundational generation of Nuyoricans, Chalí immediately shook his head no, clarifying that his father would never have identified as a "Nuyorican." Revealing the lingering negative associations of the term as a derogatory and subordinate status for Puerto Ricans outside the island, Chalí's refusal to even consider his father as perhaps a pioneering or proto-Nuyorican attests to the disavowals and boundaries that still linger in the national imaginaries of middle-class islanders. While recognizing the anxieties still evident among island Puerto Ricans regarding Nuyorican as abject, and yet respecting the opinions of the Hernández family, here I propose a historical continuity, a sort of alternative genealogy, that connects the Black Puerto Rican composer Rafael Hernández with Marc Anthony, who was born in 1968, thirty years after Hernández composed "Preciosa" in Mexico in 1937.

Thus, my critical analysis of the song and its multiple iterations reveals that the nation resides in the experience of displacement, just like Hernández in New York and Mexico, and Marc Anthony singing from New York to the world. When Marc Anthony pays homage to Rafael Hernández in the concluding verses of the song and refers to him as "ese noble jíbarito Rafael" [that noble country fellow Rafael], he proposes a long tradition of Puerto Rican music-making and singing that connects the Nuyorican Marc to the Black Puerto Rican composer Don Rafael Hernández, better known, ironically, as "el Jíbarito."[10] The fact that el Marc has repeatedly sung "Preciosa" in major Boricua urban centers across the Americas, most poignantly in New York, Chicago, Orlando, and in San Juan, Puerto Rico, evinces how songs can be, in the process of globalization, recanonized and reinvigorated with new

---

10. I note the irony of this epithet since the jíbaro figure has been the embodiment of a Creole-based whiteness in Puerto Rico, an identity that erases Rafael Hernández's Blackness. I will address the racial dilemmas that Hernández faced in the following sections of this chapter.

meanings and new listening audiences throughout history. This reiteration, across time, allows for an ongoing relevance of a song that has, since its early performances after 1937, been affectively and politically associated with the love for the nation of Puerto Rico and that triggers such love during times of crisis. As Alejandro Chalí Hernández commented, "tanto 'Preciosa' como 'El Lamento Borincano' toman vigencia en diferentes momentos históricos en Puerto Rico" [both songs, "Preciosa" and "El Lamento Borincano," become relevant during different historical moments in Puerto Rico].[11] These historical moments include, among others, the mobilization against the US Navy occupation of Vieques in 2000, the fundraisers after the devastation caused by Hurricanes Irma and María in 2017, and the 2019 mobilization that removed then Governor Ricardo Rosselló from office (Collado Schwarz 2008). The song, long deemed a patriotic text, also voices a nostalgia for the patria that can be most felt outside, in displacement, in the nomadism and migratory flows that have been fueled not only by the imperial political economy that has displaced workers and laborers on the island since the 1940s but also by the dreams of artists like Rafael Hernández, who left the island in search of better opportunities. If Hernández's sister, Victoria, "maintained that her brother was the first Latino to sound a Latin musical note in New York in 1919, when his trio performed at a house party" (Salazar 2002, chap. 1), Rafael's compositions, singing, and performances pioneered the long and rich history of Puerto Rican music-making in and from New York.[12] In addition, as Cristóbal Díaz Ayala writes, Rafael Hernández transformed the traditional Cuban bolero from exclusively romantic songs to a bolero that enunciates his love for the country: "Es posiblemente Rafael el que primero siente que su público pide algo más que el simple tema amoroso; que hay que hablar de la patria" [Possibly, Rafael was the first one who sensed that his listening audience asked for more than the love theme; that he had to sing to his country] (2009, 54).[13] As the late Vanessa Knights reiterated, "with Hernández, the bolero returns to its origins in the traditional Cuban trova whose songs were often dedicated to the fatherland (Patria) or to political figures" (2008, 396). The fact that

---

11. Alejandro Chalí Hernández, interview with the author, Interamerican University, San Juan, Puerto Rico, February 19, 2020.

12. In the early years of the emerging Puerto Rican and Latinx community in New York, house parties became the sites for these initial Puerto Rican and Cuban musical performances. Max Salazar described house parties in Latinx New York as follows: "Cubans and Puerto Ricans who were unemployed raised rent and food money by holding dances in their apartments. The entrance fee was twenty-five cents. Musicians were paid with the money earned from the sale of beer, maví, pastelillos, alcapurrias, and pasteles" (2002, chap. 1).

13. I thank Omar Ruiz Vega for the reference to Cristobal Díaz Ayala's book, which he shared with me as well.

younger Puerto Ricans on the island have erroneously credited Marc Anthony as composer of "Preciosa"[14] also signals the powerful role that the Nuyorican salsa singer has had in maintaining the song's relevance and vigor across younger generations of listeners, thus transforming it into a political anthem.

Rafael Hernández, the most renowned Puerto Rican composer of all times, authored over two thousand songs, including boleros, guarachas, danzas, and classical music, and his songs circulated throughout the Americas. Most notably, he embodied the itinerant musician as he traveled and lived in France, Cuba, Mexico, and New York. Born in Aguadilla, Puerto Rico, on October 24, 1891, in his youth he learned to play the violin, the cornet, and later the trombone and the bombardino (euphonium). Like many other young Afro–Puerto Rican men with musical talent, he was able to perform mostly in bandas or musical youth bands during a time when there were very limited, if any, opportunities for musical training and no infrastructure that allowed them visibility and, ultimately, fame.[15] In fact, Hernández played the trombone in the Orquesta de Paco Tizol, an ensemble made up of eleven musicians, of whom seven were Black or mulatto (Allende-Goitía 2014, 279). For two years, between 1910 and 1912, Hernández toured the island of Puerto Rico with a Japanese circus. He then moved to Puerta de Tierra in San Juan, where he joined the Banda Municipal. James Reese Europe, who was in Puerto Rico recruiting musicians for his military band of the 369th Regiment, invited Rafael and his brother Jesús to join this ensemble, also known as the Harlem Hellfighters. They both traveled to France and Europe, but not before doing military training in North Carolina, where Rafael experienced the brutality of racism in the Jim Crow segregated South. As Juan F. Correa-Luna (2020) writes, they were "víctimas de muchos ataques físicos y abusos verbales raciales" [victims

---

14. Alejandro Chalí Hernández, interview with the author, Interamerican University, San Juan, Puerto Rico, February 19, 2020.

15. As Noel Allende-Goitía documents, in 1911 Rafael Hernández played in the Banda Municipal de Aguadilla "bajo la dirección de José Ruellán Lequerica," a bandleader well known for "recoger en su casa y en su banda a niños pobres" [sheltering and saving poor children in his home and band] (2014, 247). These bands, according to Allende-Goitía, constituted the infrastructure for musical education at the time, as they became the "centro de formación de músicos" [center for the formation of musicians] and the

> máquina en la que se forjan y desarrollan prácticas de ejecución y una literatura musical que para todo fin práctico forman el capital de conocimiento musical de intérpretes y compositores y fijan preferencias por formas y géneros musicales y formaciones instrumentales particulares.
>
> [machine in which musical execution and a musical corpus is developed, all of which for practical purposes constitute the capital of musical knowledge of interpreters and composers and it establishes preferred forms and musical genres, and specific instrumental formations]. (266–67)

of many physical attacks as well as racial verbal abuse] in the US South.[16] As has been written but perhaps not remembered enough, James Reese Europe's band introduced jazz to European listening communities, a historic contribution that situates Rafael Hernández at the center of African American music-making during World War I and as a central actor in the early globalization of jazz.[17] Moreover, it also positioned him as a Black male body who faced segregation and discrimination in the army, a racialization that must have had an imprint on his psyche.[18] Yet, despite these traumatic experiences, he managed to become a sergeant in France, where he received the Croix de Guerre, never shot a gun, helped to heal the wounded, and played concerts.[19] Upon his return to the United States, he stayed in New York playing in jazz bands and working in a factory, where he lost a finger in an accident (Glasser 1995). From 1920 to 1925, Hernández traveled to Cuba to work in theaters, playing in the orchestras that accompanied the silent films of teatro bufo (buffo theater, like guarachas). In 1925, he returned to New York City, where he worked with Manuel Jiménez ("El Canario") as well as Trío Borinquen, Cuarteto Victoria, and other ensembles made up of Cuban and Puerto Rican musicians. These are the years described as "bohemios" by scholars and historians, for Hernández shared late nights of bohemian life with then young Luis Muñoz Marín, Pedro Flores, and Luis Lloréns Torres (Glasser 1995). During these years, Hernández (see fig. 1.1) composed the classic song "Lamento Borincano," an homage to the Puerto Rican jíbaro during the Depression years.

---

16. Correa-Luna notes that the 369th Regiment distinguished themselves in the war front for more than 191 days, longer than any other US military unit, for which they received the French Croix de Guerre.

17. As Elena Martínez (2015) writes,

> Rafael Hernández was recruited into Europe's 369th Regiment band as a trombone player and became a sergeant during World War I. Other musicians who were recruited from Puerto Rico included Rafael Duchesne Mondríguez from Fajardo, who played first clarinet, and Rafael Hernández's brother Jesús. Hernández and the others went to North Carolina for basic training. Europe's 369th Regiment, which became known as the "Hellfighters," was considered to have introduced jazz to the European continent. They gained the nickname during their tour of duty for their bravery on the battlefield. After the war the 369th US Infantry band began recording for the Pathé label and toured briefly until James Reese Europe was tragically murdered after a concert by his drummer. The group disbanded and the musicians had to strike out on their own." For more historical details on the numerous Puerto Rican musicians who performed during the early years of jazz, see Basilio Serrano. (2007)

18. Juan Correa-Luna states that this experience of racism in the United States clearly positioned Rafael Hernández against US imperialism and racism, and thus is expressed in the much-debated reference in "Preciosa" to the "tirano" as well as in the concluding verses referring to "los hijos de la libertad."

19. Interview with Alejandro Hernández, 2020.

FIGURE 1.1. Rafael Hernández professional portrait. Wikipedia / public domain.

Manuel Canario recorded the song even before Hernández had completed the composition. It is notable as well that "Lamento Borincano" appears in Guillermo Cotto-Thorner's 1951 novel *Trópico en Manhattan* as a reference to the common experience of economic struggles that Puerto Ricans faced both on the island and in New York ([1951] 2019, 15).[20]

In 1932 a Puerto Rican entrepreneur invited Rafael to work in Mexico, sponsored by Laboratorios Picot, a manufacturing company that produced Sales Picot, similar to today's Alka-Seltzer. What initially was a three-month contract turned into fifteen years of residency in Mexico City. There, Rafael married María Pérez in 1940, with whom he had four sons (Alejandro, the youngest, was born in Puerto Rico). During his fifteen years in Mexico, Hernández worked assiduously composing, conducting orchestras, and performing for film and radio during Mexico's golden age of film. He was known

---

20. *Trópico en Manhattan* was translated into English by J. Bret Maney and published by Arte Público Press as part of the Recovering the US Hispanic Literary Heritage initiative. The English translation, titled *Manhattan Tropics,* includes an introduction by Cristina Pérez Jiménez (Cotto-Thorner [1951] 2019).

as "el jíbaro mexicano" and was frequently confused for Mexican or Cuban. His song dedicated to Puebla, "Qué Chula es Puebla," has become the city's official anthem and is performed every May 5 in the region. Not all Mexicans know that a Puerto Rican composer wrote their song, yet this fact unveils the very transcultural Mexicanization that Hernández experienced. He also completed a master's degree in harmony, counterpoint, and conducting at the Conservatorio Nacional de Música. His thesis was "Danza Capricho #7," an example of one of his many but less well-known incursions into classical music. He arranged music for the Orquesta Sinfónica de Oaxaca, among others.

In 1947 he returned to Puerto Rico on tour with the Revista de Artistas Mexicanos, evincing the transnational exchanges between Mexico, Puerto Rico, and Cuba that led to what ethnomusicologists have recently framed as the transcultural sounds of the circum-Caribbean.[21] His long-term friend, Luis Muñoz Marín, then governor of Puerto Rico, convinced Rafael to stay in Puerto Rico and offered him work at WIPR, the public television channel, an offer fueled by the official government's national campaign to "rescue" and bring home émigré Puerto Rican artists. Back in Puerto Rico, Hernández composed children's songs and classical music for piano while he became manager of a Little League baseball team on which his sons played.

Rafael Hernández died of cancer on December 11, 1965. Having composed over two thousand songs, he remains the most renowned and loved composer among all Puerto Ricans. Today his youngest son, Alejandro Chalí Hernández, manages his father's archive and permanent exhibit in the Sala Museo Rafael Hernández at the Universidad Interamericana Metropolitan Campus in San Juan, Puerto Rico.

This brief biographical summary of Rafael Hernández illustrates the imperative that Puerto Rican, and Black, musicians felt to move in search of better professional opportunities. Indeed, his formative and most productive years as a composer and musician were fueled by his travels to Europe and later his circulation among New York, Puerto Rico, Cuba, and Mexico.[22] Given the central function of Puerto Rican popular music as a site for engaging the colonial displacements and the itinerancies of our communities, the

---

21. Alejandro Madrid and Robin Moore (2013, 15–17) propose a rethinking of the term "transnationalism" as it is used loosely as a synonym of border-crossing. They analyze the danzón as it articulates "notions of space and circulation implied in the term 'circum-Caribbean,' a geocultural region that encompasses the West Indies, the northern coast of South America, the Florida and Yucatan peninsulas, as well as New Orleans and Veracruz" (17).

22. Alejandro Chalí Hernández, interview with the author, Interamerican University, San Juan, Puerto Rico, February 19, 2020.

connection between Rafael Hernández and Marc Anthony as composers and interpreters of sounds of itinerancy is not fortuitous.

It is no coincidence, then, that Marc Anthony is featured singing both "Preciosa" and "Lamento Borincano" in the 1998 edition of Banco Popular de Puerto Rico's annual holiday cultural video, which paid homage to Rafael Hernández. Marc Anthony's inclusion in *Romance del Cumbanchero* strategically marks him as a metonym for the thousands of Puerto Ricans who, like Marc Anthony's own parents, had left the island since the 1940s and moved to New York for better opportunities. In the video, Gilberto Santa Rosa and Ednita Nazario, two renowned singers from the island, converse with Marc Anthony, who was less known in Puerto Rico than his two interlocutors and speaks to the affective consequences of displacement. The video thus initiates the public conflation of and associations between Rafael Hernández and Marc Anthony.

As Arlene Dávila (1997) has claimed, the Banco Popular de Puerto Rico cultural videos, produced for years every holiday season, for las Navidades, constitute meaningful cultural interventions that exemplify what she calls "sponsored identities," that is, cultural productions that stem from the neoliberal and capitalist interests of private corporations and illustrate the increasing power of corporations in defining and redefining the paradigms of cultural and national identity on the island. These musical, historical, and cultural videos have gradually contributed to the legitimation of Puerto Rican musical traditions, styles, and singers as well as to the inclusion of Puerto Rican migrants as members of the nation.

Romance del Cumbanchero is a meaningful text that performs the sounds of itinerancy. The conversation among Gilberto Santa Rosa, Ednita Nazario, and Marc Anthony, which frames the production, also structures these performers *as listeners* and as an ideal audience to the various interpretations in the video. As the only Nuyorican, Marc Anthony stands out as different from his island-based interlocutors, for he embodies the displaced Puerto Rican community, the Nuyorican abjects, the Diasporicans of today. After watching the footage of Rafael Hernández's funeral in 1965, Marc Anthony poignantly comments:

cómo él [Rafael Hernández] describe que el amor que él siente por su patria, uno tiene que estar lejos, y yo entiendo exactamente lo que él escribe en esa canción ["Preciosa"]. . . . Cuando yo me senté por primera vez y leí la letra lo oí, me mató, me siento en cantar esa canción mi declaración de amor a mi patria, y cuando joven ni sabía que existía esa clase de amor.

[just like he (Rafael Hernández) described the love he felt for his home country, one has to be far away, and I understand exactly what he writes in this song ("Preciosa"). . . . When I sat and listened to the lyrics for the first time, it killed me, while singing that song I feel my declaration of love to my country, and when I was young I had no idea that that kind of love existed.]

These comments regarding the love for the nation, one's bond and affective, nostalgic connection to the homeland, are fascinating in the ways that their wording—"me mató" [it killed me]—echo the dynamics of the singer as listener present in "Killing Me Softly With His Song." They also preface Marc Anthony's own interpretation of "Preciosa," one that inaugurates in the Banco Popular video the innumerable iterations of the song that will characterize Marc Anthony's concerts for future decades. If, as he stated, "la música de Rafael Hernández es para siempre" [Rafael Hernández's music is forever], his own renderings have been responsible for facilitating such immortality by voicing and interpreting this canonical song to many younger listening audiences, both in Puerto Rico and all over the Americas. Most notably, his statement about distance from home as a prerequisite for feeling that patriotic love—"uno tiene que estar lejos" [one has to be far away]—inscribes the centrality of displaced communities, the Nuyoricans and Diasporicans, as the site from which Puerto Ricans can love and, thus, acknowledge the nation and be acknowledged by it. For Marc Anthony, as a self-declared Nuyorican, this short phrase constitutes his reclaiming and legitimating gesture for belonging to the Puerto Rican nation, particularly within the setting of an island-based video production. As he commented, "Las canciones sobre Puerto Rico todas fueron escritas fuera de Puerto Rico y yo me identifico con eso" [All songs about Puerto Rico were composed outside the island and I identify with that].

Marc Anthony's statement also signals another major role: that of *listener*. In fact, he highlights the significance of the act of listening to "Preciosa" that triggered his reflection on the affective power of love for one's nation. As listener, Marc Anthony expands his repertoire and gradually transforms his earlier and perhaps more circumscribed relationship to the island as a New York–born, second-generation Diasporican, who rejected his parents' salsa music during his youth. Through the act of listening to "Preciosa," Marc Anthony reconnects to the analogous love for Puerto Rico that Hernández articulated in the lyrics and bolero sonorities of the song and that was profoundly rooted in the latter's personal experiences as an itinerant musician, as a racial exile who penned the song while far away from his country. As a listener of "Preciosa," Marc Anthony reclaims Puerto Rico the island as his native land, a political gesture and contestatory experience that, in the larger context of settler colonialism in Puerto Rico, resists the dominant imperial interventions of what Indigenous scholar Dylan Robinson (2020) has termed "the hungry listener." If, as Robinson suggests, "listening is perhaps always a listening through, or in relation to land" (53), then Marc Anthony's personal interpretations of "Preciosa," fueled by his own personal experience as a decolonial listener of Hernández, and throughout their numerous iterations, reveal the potential for this public act of sounding to serve as a "sovereign structure of performance" or, at least, as a form of exhortation to his listening audiences that invites us to a resurgent form of listening. This liberatory form of listening constitutes an instance of "sovereign reception" (Robinson 2020, 62–73), for it contests the more normative neoliberal modes of an extractive listening fueled by the settler-colonial drive to accumulate knowledge and appropriate cultures. Instead, Marc Anthony's political possibilities of his own performances of "Preciosa"—informed by affect, nostalgia, and love—cannot be separated from his own praxis of a decolonial "critical listening positionality" (Robinson 2020, 51) as he moves "beyond hungry listening toward anticolonial listening practices" that "require[s] that the 'fevered' pace of consumption for knowledge resources be placed aside in favor of new temporalities of wonder dis-oriented from antirelational and nonsituated settler colonial positions of certainty" (53).

For instance, in *Romance del Cumbanchero*, Marc's intervention, voice, and presence unsettle the dominant modes of reception exercised by the white elite sector in Puerto Rico. His presence is structured not only as a performer of Rafael Hernández but, most significantly, as a "guest listener" (Robinson 2020, 53) who shares the experience of displacement with the composer and is witness to his oeuvre. By suggesting that listening is also an act of witnessing, as the video clearly frames, Banco Popular's production may have inscribed the enduring values of Rafael Hernández's cultural meanings for all Puerto Ricans across generations and geographical locations. In a more nuanced and perhaps unplanned mode, framing Marc Anthony as also a listener-witness pushes us to rethink how singers (like Marc Anthony, Gilberto Santa Rosa, and Ednita Nazario) are also listeners who enter a "sound territory" (Robinson 2020, 53) and thus become witnesses of the sounds of their elders and their antecedents, musically speaking, and voices that create musical genealogies linking the past to the present.

"Preciosa," Race, and Blackness

The lyrics of "Preciosa," easily available on the internet, serve as an entryway into a critical discussion about the racial politics inscribed in the song. Despite what is a traditional approach to lyrics in particular, my discussion of two verses in the song will center on the racial ambiguity that Hernández deployed to accommodate to the racial politics of the 1930s in Puerto Rico while building on, and not risking, his own public image as a nationalist and a patriot.[23]

Given the composer's numerous departures and itinerancies to other countries, the question emerges regarding why he didn't remain in Puerto Rico during the 1930s and later. Why was "Preciosa" composed in Mexico City and not on the island? Would it have been composed at all if Hernández had not been in what perhaps we could describe as *a racial exile* from his homeland?[24] A review of the prevalent racial discourses in 1930s Puerto Rico that privileged whiteness suggests that he may have left not only to find better professional opportunities but also to escape the systematic and structural erasures of Blackness on the island at the time. The canonical essays of Antonio Pedreira (1942) and Tomás Blanco (1935), among others, became foundational in cementing and mainstreaming the social constructions of Puerto Rican cultural and racial identity as a benign mestizaje, reproducing the dominant enduring myths and false claims that there is no racism on the island given our mixed racial heritage. The traditional icon of the tripartite ethnicity—the Indigenous, the Spanish, and the African—has long served as a dominant discourse that privileges mestizaje as a tool for whitening. By situating the Black and the Indigenous exclusively as a root or influence bracketed in the past, the mainstream and racist reading of this tripartite icon (the Spanish, European, and White presence) continues unabated as the dominant racial, ethnic, and cultural identity among Puerto Ricans. It was during the 1930s that Puerto Ricans witnessed the debates about Blackness centered on the Afro-Antillean sounds and rhythms of poet Luis Palés Matos, an instance of how Puerto

---

23. When asked whether his father was a nationalist, Rafael Hernández's son Alejandro Chalí Hernández responded: "Sí, todos lo somos" [Yes, we all are]. He also added that, in 1947, students in Puerto Rico protested the fact that their composer was living abroad. Perhaps this was one of the factors that led to his father's permanent return to the island that year (Collado Schwarz 2008).

24. Here I deploy the term "racial exile" based on the discussions about exile and diaspora proposed by Hamid Naficy, in which he affirms how the term "exile" has been transformed "from a strictly political expulsion and banishment to a more nuanced, culturally driven displacement" (2001, 9). Naficy argues that "diaspora, exile and ethnicity" are no longer clearly segmented states but, rather, "fluid." He highlights the collective memory and the idealized homeland that frame diasporic and exilic identities, while arguing that "this idealization may be state-based involving love for an existing homeland, or it may be stateless, based on a desire for a homeland yet to come" (2001, 14). This merging of exile and diaspora, indeed, can be easily applied to displaced Puerto Ricans who long for the lost island territory as much as they hope for an increasingly autonomous nation in the future. See also John Durham Peters's chapter "Exile, Nomadism and Diaspora" (pp. 17–41 in Naficy 1999) for a clearer differentiation and tracing of exile, diaspora, and nomadism in Western literature and arts.

Rican Creole white writers "invented to represent something they thought of as black speech" and "strongly suggest a hysterical rendition of the black subject" (Allende-Goitía 2014, 82–83). As Noel Allende-Goitía summarizes the 1930s,

> Lo negroide como valor humano y la negritud como construcción de un ideario e identificación positiva del ser son conceptos problemáticos para los letrados de esta generación y presentan la dificultad que tiene la sociedad letrada puertorriqueña de la década de 1930 de identificar la negritud, lo africano, como parte distinguible y característica de sí misma.

> [Blackness as a human value and being Black as an ideal and positive identification of the self are problematic concepts for the elite and lettered sectors of this generation and they reveal the difficulty that the Puerto Rican intellectual society of the 1930s had of identifying Blackness, the African, as a distinguishable part and a characteristic in itself.] (217)

Within this social, political, and racial construction of puertorriqueñidad, how do we understand the racial erasures that Hernández faced as an Afro–Puerto Rican musician?

Hernández composed popular music based on rhythms associated with Blackness and its concomitantly constructed African origin in "primitivism," and he also composed classical pieces for piano, arranged for symphony orchestras, and contributed to a classical corpus and canon as well. Another Black Puerto Rican figure in the music industry at the time, Ruth Fernández, grappled with mediating her repertoire through "semiclassical" styles (Fiol-Matta 2017, 78) and performed her Blackness as "acousmatic," that is, tamed, veiled, and framed as music for listening and not for dancing (84–85). Rafael Hernández and his vast repertoire evince these very same racial dilemmas and negotiations through sonic categories and valorations. Hernández's in-betweenness, as a composer who straddled the world of Eurocentric classical structures of sounds for the white elite, and the mass popularity of his most recognizable songs and melodies may be explained precisely by his putative awareness of the discursive narratives around sounds and rhythms and their categorical evaluations prevalent at the time. If, in 1937, writer Erasto Arjona Siaca described the most well-known composer of danzas, Juan Morel Campos, as a "prócer" [noble leader] while erasing his identity as a mulatto and as an artisanal laborer, what would he have written about Rafael Hernández? When Hernández was composing "Preciosa" in Mexico City, the lettered elite thinkers on the island—Antonio Pedreira, Tomás Blanco, and Arjona

Siaca—were publicly expressing their anxiety over the creolization of European dance forms such as "la danza" (Aparicio 1998). Allende-Goitía echoes the language of Arjona Siaca as he refers to the "contemporary Antillean popular music" in terms of its "tendencia degenerativa" [degenerative tendency], "degeneración musical" [musical degeneration], and "tendencia mórbida" [morbid tendency], evaluative ascriptions that equate the syncopated rhythms of the bolero-son and of the danzón with the "gregarismo de la masa" [gregarious masses] and with an "africanización de la música" [Africanization of the music] (2014, 185). As Allende-Goitía wrote, "Dentro de una sociedad que inhibía la exteriorización de expresiones abiertamente negras, africanas, la vigilia tenía que ser constante" [In a society that repressed any openly outward expression of Blackness and of Africanity, the vigil had to be constant] (292). This was the world that Hernández escaped as he searched for better professional opportunities.

Within this racial and social context of public anxiety over the "contamination" of white musical structures and dance forms, we can better understand, engage, and reflect on Rafael Hernández's own controversial racial erasure of Blacks in Puerto Rico, as his "Preciosa" verses sing: "Y tienes la noble hidalguía / De la madre España / Y el fiero cantío del indio bravío / Lo tienes también" [And you have the noble chivalry / of our Mother Spain / And the fiery song of the brave Indian / You also possess]. This erasure of Puerto Rican Blackness within the official tripartite Puerto Rican cultural paradigm glaringly essentializes Spain as nobility and the Indigenous communities, the Taínos, as brave and courageous, traits that can easily slip into egregious Eurocentric constructions of civilization versus savagery. These lyrics reveal that Hernández, as a man of his times, had to negotiate these dominant racial discourses in his songs. Does he conform to the systematic erasure of Blackness in the national Puerto Rican imaginary of the times? Should he be deemed as one of many "cantautores negros [que] legitiman el discrimen y caen en la autodiscriminación" (Choco Orta, quoted in Abadía-Rexach 2012, 18)? While Hernández assumes a safe racial language for his times, it is imperative to understand that songs, like other cultural texts, are open to multiple significations and rewritings.

In this vein, Afro–Puerto Rican singer and performer Choco Orta offers us an alternative explanation to this problematic erasure in "Preciosa." She reads this as a possible inscription of the belief that there are ethnic differences among Puerto Ricans, but no racial ones:

> si él [Rafael Hernández] hizo una exclusión, sacó de contexto, al resaltar, significar, reseñar nuestra negritud en esta canción que se convirtió eventualmente en otro himno nacional, "Preciosa," pues yo no lo puedo a él señalar

por el hecho de que no haya incluido nuestro grupo étnico porque raza es solo una.

[if he (Rafael Hernández) excluded and decontextualized, by highlighting, giving meaning, and reviewing our Blackness in this song that eventually became another national hymn, "Preciosa," well, then I cannot accuse him of not having included our ethnic group because there is only one race]. (quoted in Abadía-Rexach 2012, 49)

Orta's quote is meaningful as it attempts to grapple with this contradictory and controversial erasure of Blackness by an Afro–Puerto Rican composer. For her, this exclusion can be read, a posteriori, as either the result of an ideology of color blindness or by a more current scientific knowledge that has concluded that there are no genetic differences among the so-called racial groups. Rather than assume that Hernández has internalized racism, and informed by Choco Orta's reflection, I would conclude that in his songs, particularly in these verses from "Preciosa," he discursively negotiates race through racial ambiguity, or through "acousmatic blackness," as Fiol-Matta (2017) has suggested in her brilliant analysis of Ruth Fernández.[25]

Unsurprisingly, Rafael Hernández's own Blackness has also been long erased in Puerto Rican public discourse, a discursive deletion that facilitates his status as a national icon through sanitizing strategies. In 1939 Margot Arce published an article titled "Puerto Rico en las canciones de Rafael Hernández" in the first volume of the journal *Isla* (Allende-Goitía 2014, 215), and its language equally silences the composer's Blackness. Allende-Goitía remarks:

Aunque el silencio sobre la negritud de Rafael Hernández es ensordecedor, la realidad de que la producción musical de un afropuertorriqueño sea identificada como "tan nuestras," y que en ellas "canta el corazón de toda la América Latina," no deja de atraer la atención al hecho de cómo la existencia se impone al hecho discursivo.

[Although the silencing of Rafael Hernández's Blackness is deafening, the fact that the musical work of an Afro–Puerto Rican is identified as "ours"

---

25. In *The Great Woman Singer: Gender and Voice in Puerto Rican Music* (2017), Licia Fiol-Matta examines the mechanisms, rhetoric, and sonic and rhythmic negotiations that Ruth Fernández deployed in order to be accepted, as a Black female performing body and voice, by white elite listening audiences. To escape being racialized as an Afro–Puerto Rican singer who only sang Black popular genres like bombas and plenas, Fernández performed a diverse gamut of musical styles, even when she found herself serving as the authenticating Black body on Caribbean stages.

and that in his songs "the heart of all Latin America sings," does not distract us from the ways in which the existence overwhelms the discourse.] (215)

In his critical reading of Arce's celebratory yet racist comments about Rafael Hernández, Allende-Goitía highlights the Eurocentric discourse that naturalizes the power of European civilization to assimilate and absorb the Indigenous and Black sectors, both of whom are required to "abandon their culture" to be embraced and accepted by the mainstream (2014, 216–17). When Arce writes that Hernández's music is the "voz de su propio corazón y allí (en su música) se mira como en un espejo" [the voice of his own heart and his music serves as a mirror to himself] (215), in reference to all of Puerto Rico, she proposes that Hernández, as an Afro–Puerto Rican subject, becomes a symbol of all Puerto Rico. Thus, as Allende-Goitía lucidly indicates, Arce naturalizes, homologizes, and essentializes puertorriqueñidad from the prism of Eurocentric whiteness (215). It therefore makes sense that Hernández would be referred to by the Puerto Rican elite as "el jibarito," a figure whose own racial and social construction and appropriation by the Creoles remits us to a complex web of ideologies and social projects for national and racial identities (Scarano 1996). Given the white iconicity of national images of the jíbaro in Puerto Rico, this epithet erases his Blackness and makes him palatable and safe enough to be embraced by all social and racial sectors in Puerto Rico, most notably the white elites.

It is imperative to acknowledge the potential for the semantic transformations of a song such as "Preciosa" to identify and trace the shifting meanings of its performances. Performers like Choco Orta and Marc Anthony, among others, have reclaimed the Blackness erased in the lyrics of "Preciosa." Orta, who is a salsa singer, percussionist, actor, secretary, librarian, and teacher of drama and theater, and who is aware of the race and gender discrimination in the musical industry (Abadía-Rexach 2012, 88), rewrites the lyrics when she performs "Preciosa." She replaces "no importa el tirano te trate con negra maldad" [no matter if the tyrant treats you with Black malice] with "tanta maldad" [so much malice], thus avoiding the negative association between Black/negra and malice. She also has replaced "y tienes la noble hidalguía de la madre España y el fiero cantío del indio bravío lo tienes también" [you embody the noble chivalry of our mother Spain and the courageous song of the brave Indian you also hold] with "del negro taíno lo tienes también" [of the Black taíno you also hold]. As Abadía-Rexach explains, Choco Orta

> se detiene a analizar las letras de las canciones que interpreta y asume la responsabilidad de alterar los textos musicales que entiende excluyen a los

miembros de su etnia. Por tanto, en ocasiones, se lleva a cabo una colonización de las letras o bien se construye un nuevo texto, pues a través de la elusividad semántica Orta elimina, por un lado, e incluye, por el otro, la palabra "negro."

[stops to analyze the song lyrics that she interprets and she assumes the responsibility of altering the musical texts that, according to her understanding, exclude the members of her ethnicity. Thus, at times, there is a colonization of the lyrics or she writes a new text, as Orta eliminates, or includes, through a semantic elusiveness, the word "Black"]. (2012, 49)

This example illustrates the open-ended nature of all cultural texts, including songs and their lyrics, and highlights the potential for rewriting across temporalities.

Marc Anthony also transforms "Preciosa" as a bolero canción and participates in the dialogic texture around Blackness and Puerto Rican cultural and national identity through a different and less direct process, most notably, from his vantage point as a Nuyorican. He does so by reclaiming his Nuyorican abject subjectivity through the sonic traditions of salsa music, which are intimately intertwined with Puerto Rican Blackness. As Marisol Berríos-Miranda and Shannon Dudley (2008) have documented, the "musical geography" of Santurce, Puerto Rico, where beloved Black musician Rafael Cortijo and singer Ismael Rivera lived and which established the Black diasporic sounds of salsa music proper, was characterized by an Afro-Caribbean transnational and maroon community. Santurce—an urban barrio that was previously known as San Mateo de Cangrejos, Puerto Rico—would thus become a major center for the sonic and rhythmic traditions that Rafael Cortijo y su Combo and El Gran Combo de Puerto Rico and other salsa ensembles and musicians would later develop.[26] This longer history of a circum-Caribbean Black sonic tradition in Puerto Rico needs to be acknowledged as a major

---

26. In "El Gran Combo, Cortijo, and the Musical Geography of Cangrejos/Santurce, Puerto Rico," Marisol Berríos-Miranda and Shannon Dudley (2018) explore the rich hybrid sonic traditions that emerged in Santurce around the 1950s. These pan-Caribbean and Afro-diasporic sounds and rhythms were the result of

> 1) centuries of immigration from other islands that created a hybrid and inclusive musical culture in Cangrejos; and 2) 20th century economic developments that positioned Santurce at the crossroads of international entertainment, media, and labor migration. These flows of people and music constitute a "musical geography" that connects local neighborhoods and musicians in Santurce to transnational networks, and that locates Puerto Rico in Latin America as much as in the United States. (121)

precursor to salsa music-making in New York City. If a young Marc Anthony, who grew up in Spanish Harlem, would frequent the local clubs where African Americans and Puerto Ricans would gather and where the sounds of freestyle, house, R&B, and hip-hop informed his musical imagination later, his performances of "Preciosa," among many others, serve as a continuation of Afro rhythms and sounds in Puerto Rican popular music.[27] This antiracist framing disrupts the Black-white binary constructed by the ideologies of white supremacy that position US Latinx communities as mixed race, mestizos, or whitened.

Nuyoricans have grappled with Blackness in complicated ways. Historically, their social, racial, and political alliances and solidarities with their African American neighbors were publicly articulated during the civil rights struggles of the 1960s and 1970s, radical values that informed the political resonances of boogaloo and salsa music. As Felipe Luciano, a former Young Lords member, explains cultural nationalism, "We believed in the Black Arts Movement and declared that we hear, see, feel, and think differently from whites" (2024, 98). The movements for Puerto Rican studies in New York City that led to the establishment of departments and research centers in public universities in the 1970s succeeded because of the collaboration of these two racial communities. The salsa music produced during the 1960s and '70s powerfully articulated this alliance fostered by the shared values of the Black Arts Movement and its Nuyorican counterpart. The poetry of Tato Laviera, among other Nuyorican voices, stands out as a radical celebration of Blackness in Puerto Rican culture and music, not to mention among Nuyoricans themselves.

Yet Nuyoricans also grappled with the contradictions in how their ethnicity as Puerto Ricans differentiated them from African Americans in New York and tended to erase their dark skin color and their racial subordination. As Miriam Jiménez-Román has written about writer Piri Thomas, whose autobiographical *Down These Mean Streets* stands as one of the most sophisticated life stories of an Afro-Nuyorican, "[he was] stuck between the myth of racial

---

27. See David García (2006) for a historical documentation of the role of local clubs in El Barrio and the Bronx as social spaces that contributed to the "local music culture" of these neighborhoods. They constituted "a shared identity of community among dancers and musicians as well as a sense of cultural resistance to modern or Americanized mambo styles" (91). These local clubs offered African American, Puerto Rican, and Cuban dancers and listeners, mostly "skilled workers, and from middle to working-class backgrounds," a space where they could enjoy the mambo, as performed by Arsenio Rodríguez, for instance, away from the "internationalized" styles of the mambo as it was performed at the Palladium. This earlier history continues to play a major role during Marc Anthony's youth growing up in Spanish Harlem.

democracy with its implicit preference for mestizaje, and the reality of African descent and racism ... between the myth of race-free color blackness and the reality of white supremacy" (2001, 12; my translation).

The ethnoracial dilemma of Nuyorican subjectivities situates them both within and outside Blackness. As Nuyoricans returned to the island in the 1970s, islanders who had internalized the myth of racial democracy critiqued the newcomers' racial awareness as minorities in the United States who unsettled the whitening logics of the official Puerto Rican cultural identity and performed their Blackness in the public sphere, thus deploying Blackness as a political identity (Findlay 2012, 22; Jiménez-Román 2001, 11). The common experience of being "racialized" by mainstream institutions in the United States, whether by being denied their Blackness as Puerto Ricans (Findlay 2012, 32) or by being criminalized, marginalized, or exploited, placed "them on par with African Americans, with whom (in the Bronx in the 1960s) they lived, worked, studied and shared leisure time. In turn, this shared oppression could be the basis for a deep inter-racial solidarity" (Findlay 2012, 36). Marc Anthony's close collaboration with Afro-Nuyorican music producers like Sergio George and African American composers like Cory Rooney are extensions of these ties to Blackness that began in his childhood and youth in El Barrio and continue to inform his sonic engagement with Black sounds and rhythms.

The Nuyorican Montuno

As Christopher Small argues, "performance is for performers and for listeners, not for composers and certainly not for their works and not for musicologists either. The performer's obligation, in other words, is not to the composer (who is quite likely dead anyway and can make no protest) or to the work but to his own enjoyment and to that of his or her listeners, if there are any. The performer has the right to make any changes he or she feels like making in the work and to interpret the written or printed score any way he or she chooses" (1998, 217). Practicing the freedom of performers to transform the original song, the signature element of Marc Anthony's renderings of "Preciosa" is not only his vocal intensity and passion but his addition of the son and montuno. If the original constitutes a bolero canción, Marc Anthony rewrites the song by adding an upbeat salsa arrangement that functions as a concluding coda and that I would deem a Nuyorican montuno. Among its various definitions, *montuno* refers to the final section of the song, which is also distinguishable by its "faster, brasher, semi-improvised instrumental section" and by a piano ostinato figure constituted by a "repeated syncopated piano vamp, often with chromatic root movement."[28] The shift that marks the entry into the Nuyorican montuno is noted by the up-tempo, syncopated rhythms of the congas and percussion, which augment the sonic intensity of the previous guitar- and cuatro-led, trio-textured bolero and lead listeners into what sounds like an improvisatory son of strong affective power and a sonic space of current urban culture, in stark contrast to the lyrical nature of the original bolero song.

The coda or montuno profoundly restructures the sonic experience of the listening audience, which, during the bolero canción, travels back in time to the 1930s, 1940s, and 1950s, or relocates itself on the island. Instead, these added lyrics—"Preciosa te llevo dentro / Muy dentro de mi corazón" [Precious island I carry you in me / very deeply within my heart]—and rhythmic section transport Puerto Rican listeners to New York, to the early years of salsa dura, to the 1960s and 1970s, and to the Blackness of the working-poor Boricua families that had been displaced from the island since the 1940s. The salsa rhythms of the montuno remit us to the cultural agency of second-generation Boricuas, who articulated their racialized experiences as ethnic minorities in New York City, what we now refer to as "salsa dura" precisely because of the harsh brass instrumental sounds that articulated urban life.

The percussive syncopated rhythms of the Nuyorican montuno make audible this long history of racial solidarity and disavowal among Nuyoricans. Marc Anthony leads us into words that reclaim his puertorriqueñidad from the position of his love for his heritage: "porque lo llevo en la sangre / por herencia de mis padres" [for I carry it in my blood / by my parents' heritage]. Marc Anthony thus not only reclaims Blackness in his performances of "Preciosa" through the salsa brass instrumentation and rhythmic arrangements, he also reclaims the experiences of displacement, migration, and exile that constitutes puertorriqueñidad up to now. The fact that Ángel "Cucco" Peña, who resides on the island and is the musical director of *Romance del Cumbanchero*, penned and composed the lyrics to the Nuyorican montuno, is a fascinating factor that allows us to question the island/diaspora binary once more. If these lyrics articulate the affective energy and power of displaced Puerto Ricans toward the island as the nation, then what does it mean that they were composed by an island-based composer and musical producer? The collaboration between Marc Anthony, who is an interpreter of songs and not a composer, and Cucco Peña, a long-term collaborator, merits attention as a notable instance of the transnational exchange between musicians that unsettle the by now cemented binary of island versus the diaspora. In brief, these

---

28. Wikipedia, s.v. "montuno," https://en.wikipedia.org/wiki/Montuno.

collaborations unearth the complexities of identity and territoriality. While identity transcends territoriality, as the case of the displaced subjectivities illustrate, identity is already always embedded in the specificity of geographical spaces.

Returning to the racial politics of the 1930s on the island and revisiting the dominant racial discourses that framed Rafael Hernández's Blackness as erased, ambiguous, and, ultimately, negotiated are meaningful if not imperative interventions in understanding our current racial moment. The newly invigorated political interventions of Black Lives Matter activism in 2020, and the marches across the United States denouncing police brutality against Black males as modern forms of lynching and disposing of Black lives and of their humanity, connect the past with the present in my analysis. Puerto Rico's own racial discourses, which have consistently erased the presence of Afro–Puerto Rican people in a society that aspires to whiteness through its dominant Hispanophilia, have not disappeared. As Marisol Negrón (2024) brilliantly argues in *Made in NuyoRico,* the dominant co-optation and ensuing whitening of Puerto Rican salsa music became most evident in 1992, when then Puerto Rico Governor Rafael Hernández Colón sponsored a performance of El Gran Combo de Puerto Rico in the Puerto Rican Pavilion in Spain during the celebration of the five-hundredth anniversary of the "discovery of America." Negrón claims that salsa then was "deterritorialized from its Black, diasporic, poor, and working-class roots" and "became a receptacle for Puerto Rico's global nationalism" (172). While much has changed on the island because of the progressive activism of Afro-Boricua activists and educators, there are still profoundly entrenched racial attitudes and white privileges that resist these interventions. Ongoing debates and conflicts between elite white cisgender male intellectuals and Afro-Boricua queer women, for instance, are now publicly articulated through social media and have become sites for a more profound acknowledgment of the longevity of these racial discourses, painful reminders of the social marginality, colonial violence, and systematic invisibility that continue to dehumanize Afro-Boricuas. This small but necessary analysis of the racial dilemmas of Rafael Hernández, as articulated in "Preciosa," pushes us to understand the present in continuity with our past. Recent social media debates in Puerto Rico clearly illustrate the virulent racial and gender subordinations that linger in our society and call for the imperative of self-critical reflections as a nation regarding racial, gender, and class marginalizations.[29]

---

29. See Marissel Hernández Romero (2020) for a critical review of one such controversy.

Performing "Preciosa": Aesthetic Iterations, Anticolonial Interventions

Marc Anthony's contribution to the longevity of "Preciosa" is without question. That he is often erroneously thought to be its composer reveals, at the risk of Rafael Hernández's historical erasure, the direct connection that younger listeners have established between the Nuyorican singer and the song itself. Since the 1998 release of *Romance del Cumbanchero,* which cemented Marc Anthony's authority as the most influential singer of "Preciosa" among Puerto Ricans everywhere, his continuing tradition of singing "Preciosa" at concerts allows for the powerful possibility of unearthing the affective impact that the sounds, the embodied performances, and the listening audiences' participation have had on the ongoing national imaginaries of Puerto Rico and the sense of collective belonging and endurance critical in the face of the multiple crises that Puerto Ricans have experienced. If in *Romance del Cumbanchero* the younger Marc Anthony, dressed in a traditional vest that hearkens back to the early twentieth century, performs "Preciosa" with the official seriousness of an homage to Rafael Hernández and in a most deservedly proper and respectable performative style, he is already prefiguring, through the rhythmic movement of his hands and fists as he moves his hand near his heart as he sings "Yo te quiero, Puerto Rico" [I love you, Puerto Rico], the performative body movements that in the new millennium will become, in the face of critical adversities, even more powerfully suggestive. If the addition of the Nuyorican montuno has racially, geographically, and temporally transformed the significations of the original text, Marc Anthony's nationalism and patriotic fervor for the island and the nation became even more pronounced and meaningful on three occasions when he performed: in San Juan, in New York, and in 2017 during a fundraiser in the aftermath of Hurricanes Irma and María. In fact, a review of a 2005 concert at Madison Square Garden, in which Marc Anthony shared the stage with Chayanne and Alejandro Fernández, clearly noted the outstanding popularity of "Preciosa" among other songs in his repertoire: "But in this heavily Puerto Rican crowd, the climax may have come some moments before, when Mr. Anthony did his version of 'Preciosa.' It may have been the night's most popular love song, precisely because it's not about a woman: it's about a whole island, instead" (Sanneh 2005). The aesthetics of the song, as performed on various stages, cannot be separated from the performances themselves as instantiations of a political and anticolonial intervention that denounces the multiple crises facing Puerto Ricans, while reclaiming the artistic and cultural agency of the Diasporican subject.

As Alexandra T. Vázquez (2013) proposes in *Listening in Detail,* things that "you might first dismiss as idiosyncrasies" (19) in musical events may be significant as, to quote Vijay Iyer, "minute laborious acts that make up musical activity" (19) and that may lead to a "transformative exercise that enables performative relationships to music and writing" (19). For Vázquez, details could be "saludos, refusals, lyrics, arrangements, sounds, grunts, gestures, bends in voice" that "can be engaged as creative work" (19). In addition to the added Nuyorican montuno that Marc Anthony has performed in "Preciosa," I now turn to specific body gestures that he enacts onstage in different performances of the song and that suggest "sovereign" modes of listening and reception through the power of embodied affect and emotion.

Marc Anthony's Boricua power is clearly at work in his October 5, 2013, performance of "Preciosa" in San Juan, Puerto Rico. The song is a most poignant selection to conclude the concert, as most of the listening audience are island residents. From the beginning of the song, we hear the audience singing along, a collective instance that is not uncommon in Marc Anthony's concerts throughout the Americas, from Viña del Mar, Chile, to Madison Square Garden in New York. El Marc's concerts are instances of collective singing and affective dialogues between the singer and his listeners. Despite the large dimensions of his megaconcerts, Marc Anthony successfully creates a sense of intimacy between his listeners and himself.

While Marc's rendition is quite conventional for a bolero singer, initiated by the traditional string sounds of the guitar and Puerto Rican cuatro (which produce the sounds of the traditional trio ensemble) and characterized by an almost operatic singing voice that projects passion and lyrical subtlety, at the end of the bolero, Marc Anthony wants us to pause. He utters the closing lyrics of the original song—"los hijos de la libertad"—through a fermata, that is, a very elongated singing of one note and syllable, in this case, the "jos" in "hijos," and in "tad," the last syllable of "libertad." Derived from the Italian *fermare,* which means to stay or to stop, this elongation is a stylistic detail that merits critical attention (see fig. 1.2). This pause, whose length and duration are left up to the performer, can be twice as long as the original note's temporal value, or even longer.

The fermata allows a singer to exhibit the virtuosity of their voice in maintaining that note for an impressive period, a performative feat common among operatic singers. This manipulation of time, a temporality stilled and paused, can also be framed as the colonial subject's performativity that contests the historical, linear, and imperial time of progress. According to Sandra Ruiz (2019), Puerto Rican anticolonial performers such as Papo Colo and

FIGURE 1.2. The fermata in musical notation. © Hyacinth / Wikipedia / CC BY-SA 3.0.

Pedro Pietri create spaces "in which the social and psychic merge at the site of aesthetics, uncovering what's really at stake politically for the enduring body" (10). Indeed, the conditions of coloniality that Puerto Ricans experience lead to "the sensation of time standing immobile" (81), which in turn remits us to the imperative endurance as colonial subjects. Let us not forget the national paralysis of the government and of society in the aftermath of Hurricane María and the durability of the colonial violence on the part of the US government (Ruiz 2019, 115). Marc's performance of the fermata, then, may transcend the very structures of musical notation and take on a political signification, as suggested by Ruiz's critical engagement with "enduring time." This manipulation and control over time is not unique to Marc Anthony's "Preciosa"; in fact, syncopations, the clave rhythms, and polyrhythmic structures central to salsa and Afro-Caribbean musical traditions across the archipelago are instances of what Anna Monroe Teague (2015) analyzes as "metrical dissonances." Teague charts examples of how "salsa's rhythm motivates energetic perceptions and associations of musical energy" (iv). If metrical dissonance "emphasizes beats other than metrically strong ones" (3), then salsa music is full of these rhythmic syncopations, these manipulations of the metric beat, that create a "metaphorical, musical energy" (30). Not only do we listen to metric distortions and resistances to the chronologies of colonial time in the clave rhythms and polyrhythms, but also in how salsa dura styles in the early Nuyorican years of salsa musical production accelerated time right before the beat, thus effecting a relationship between time and political economy and allowing for the possibility of creating an "affect" as the New York sounds of salsa dura compete with the loud volumes of the urbanscape. The visceral effect of the fermata, moreover, connects Marc Anthony to the affective pain of exile and its freezing of time. How do exile communities stop time by reimagining their homeland, by idealizing them from temporal and spatial distances? These instances of decolonial disruptions of time clearly tell stories about displaced communities. By departing from and disobeying the colonialist imposition of the Spanish lineage of the coplas and the décimas, for instance, the montuno, the fermatas, the soneos, and the syncopated clave rhythms in salsa all disrupt the colonialist, imposed time of the Western world.[30]

Beyond this performative feat, in the case of "Preciosa," the two pauses in the closing verse exhort listeners to listen to el Marc exclusively as this pause marks the transition into the Nuyorican montuno. In his concerts, which are examples of what Thomas Turino (2008) names "presentational music," the attention to structures, repertoire, and details are meant to "sustain audience interest" (58). Thus, in concerts "planned contrasts" function precisely "as indexical nows that draw listeners' attention back to the moment of performance" (58). The fermata freezes the listener's sense of time and rhythm, increasing the anticipation for what is next, perhaps the uncertainty of a future that is tied to the long history of coloniality for Puerto Ricans, a sense of a future not unlike the anticolonial texture of Marc's performance. What follows musically, however, is the acceleration of the rhythm, as the song metamorphizes from a bolero to a salsa arrangement, thus introducing the repeatedly syncopated percussive rhythms that allow listeners and singer to enter a different temporality and a different communal space altogether. This transition becomes even more meaningful when performed in San Juan, the capital city, as the audience embraces salsa as Nuyorican music and, ultimately, as a Puerto Rican sonic contribution to the world. The elongated notes, this stopping of time, facilitate an expansive and collective sense of belonging among the listeners. While it reaffirms the present moment of the performance, it also remits the audience to the anticolonial liberatory values of the song and its composer, as much as it moves listeners into the temporal space of the early years of salsa music in New York. The fermata, as a "detail" in notation (Vázquez 2013), thus carries a powerful aesthetic and political import that allows for the song's performance, and its listeners, to establish a space of belonging and home, both for the island listeners and Diasporican cohorts, through the trope of anticolonial endurance. This, to be sure, does not diminish the performative virtuosity of Marc's vocal skills.

---

30. I want to thank Wilson Valentín-Escobar for a fruitful discussion on the relationship between metric dissonance and anticolonial gestures.

As Marc Anthony concludes the concert and his rendering of "Preciosa," he kneels on the stage and kisses the floor as a metonym for the land, for the island, for the national geographical territory that is Puerto Rico. Unsurprisingly, this theatrical moment of patriotic love, already embodied in the selection of the song as the closing number, is visually enacted by the images of Puerto Rican flags that appear on monitors across the arena. What could be easily and correctly interpreted as a fervent performance of nationalism by his diasporic and itinerant self within the space of home and belonging, his "land" is now reconstructed, like the concert itself, as a musical collectivity and, ultimately, as a "sovereign" space (Robinson 2020, 62–65).

In 2017, after the devastation to the island caused by Hurricanes Irma and María, and following the earthquakes in Mexico City and other natural disasters in Florida and Texas, Marc Anthony, Jennifer Lopez, and Alex Rodríguez led a global fundraiser for the reconstruction of houses, neighborhoods, and infrastructure. *Somos Una Voz* (We Are One Voice) was broadcast from Los Angeles, California, and Miami, Florida, and brought together Telemundo and Univision to telecast simultaneously for the first time. The fundraiser successfully achieved its goal by attracting one billion donors and raising almost a million dollars ($968,081) in two years. The simultaneous concerts took place on Saturday, October 14, 2017, and included major singers and artists like Camila Cabello, Demi Lovato, Maroon 5, Ricky Martin, Gwen Stefani, Chris Martin, Jamie Foxx, Mary J. Blige, and others.

As in previous performances of "Preciosa," Marc Anthony performed the fermata as a bridge into the Nuyorican montuno, thus replicating the anticolonial meanings discussed above and reproducing a safe space of belonging among his listeners. Yet, during this fundraiser, and given the critical urgency of the moment, Marc Anthony unbuttoned his shirt on stage while singing the Nuyorican montuno, most specifically during the verse "en ti se vuelca mi amor" [my love tips over you]. This dramatic, performative gesture could easily be read as an erotics of nationalism, that is, expressing how his desire for Puerto Rican recovery and survival and reconstruction resides in his own body, mostly the chest as a metonym for his heart and love for the island and its people. Likewise, these erotics cannot be separated from the production of desire that the musical industry fuels among Marc's most ardent fans, which results in the sexual desirability of the singer. However, I would argue that these gestures—the fermata, the unbuttoning of his shirt, and embracing the large-sized image of the Puerto Rican flags on the monitor onstage—also signal a sort of affective urgency that takes on power and meaning given the specific moment, a month after the storm, as a denouncement of the dire conditions of the communities who survived the storm, an emphasis on the imperative to collect donations for the victims, and a moment of mourning for all those who perished during the storm, and after, as the result of government inaction and negligence.

The massive popularity and the sonic associations between "Preciosa," Marc Anthony, and the anticolonial love for the nation are clearly cemented. Aware of Marc's popularity among Puerto Ricans and Latinxs everywhere, the Biden-Harris 2020 campaign invited him to narrate a video exhorting Puerto Ricans in the diaspora to vote for the Democratic ticket. The video, titled *Prohibido olvidar* and produced by the Lincoln Project, started circulating on YouTube and social media in mid-September 2020.[31] The video includes compelling images of the material destruction as well as the solidarity and collaboration among Puerto Ricans. We hear Marc Anthony exhort viewers not to forget the strength and resilience of the Puerto Rican people, who rescued each other after the egregious, inhuman abandonment and neglect on the part of the first Trump regime. And, unsurprisingly, at the conclusion of the video, we listen to a simple piano riff, without accompaniment, voice, or lyrics, off the melody of "Preciosa," a mnemonic sound that, once again, at a time of duress and multiple crises for Diasporicans, islanders, and racial minorities in the United States, triggers in us the affective "attunements between place and people by which to survive" (LaBelle 2020, 100). Indeed, the melody of "Preciosa" sparks in listeners the memory of that "general precariousness in which mobility paradoxically locates one upon a threshold to homelessness" (LaBelle 2020, 92). This time, however, the political message was much more clearly partisan and strategic, at a moment when Trump and Biden were fighting for the Latinx vote in Florida. Biden's victory for the presidency, finally validated by the Electoral College on December 14, 2020, yet contested by Trump loyalists, may not have been possible without the Latinx vote in Florida, of which displaced Puerto Ricans formed a critical mass. That Marc Anthony was chosen for this video acknowledges the impressive power that his singing of "Preciosa" still possesses among Puerto Ricans and Latinx in the United States.

"Preciosa" and Latinidad: The Palimpsests of Exile

In a 2002 *New York Times* article titled "The Latino Cultural Wars," Seth Kugel argued that Puerto Ricans in New York City have maintained a strong cultural hegemony and have imposed their own cultural texts, rituals, and productions onto other, more recent immigrant communities from Latin America. This

---

31. Please refer to the YouTube link: https://www.youtube.com/watch?v=rRN9wnTvzro.

claim, which he describes as an example of "Latino Cultural Wars," may be analogously framed as the "horizontal hierarchies" that I proposed in *Negotiating Latinidad* (2019). In brief, given the demographic diversification of Latinx urban centers throughout the United States, the power differentials, struggles for resources, and social, political, and racial hierarchies that emerge among the various immigrant communities sharing urban and suburban spaces become meaningful sites for teasing out the complexities of Latinidad. I return to this article from 2002, which I have already examined (Aparicio 2003), because the major case study that Kugel highlights still haunts me today as I write this chapter. The figure of a then nine-year-old Guatemalan girl named Gabriela Minuenza singing "Preciosa" at a school event in New York allows me to conclude this critical analysis by troubling the national homology between "Preciosa," Puerto Rico, and Puerto Ricans. That is, "Preciosa" also sings to Latinidad if we define this identitarian term as shared experiences of "racialization and stigmatization in the United States" (Rúa 2005, 505), thus transforming its meaning from a static umbrella term to a concept of resistance that acknowledges and denounces the racialization of our communities. Gabriela's sonic performance of "Preciosa," then, embodies the "palimpsests of exile" that characterize the displacements, migrations, and itinerancies of millions of Latin Americans and US Latinx subjects. The pain of colonialism, so lyrically uttered in Rafael Hernández's "Preciosa," moves beyond the Puerto Rican and Diasporican boundaries to embrace other Latinx identities and communities analogously dehumanized and displaced by US imperialism. Marc Anthony, too, is not just a Nuyorican singer but also a Latinx performer who is profoundly loved by US Latinx fans, Mexicans, and other listeners in Latin America. His powerful embodiment of the Nuyorican subjectivity does not by any means exclude his critical importance in the public sphere of Mexican music, as he embodies a Latinidad rooted in a long history of Mexican and Puerto Rican musical exchanges. It was, indeed, Marc Anthony's interpretation of Mexican singer Juan Gabriel's original song "Hasta Que Te Conocí" that inaugurated el Marc's hemispheric voicing as a singer of love songs, ballads, and suffering and that positioned him as a voice for a hemispheric Latinidad.

CHAPTER 2

"Hasta Que Te Conocí" (1993)

Latinidad as Suffering

Toward a MexiRican Latinidad

In her 2013 memoir, Puerto Rican actor Rita Moreno recalled a moment during her early years as a starlet in Hollywood that painfully revealed the sexual violence that has long permeated the film industry, one that traumatized and wounded her. Rita recalled how as she fled a cocktail party at a stately Bel Air mansion where she was being sexually harassed, she ran into a group of Mexican gardeners:

> I was starting to remove my high heels, thinking that somehow, I would walk back miles and miles to Westwood, when a pickup truck arrived to collect the gardeners I'd seen working earlier in the day. They were Mexicans. I ran over to the truck and spoke in Spanish to one of them.
> "Please, can you take me home?" I begged.
> The men didn't ask why. They understood without a word. They sat me down on the front seat, and one of them gently put his work jacket over my shoulders. They drove me home without a word. They were the only gentlemen I met that night. (R. Moreno 2013, 135)

This poignant moment, in which a Puerto Rican female movie starlet finds unexpected solace and protection among Mexican male gardeners in Los Angeles during the early 1950s, should not be deemed an exceptional moment but rather be interpreted as an instance of social Latinidad, an encounter between individuals of different Latin American nationalities who interact with a mutual understanding of the subordinations, racializations, and colonial subjectivities that Latinx peoples have shared in the United States. Mexicans and Puerto Ricans are two communities that have been enriched by the ongoing mutual exchange of sounds, popular music, actors, and artists across decades. This artistic and sonic binational reciprocity is apparent and richly illustrated not only in the arts scenes of both countries but also, as Rita Moreno's anecdote evinces, in the everyday serendipitous encounters between individuals from both communities in the US diaspora. These spaces of encounters, synchronicities, and reciprocity between Mexicans and Puerto Ricans, examples of Latinidad[1] that "signals the mutual transculturations and horizontal hierarchies" (Aparicio 2017, 113) as well as "a shared sense of a Latino identity" (Rúa 2005, 505) between and among the different colonized ethnic communities in Latinx USA, serve as a contextual framework for my critical listening of the song "Hasta Que Te Conocí" [Until I Met You], a popular hit written and performed by Mexican singer-songwriter Juan Gabriel in 1986 and interpreted by, among many others, Marc Anthony in 1993.

Rita Moreno's anecdote beautifully encapsulates the role of trauma and suffering, hermandad [brotherhood] and solidarity, race, gender, class, and sexuality in this instantiation of Latinidad. Moreover, the encounter between Moreno and the Mexican workers reveals the role of sounds: first her oral deployment of Spanish as she requested their help allowed her to be acknowledged as a Latina in an otherwise white, Anglo, and wealthy setting. Yet the scene also subtly reveals a long history of reciprocity, mutual acknowledgment, and expressions of suffering and sentimiento [melancholia] that have taken place between both communities in the sphere of popular music. While unspoken, Rita's trauma was nonetheless acknowledged by the Mexican gardeners who cared for her. This assumed recognition of shared suffering, long articulated by singers of rancheras and boleros, may explain the quiet solidarity that Moreno felt. It also helps me delve into the genesis of Marc Anthony's decision to sing Juan Gabriel's song and the social meanings of the Nuyorican singer's interactions with, and interpellations of, his Mexican listeners. This chapter first offers a glimpse at the long history of the mutual exchanges and migrations of popular music between Mexico and Puerto Rico, a sonic history that informs Marc Anthony's own incursion into Mexican love ballads.

---

1. For a more detailed genealogy of the various meanings of "Latino/a/x" and "Latinidad/es," and attendant academic debates, see chapter 1 in Aparicio (2019).

It then discusses the centrality of Mexican sentimiento in the performances of what the late queer critic José Esteban Muñoz refers to as the "excessive affect" of Juan Gabriel's and Marc Anthony's "Hasta Que Te Conocí." After a critical listening of the numerous rewritings and adaptations of this canonical love song throughout the Americas as evidence of its hemispheric resonance with diverse communities, I close with an analysis of the multiple masculinities embodied in the singing performances of Juan Gabriel, Marc Anthony, and Willie Colón as they enact the affective associations between suffering, gender, and sexuality.

The Singing Tocayos: Marco Antonio / Marc Anthony

Marc Anthony could have been born Mexican. His birth date, September 16, 1968, coincides with the celebration of Mexican Independence in Mexico and among Mexican American communities in the United States. His birth name is Marco Antonio Muñiz, the same as the Mexican singer of romantic boleros whom his parents honored by naming their son after him, an onomastic choice that links the Nuyorican voice to the longer history of Mexican and Latin American balladeers.[2] Yet later the Nuyorican singer changed his name to the Anglo version, Marc Anthony, "in order to avoid confusion with his namesake" (Cano-Moreno and Del Río 2010). While he is proud of his Nuyorican and Boricua identity, Marc Anthony's Nuyorican identity is not mutually exclusive from his popularity in Mexico and his sense of belonging among Mexican Americans in the US Southwest. These two identities, Nuyorican and Latinx, are simultaneous and relational, yet not natural. Rather, his hemispheric Latinidad is the result of Marc Anthony's labor as a singer and interpreter who ultimately chose a repertoire dominated by love songs and ballads, a most popular genre throughout Mexico and Latin America. The uncanny and felicitous synchronicity of his name is not mera coincidencia but rather points to el Marc's location and participation within a longer, rich history of musical exchanges and flows between Mexico, Cuba, and Puerto Rico—in brief, the sonic spaces of the "circum-Caribbean," as Alejandro Madrid and

---

2. In an article for *Billboard*, Chuck Taylor (2000) erroneously identifies Marc Anthony's father, Felipe Muñiz, as a "Mexican singer." This mistake can be clearly traced to the homogenizing effects of Latinidad as a dominant construct. It is not, I believe, associated with the strong presence of Mexican music and films among New York Puerto Ricans, a historical fact that is commonly elided in music studies.

Robin Moore (2013) have framed their monumental study of the transnational flows of the Cuban danzón.³

During Marc Anthony's concert at Radio City Music Hall in New York City on August 27, 2016, I was struck by the meaningful MexiRican synchronicities of that weekend. That Saturday night, he sang to a full house, with both Jennifer Lopez and his father, Felipe Muñiz, who is a talented singer of boleros and bachatas, as guest performers. Before the performance began, I was struck by an announcement for an upcoming concert that was displayed on the walls of the theater. The Mexican "Divo de Juárez," Juan Gabriel, was scheduled to perform at Radio City Music Hall in the next few weeks as part of a US concert tour. Yet the next morning, Sunday, August 28, we woke up to the devastating news of Juan Gabriel's unexpected passing. Along with numerous Mexican listeners and fans who were profoundly upset by the loss of their beloved Juan Gabriel, Marc Anthony was also a devoted fan. Not only do Puerto Rican families and communities on the island share a long history of listening to their Mexican counterparts on television and radio, but Puerto Rican families in New York, as the Muñiz family can attest, also became an important audience to the sounds of Mexican music-making. Marco Antonio Muñiz sang in Teatro Puerto Rico in the South Bronx during the 1950s as part of La Farándula, a show of Latin American singers. He also sang in Madison Square Garden in 1970 (Muñiz 140, 142). I fondly remember growing up in San Juan, Puerto Rico, watching Mexican films featuring Miguel Aceves Mejía singing rancheras with mariachis in the background, among many other Latin American classics. As Bobby Sanabria (2021) has stated, during the 1950s and 1960s, New York Puerto Ricans watched a lot of Mexican films and listened to Mexican music in their homes, a fact that helps to explain the unexpected choice of the huapango rhythm for *West Side Story*'s "America" choreographic designs.⁴ This longer sonic history, uncannily inscribed in Marc Anthony's

---

3. Alejandro Madrid and Robin Moore (2013) map the circum-Caribbean as follows: "Linked together by a shared history of colonization, diasporic movement, and immigration, the circum-Caribbean is a geo-cultural region that encompasses the West Indies, the northern coast of South America, the Florida and Yucatan peninsulas, as well as New Orleans and Veracruz. It is precisely the revolving path of the Gulf Stream that best symbolizes the perpetual (yet always renewed) cultural flows explored in this volume and suggests a possible model for thinking about them, the notion of circularity" (17).

4. Bobby Sanabria discussed this as a panelist in "Reimagining *West Side Story*: A Critical Discussion of the Remake," a panel sponsored by Centro de Estudios Puertorriqueños, CUNY, on December 13, 2021. Other panelists included Frances Negrón Muntaner, Virginia Sánchez Korrol, and Brian Herrera. The panel was moderated by Professor Jillian Báez.

name and birth date, explains Marc Anthony's decision to sing salsa music in Spanish inspired by a Mexican bolero ranchera.

According to entertainment journalists, "Hasta Que Te Conocí," one of Juan Gabriel's most canonical and popular hits, was the song that triggered Marc Anthony, until then a singer of freestyle in English, to sing salsa in Spanish.[5] Juan Gabriel, warmly known as Juanga by his fans, was one of the most outstanding and loved singers and composers in Mexico and Latin America. He not only composed over 1,800 songs, many of them hits, but he also transformed the traditional structures of rancheras, boleros, and Latin pop. His flamboyant style of live performance broke taboos, and he managed to inspire the Mexican government to pass gay-friendly laws and policies without ever officially coming out to the public. *Hasta Que Te Conocí* was also the title of a television series Juan Gabriel produced about his life and career. In an uncanny coincidence, the series concluded the same day as his passing.

As Marc Anthony recalls, hearing this Mexican song for the first time in a car radio profoundly inspired him to produce salsa music despite his earlier misgivings—"it was old people's music"—and disidentification with salsa:

> I saw my life clearly when I heard that song.... The only way I could do it was salsa, and I just said yes immediately.... So I signed this salsa record deal and I'm thinking: What the hell am I doing? I don't even like salsa. But I need to record this song. I don't know how I'm going to do it, but I'm going to record this song....
>
> *It was in me.* Once I was in the studio and heard the rhythms, I understood it for some reason and it just fell into place. (Harrington 2002a, H6; emphasis mine)

That a Mexican love ballad, more specifically a bolero ranchera, was the song that propelled a young Marc Anthony to shift from singing freestyle in English to salsa in Spanish is not without ironies, given the strong nationalist boundaries that linger in our uncritical segmentations of musical genres in Latinx USA and the rigid categories that constrain singers to one specific ethnicity or racial identity. Yet Marc Anthony's own acknowledgment that both the salsa rhythms and the sounds of boleros were within him—"in me"— evinces the omnipresent and long historical soundscapes of Mexican musical traditions all across the Latinx diasporas in the United States, including New

---

5. Among many others, see the "Hasta Que Te Conocí" entry in Wikipedia, https://en.wikipedia.org/wiki/Hasta_Que_Te_Conoc%C3%AD.

York City well before Mexicans were deemed a settled community, as well as the long experimentations of musical hybridity in Latinx popular music.[6] It also documents the intimate entanglements between salsa music and Latin American boleros, which scholars have studied (Aparicio 1998; Knights 2008).

From then on, "Hasta Que Te Conocí" in Marc Anthony's salsa arrangement became part of a longer genealogy of Mexican and Puerto Rican musical exchanges. This longer history, inaudible and disposable outside of Latin America and the Caribbean, allows us to situate el Marc not only as a Nuyorican and "American" voice, as other chapters examine, but as a hemispheric Latino singer as well, a voice whose sonic innovations produce a sense of community and belonging throughout the Americas. In fact, when Marc Anthony first performed "Hasta Que Te Conocí" in a salsa arrangement on the international travel show *Carnival Internacional*, he "hit a homerun" singing it, "and in a flash was traveling the Spanish-speaking world to sing the sudden hit track" (Cano-Moreno and Del Río 2010).[7] By 1993, the young Nuyorican known locally for his freestyle singing was resituating himself in the Southern Hemisphere and reimagining himself as a Latinx salsa singer who would sing love ballads in Spanish to Latin America, to Latinx USA, and, eventually, to the world.

Marc Anthony's interpretation and recording of "Hasta Que Te Conocí" need to be understood within the longer history of sonic flows and mutual exchanges between Mexico and Puerto Rico and throughout the Americas. These musical crossings that contest the atomized discourses of the industry include a vast repertoire of heterogeneous musical genres, interpreters, and nationalities. The Cuban danzón has permeated the popular dancing venues in Havana as well as in Veracruz and Mexico City, and the mambo, also hailing from Cuba and brilliantly embodied in Benny Moré's arrangements, was popularized and danced to by Mexicans from South to North in the 1950s. Mexican listeners have long enjoyed the live performances and compositions of Puerto Rican and Cuban artists such as Toña la Negra, Celia Cruz and La Sonora Matancera, Rafael Hernández, Willie Colón, Ednita Nazario, and Lucecita Benítez, among many other Caribbean and Boricua figures. Willie Colón, who resided in Mexico City for many years and who opened up Salón 21 in 1999, deserves to be highlighted as an honorary Mexican. In the US Latinx diaspora, Chicano rock musician Carlos Santana popularized Nuyorican Tito Puente's "Oye Como Va," a cha-cha-cha song composed in 1963 and

---

6. See Pacini Hernández (2010) for a rich analysis and documentation of hybridizations and musical genre crossings that have characterized the history of Latino popular music in the United States and transnationally.

7. See Taylor (2000); Márquez (2001, 71); Harrington (2002a); and Cano-Moreno and Del Río (2010).

whose signature introduction comes from Afro-Cuban bassist Israel "Cachao" López (Pacini Hernández 2010). Santana resignified the song's ideal listeners by arranging it as a rock song, and in 1971 his version of the song reached number thirteen on Billboard's Top 100 chart. By 2000, "Oye Como Va" had become one of the most recognizable canonical hits in so-called American (US) music:

> In 2000, National Public Radio's All Things Considered named "Oye Como Va" one of the one hundred most important American songs of the twentieth century, a decision based on its profound influence on musical developments in the United States. Ironically, then, it was an immigrant Mexican rocker who, in pioneering the subgenre of Latin rock, introduced the U.S.-born Puente's Afro-Cuban dance music to mainstream U.S. rock audiences. This single example of multiple origins and intersecting pathways brings into focus a characteristic of U.S. Latino musical practices. Far from being defined by or limited to musical aesthetics associated with particular national groups, Latino music-making has always entailed crossing musical, geographic, racial, and ethnic boundaries. (Pacini Hernández 2010, 1–2)

Indeed, this hit, now listened to as one of the sounds of mainstream America, exemplifies the "Latin/o American hybridity" (Pacini Hernández 2010, 3) that has structured Latinx popular music through its crossings of Mexican, Cuban, Puerto Rican, Nuyorican, Dominican, and Colombian sounds and rhythms. As Pacini Hernández lucidly documents, the mixtures and sonic hybridizations in the genres of rock, Dominican bachata and merengue, and the circuits of Colombian cumbia now Mexicanized oblige us to reconsider national boundaries and sonic ethnic traditions as imposed, untimely, and constraining when we acknowledge the rich sounds, rhythms, and melodies of Latinx popular music as they circulate and transculturate each other hemispherically.

Within these long and rich mutual exchanges of music, songs, and singers, Marc Anthony cannot be understood without his tocayo [namesake], the Mexican balladeer Marco Antonio Muñiz, aptly known as "El Embajador del Romanticismo" and whose name he carries as homage to the long and rich history of MexiRican musical reciprocities.

If you ask any older Puerto Rican on the island and the diaspora about Marco Antonio Muñiz, most surely the response will be an affirmative and loving statement about his romantic ballads and his honorary presence in Puerto Rico. Marco Antonio loved Puerto Rico as his "second country," and Puerto Rican listening audiences loved him back. The love and respect for, and presence of, Marco Antonio lasted for decades on the island. He visited every Christmas holiday, singing at the Club Caribe in the Caribe Hilton and at the

La Concha Hotel, among many others; visiting patients in hospitals; volunteering for fundraisers, including one for the Girl Scouts in Puerto Rico; and sharing with his own family and with local friends and social networks. As a young girl, I warmly remember his singing on television and his friendly smile as he greeted his fans and listeners. I also have vivid memories of my father and mother dressing up to go to the Club Caribe for dinner and drinks with friends to listen to Marco Antonio.

As the late Enrique "Quique" Talavera indicates, between 1960 and 1980, Puerto Rico became the epicenter of night clubs and entertainment in the Hispanic Caribbean after the 1959 Cuban Revolution and the closing of Havana as the entertainment capital for the US elite. Major hotels, such as the Caribe Hilton, Normandie, Condado Vanderbilt, Ponce Intercontinental, Hotel San Juan, Hotel La Concha, Club Escambrón, and the Mayaguez Hilton, became venues for musical shows and social dancing all week long (Talavera 2021, 8). Those twenty years, 1960–80, are considered the "época de mayor esplendor de los clubes nocturnos y cabarets, tal como lo fue para la música en general" [the most splendorous years for nightclubs and cabarets, as it was for music in general] (Talavera 2021, 12). Among the numerous singers and interpreters who performed in San Juan were notable Black US singers like Roberta Flack, Sammy Davis Jr., Ella Fitzgerald, the Supremes, the Temptations, and Eartha Kitt (Talavera 2021, 110). The high demand for Puerto Rican musicians allowed local instrumentalists to be well paid and employed. After 1980, however, a combination of factors—including the increase in criminality, the arrival of cable television and MTV, and the folding of the musicians' labor union, the Federación de Músicos de Puerto Rico, which significantly diminished the salaries and labor rights of musicians—led many nightclubs and hotel shows to close (Talavera 2021, 243).

It was during these decades that Marco Antonio Muñiz performed in Puerto Rico, notably in the Club Caribe at the Caribe Hilton, which opened its doors in 1948 (Talavera 2021, 113). The Club Caribe, considered the best work environment for musicians (51), operated as a dinner salon and dancing and show venue from 1949 to 1988 (34). Marco Antonio Muñiz, called the Lujo de México, performed at the Club Caribe for about twenty-five years, although he continued performing in Puerto Rico until 2013 (53). His annual shows, scheduled for the Navidades holiday season, were always fully attended and well received. During a gala for the Girl Scouts, Afro–Puerto Rican singer Ruth Fernández accompanied Marco Antonio in singing "Preciosa," which received an "efusiva ovación de pie" [effusive standing applause] (Talavera 2021, 94).

Muñiz himself has credited his island listeners with his "nacimiento a nivel internacional" [birth at the international level], given that Puerto Rico was the first country to embrace him as a soloist after he left the group Los Tres Aces in Mexico. This symbolic and affective adoption is clear in his public statements regarding his profound sense of "identificación" with the island. In a 1986 interview with Annie Alfaro, he said Puerto Rico is "parte de mi corazón" [part of my heart] and that "posiblemente yo había nacido aquí" (it's possible that I was born here]. Given Marco Antonio's iconic presence in Puerto Rico and his rich contributions to the entertainment industry there, he clearly embodies the long history of hermandad and mutual sharing between Mexican and Puerto Rican musicians and singers. It is almost as if Mexico had gifted Muñiz to Puerto Rico as a gesture of reciprocity for the long presence of Rafael Hernández's thirty years in Mexico, where he contributed his talents and compositions to the national soundscape. Marco Antonio Muñiz returned this gift by sharing his boleros and love ballads with Puerto Rican listeners.

Yet highlighting Muñiz as a Mexican celebrity in Puerto Rico should not overshadow the longer presence of Mexicans in Puerto Rico. Archival documents have evinced the circulation of Mexicans in Puerto Rico and of Puerto Ricans in Mexico for centuries. Since the mid-seventeenth century, Puerto Ricans have moved to Mexico to study or work, and historians have been able to identify marriages of Mexican men and Puerto Rican women since before 1810, the beginning of the Mexican Revolution. However, less attention is paid to the few Mexicans who lived in Puerto Rico during the nineteenth century, yet trade and commerce between both countries were fundamental to the "desarrollo económico de Puerto Rico" [the economic development of Puerto Rico] (Picó 1994). The fact that residents in Ponce adopted the Virgen de Guadalupe as their patron saint can be explained by a Mexican presence in the southern island city. As the late historian Fernando Picó (1994) argues, if during the eighteenth century Puerto Rico "no era tierra de oportunidad económica, pero sí de aceptación social" [was not considered a place for economic opportunities but for social acceptance], this need for social acceptance may have motivated the emergence of a small but solid and historically settled Mexican community on the island. Today, news articles describe the increasing presence of agricultural Mexican workers in Puerto Rico, laboring in local farms and harvesting fruits and vegetables (*RTL Today* 2021). This long but neglected history of MexiRican affiliations emerges also in the diaspora as "chicanos y boricuas" (Rodríguez 1997, 34) mobilized during the Chicano Movement in solidarity to struggle against their analogous forms of colonization. A 1979 photo of Chicano/as showing solidarity with Puerto Rican Independence (Rodríguez 1997) reaffirms the US Latinx diasporas as communities that came together in the Civil Rights Movements in the north. More recently, US demographics reveal an increasing number of MexiRican marriages and intra-Latinx families that embody the tenets of Latinidad within the domestic spheres of home and family, an intimate Latinidad that reveals the longer history of sharing in the workplace and in neighborhoods (Aparicio 2019). That Marc Anthony's name is an onomastic trace of his migrant Puerto Rican parents' love for Mexican music suggests the very strong affiliations, reciprocities, and mutual acknowledgments between these two national communities, an underlying solidarity that saved Rita Moreno on that terror-filled evening in Bel Air.

Latinidad, Brownness, Suffering

In response to Juan Gabriel's passing in 2016, Marc Anthony publicly commented to Univision (2016), "Me doy cuenta cada día lo que él tuvo que ver con quien soy como artista. Su gusto, su sensibilidad, interpretación y pasión . . . me crié con la música de él y jamás en la vida hubiera pensado que grabaría en español" [Every day I realize what he had to do with who I am as an artist. His taste, his sensibility, interpretation and passion . . . I grew up with his music and I never imagined that I would record music in Spanish]. Indeed, Juan Gabriel, one of the most important musical icons in Mexico and Latin America, was a prolific composer who penned more than 1,800 songs and a singer-interpreter who transformed traditional Mexican musical genres into his unique musical style. Born in Michoacán, Juan Gabriel became a pop icon in Mexico and throughout Latin America.

Marc Anthony's public acknowledgment of Juan Gabriel's impact on him not only reaffirms the exposure that Marc Anthony had to Mexican music in his early years through his parents' listening predilections, but also, and most pertinent to my analysis in this chapter, places strong emphasis on the artistry defined by "passion," "sensibility," and "interpretation." Yet what has gone unnoticed is that Juan Gabriel's classic hit "Hasta Que Te Conocí" also inspired Marc Anthony to experiment with his interpretative style, thus performing "excessive affect," as José Esteban Muñoz (2020, chap. 2) writes in his brilliant incursions into Latinx and queer performance artists and how they counter the dominant normative affect of whiteness.[8] Dismissing the

---

8. Muñoz further discusses the power of the national affect—whiteness—situated as the norm, and against which Latinx affect "appears over the top and excessive. . . . Such mainstream depictions of Latino affect serve to reduce, simplify, and contain ethnic difference" (2020, chap. 2). Later, he clarifies his argument: "Rather than saying that Latina/o affect is too much, I want to suggest that the presence of Latina/o affect puts a great deal of pressure on the affective base of whiteness insofar as it instructs us in a reading of the affect of whiteness as underdeveloped and impoverished" (chap. 2).

traditional, linear, and hierarchical approach of musical influences, my critical listening into Juan Gabriel's and Marc Anthony's performances of "Hasta Que Te Conocí" is inspired by Muñoz's proposed critical concept of brownness, which deploys affect and queerness in the process of resituating Latinidad from its impasse as an identitarian term into the political possibilities of collectivity as "antinormative affect" (chap. 7). Muñoz discusses Latinidad this way: "The term 'Latinidad,' a theoretical catalog of different modes of Latina/o self-fashioning, demarcates a set of affective performances that help delineate Latina/o particularity. Latinidad is not about race, region, nation, gender, language, or any other easily identifiable demarcation of difference. Rather, it is an anti-identitarian concept that nonetheless permits us to talk about Latinas/os as having a group identity which is necessary for social activism. Thinking of Latinidad as antinormative affect offers a model of group identity that is coherent without being exclusionary" (chap. 7).

Thus, approaching Latinidad in its aesthetic dimensions and focusing on the affective realms that Latinidad performs allows me to engage with the dyad of Juanga and el Marc as they perform and transform their listeners' sense of relationality with others based on a shared sense of affect as they acknowledge suffering, an otherwise unspoken recognition as we witnessed in Rita Moreno's anecdote. This suffering, brilliantly examined by Lorena Alvarado (2012) as the long tradition of sentimiento in Mexican music, opens the possibilities of Latinidad as an experience of collectivity for listeners of "Hasta Que Te Conocí" as a song that has been performed in Mexico, New York, Chile, and throughout the Americas. As Muñoz clarifies, "this sense [of brownness] often comes to us through the aesthetic experience and especially in the always already relational scene of a performance" (2020, editor's introduction). Singing about suffering, singing in suffering, and singing through suffering, then, produces the shared and relational spaces of Latinidad for a "public that knows itself through shared emotion" (chap. 6). Thus, the sonic, vocal, and corporeal performances and movements of Juan Gabriel and Marc Anthony in their respective interpretations of "Hasta Que Te Conocí" should be explored as sites of "brownness" in their articulations of individual and communal woundedness, pain, and suffering.

These sonic events, analogous to the melodramas long associated with Latin American television and to the rich tradition of the Mexican rancheras, also facilitate the interrogation of dominant gender identities, such as masculinity, in the possibly queered sounds of the love ballads. Juan Gabriel's "secreto a voces," as Alejandro Madrid (2018) writes, his jotería [gayness], inevitably interrogates and interrupts the "patriotism and hypermasculinity" (Alvarado 2012, ii) long associated with the Mexican ranchera, a national musical genre that produced cultural nationalism after the Mexican Revolution and underwent "massive commercial transformation" as it was disseminated through film and radio (Alvarado 2012, 4). Long embodied in the masculine voices and bodies of Pedro Infante and Jorge Negrete, among many other male interpreters, the Mexican ranchera assumes new gender meanings when sung by female artists such as Lucha Reyes, Chavela Vargas, and Lila Downs (Alvarado 2012). In their bodily performativities and in their vocal registers, these women's singing of rancheras propose a "struggle for meaning and representation of sentimiento and the Mexicana singing body" that "is driven by a colonial imaginary that deposits feelings associated with de-privileged excess onto the gendered body" (Alvarado 2012, 2). If Alvarado traces "how sentimiento is rationalized as a bodily inscription of personal and gendered tragedy, as the manifestation of exotic suffering, or as an ancestral and racial condition of melancholy" (2012, 3) in the performances of female artists, here I attempt to offer my own reading of Juan Gabriel's and Marc Anthony's performances of "Hasta Que Te Conocí" as sites of "antinormative affect" (Muñoz 2020, chap. 7), brownness, and Latinidad, yet as very specific and different public gestures that contest to varying degrees traditionally gendered bodies and voices and the normative masculinities embedded wherein. If Juan Gabriel "queers" the traditionally masculine sonic traditions of the ranchera and engages in "acting queer" on stage as an aesthetic "strategy" (Rivera-Servera 2012, 27), Marc Anthony performs "excessive affect" through his body gestures and movements, yet without troubling dominant modes of masculinity and, most problematically, by reproducing the patriarchal discourses of heteronormative sonic traditions.

Singing Excessive Affect

If, as Simone Weil ([1947] 1999) wrote, "suffering and enjoyment" can together be considered "sources of knowledge," "Hasta Que Te Conocí," as performed by both Juan Gabriel and Marc Anthony, proposes a sort of epistemology of suffering that accounts for the affective pain and wounded subjectivity that the song utters, without eliding the pleasure and "gozo" that the song's performance simultaneously evokes among its listeners. In "Secreto a Voces: Excess, Performance, and *Jotería* in Juan Gabriel's Vocality," Alejandro Madrid (2018) highlights the "carnivalesque quality of the ending" of the song and "el gozo" as "a moment of true enjoyment or jouissance" (104). Rather than a contradiction located between the lyrics and the performance, this simultaneity of suffering and pleasure can be understood as the consequences of the "nonnormative affect" with which Juan Gabriel's bodily movements and "gay voice" interpellate (or hail) the audience, as Madrid argues for how El Divo de Juárez "jotea de lo lindo" [queers beautifully], thus breaking "conventions" of masculinity and of the ranchera tradition in his "desacralization of the type of elite, highbrow tradition and space represented by the Palacio de Bellas Artes" in Mexico City, the venue for his landmark concert in 1990 (94). Not only does his "excess and certain camp sensibility" (95) unsettle the formal and official spaces of the Palacio, but his "corruption of the mariachi ensemble with the introduction of norteña musical symbols" also transgresses the normative sounds of cultural nationalism, long entangled with icons of normative and dominant masculinity, that the accompanying ensembles are supposed to represent and perform (94). Yet, as Madrid asks, how can Juan Gabriel's queer sensibility and gayness be so highly embraced by "the largely homophobic atmosphere of mainstream Mexican society" (99)? Madrid explores this "paradox" by arguing that "excess and performance are the common grounds shared by jotería and hypermasculinity; this is a type of excess that reveals both an emotional experience and a social exposure" (101). If excess, as Madrid examines, is considered surplus value in the logic of capitalism, it is also meaningful as "queer futurity" in the critical writings of José Esteban Muñoz. The "dramatic and mannered gestures," "the emblematic vocality," and the "unrestrained character of the performance" (Madrid 2018, 86) are all examples of the "excessive affect" through which Juan Gabriel performs his queerness to a mainstream Mexican community of listeners that while predominantly Catholic and conservative, is, as Madrid suggests, also unpredictably heterogeneous in their ideologies, values, and gender positionalities.

"Hasta Que Te Conocí" is, like countless rancheras and boleros, a song about suffering, pain, and unrequited love. Composed by Juan Gabriel in D minor, the tonality of the melody evokes sadness, intimacy, and loss. Likewise, its lento tempo produces a contemplative tone and situates the song as a ballad meant for a sort of centripetal dancing, the slowness of two bodies close to each other "within the eternity of a floor tile," as Puerto Rican queer writer Luis Rafael Sánchez has poetically described it (1988, 104). The song begins describing a joyful and loving childhood, free of pain and full of innocence, a condition that is subtly performed in the isolated and singular sounds of the guitar in some performances and of the electric piano in others. Then the rupture emerges, when the singer's persona meets the lover, presumably a woman yet also highly suggestive of same-sex desire, who instills suffering in him. "Hasta Que Te Conocí" marks this encounter as the beginning of a wound, a personal pain instigated by the lover's cruelty. The song is structured in a temporal binary: the before and the after, the antes y después. "Hasta que," the prepositional phrase that initiates the title and the refrain, marks the end of the idyllic childhood and youth, one described as full of cariño and ternura, "feliz" [full of warmth and tenderness, "joyful"], as a time when the singer "no sabía de tristezas" [did not know about sadness]. Notable is the definition of sadness and affect (tristezas) as entangled with its own awareness, with a knowledge in "sabía" that suggests an epistemology of pain. The "hasta que te conocí," the recollection of the lovers' encounter, enunciated from the diegetic present, which is also the future, is described as cruel, painful, and wounding. The temporal fissure suggests that the song is an act of memory, a critical remembering of a past relationship from which the singer is now freeing and liberating him- or herself. The "tristezas" and the "lágrimas" and the "muy poco amor" are now framed in the past, but a past that has produced a desire for a lover now gone: "porque ahora pienso en ti, mucho más." His yearning for his absent lover is the motivation for a bolero ranchera that allows the lover-singer to enunciate and express his suffering. Within the tradition of rancheras and boleros, these songs blame the woman for the man's suffering, a patriarchal discourse evident throughout Latin American and Latinx musical genres.[9]

Juan Gabriel and Marc Anthony perform this temporal fissure between the joyful past and the painful present in uncannily similar ways.[10] They both produce a pause in their singing, thereby proposing a bridge (musical and metaphorical) into the second part, the body of the song. "Hasta que" is followed by a silent moment, a pause which, like Alexandra Vázquez has theorized, could be examined as a "detail," as an "event that instantly reveals and honors what can't be said" (2013, 21). If Juan Gabriel pauses after repeating "hasta que," el Marc pauses after the first utterance of "hasta que." Both pauses can be read as an anticipation of what is to come: the singer's realization and acknowledgment of the heartbreak, of the wound. The audience, in all performances that I have examined, rises emotionally at the end of the pause, responding with intense applause, with screams, with howls, to the beginning of the singer's anagnórisis: "vi la vida con dolor" [I saw life with pain]. While numerous concerts feature audience participation, a collective singing or dancing that performs an imagined community during the musical event, a sort of musicking, Juan Gabriel's dialogue with his listeners is

---

9. See Aparicio (1998) for a feminist critical analysis of patriarchy and misogyny in Latino popular music, as well as the potential for queer readings of canonical love songs and ballads otherwise categorized as heteronormative.

10. Among the numerous YouTube videos of Juan Gabriel's singing, I focused on the early 1987 performance, the 1990 concert that Alejandro Madrid also examined in his cited article, and his 2002 Viña del Mar concert. In the case of Marc Anthony, I critically listened to his 1994 performance and, later, to the 2012 concert in Viña del Mar.

clear throughout all his performances. His audiences sing to the same phrase the singer has vocalized or respond to the singer with the lyrics that follow, or wave scarves or pañuelos in the air, as in a 1989 performance in Mexico. These are but some examples of what Zizi Papacharissi (2015) terms "affective publics," forms of collective agency and participation fueled by the affective energy that produces a sense of collectivity. As Papacharissi explains, "the affective attunement to music sustains moods and modes of engagement for individuals of varying ideological orientations, leading to both a unifying effect and an impression of engagement" (22). The pause, I argue, prepares the audience for the shared experience of suffering, an affect that is as collective as it is individual, sounded in the call-and-response sections between Juan Gabriel and the audience, mostly evident in the 2002 Viña del Mar concert.

In brief, the song indexes the collective pain of Mexican and Latin American listeners, Juan Gabriel's audiences, as they reflect on the futurity at stake for themselves, the nation, their brothers and sisters, the younger generations, the Global South. It is this affective energy of articulating pain—as affect is not equivalent to emotions (Papacharissi 2015, 21)—that produces the spaces of Latinidad and brownness so poignantly theorized by Muñoz. This cathartic song exposes experiences of vulnerability and dehumanization that scholars have likewise highlighted: from Gloria Anzaldúa's (1987) definition of the border as a "wound" to her theorizations of "nepantla" and the "shadow-beast" as colonial abjection (4);[11] melancholia and necropolitics, social death (Cacho 2012), the "migrant melodramas" that Ana Elena Puga and Víctor M. Espinosa (2020) examine about refugees and border crossers. It attends to ecological crises, displacements, linguistic terrorism, the numerous precarities we have and continue to face, not to mention the "harm" faced by US Latinas (Halperin 2015), such as reproductive violence, detentions and deportations, our children in cages, family separations, the more recent ethnic cleansings under the Trump regime, the lack of access to health care, the disproportionate cases of physical illness such as COVID, and much more. As Laura Halperin has written, the concept of "harm" highlights "the relation among individual suffering, the catalysts that produce such hurt, and the collective wounding that ensues from such injury" (2015, 2). These harms call for the need for "rectification and recognition" (3), processes that, I would argue, popular music enacts and facilitates and that, in common parlance, we may refer to as "healing" or "cathartic." In effect, as Joshua Chambers-Letson writes in his introduction to *The Sense of Brown*, these innumerable experiences of suffering and pain

---

11. See Lorena Alvarado (2012, 44) for lucid reflections on both terms, *nepantla* and *shadow-beast*, as metaphors for colonial abjection.

constitute Muñoz's "brownness": "Here, brownness surfaces as the stain of enduring historical violence; a stain deeply felt at the level of the body that is subject to the ongoing history of colonialism and empire, as well as the inherent violence of migration, displacement, refusal and removal" (Introduction).

The performative production of pain as communal, experienced by the listening audiences as an index of their nondiegetic lives, is facilitated by the tones of intimacy that characterize Juan Gabriel's staged interpretation of this classic. This intimacy is not natural but staged within the registers of the singer's vocality, a term that refers to "the physical manifestation of the voice in the construction of meaning" (Alvarado 2012, 29). The "intimacy," as Madrid argues, offers "a sense of security, ease, and familiarity" (2018, 98). It is constructed at the beginning of the song, as the indications of the lento tempo and the mezzo forte volume thus frame the melody. The iterative effects of the repeated half-steps or half-intervals, from the note A to the B-flat that initiate the melody and that later unfold into a full step from G to A, frame the song as lyrical rather than epic, truly powerful in its intimacy. They create the sonic textures that exhort the singer to whisper, to speak softly, thus "tender" (Madrid 2018, 97) and vulnerably. As Alvarado writes about "effective affect" and "sentimiento," "it moves one to tears, to attention, to vulnerability, to memory, to recognition of the self" (2012, 7). This "prized emotional transparency" (Alvarado 2012, 7), in brief, the effects of this aesthetic labor on the listening audiences, produces what Madrid describes as "home": "Juanga is home. His vocality offers a sense of intimate security; it creates a space in which they are able to be themselves and revel in their emotions free from social constraints" (2018, 98).

Madrid's intervention, through his critical analysis of Juan Gabriel's 1990 performance of "Hasta Que Te Conocí" at the Palacio de Bellas Artes, concludes with a proposed rewriting and rethinking of the term "jotería," which in Mexico is a pejorative term to refer to gay men and is also associated with cowardice. Juan Gabriel's vocality invites Madrid to "theorize the notion of jotería as a libidinal economy of excesses that puts in evidence a series of contradictions and problems in the Mexican and Latin American heteronormative fantasy" (2018, 87). Jotería, in Madrid's reflection, is expanded into a "dialogic performance complex" that also embraces "cowardice and the fear such condition implies" as "active components of jotería" (88). Echoing Madrid's notion of "home," one of Juan Gabriel's gay listeners who migrated to the US has in fact reaffirmed this proposal: "for many of us who identify as immigrant and/or queer, he [Juan Gabriel] was also an important connection to a homeland, a language, and a cultural landscape that we reached for during our loneliest and most vulnerable moments, but also during moments of triumph and joy. Gracias, Juanga" (R. González 2017). If Juan Gabriel "transcended the fear of ridicule and exposure and somehow he was and is still cherished" (R. González 2017), by becoming "Mexico's voice and inexplicably, there was no shame" (Benjamin Aline Sáez, in R. González 2017), in his own performance of "Hasta Que Te Conocí," el Marc chooses to leave untouched the normative masculinities that Juan Gabriel unsettled in his joto performances of the song.

Untouched Masculinity

Despite their overdramatic gestures, Marc Anthony's interpretations of "Hasta Que Te Conocí" inscribe themselves as different from the Divo de Juárez's original and stylistic "excessive affect." First, in his 1994 performance of the song, which he recorded a year earlier in *Otra Nota*, a young Marc Anthony, wearing wire-rimmed glasses and with his long hair pulled back into a ponytail, takes time in the middle of his characteristic soneo improvisation to speak to the audience: He says, "Soy joven y puertorriqueño, y además de ser puertorriqueño soy latino, y quiero que ustedes sepan que adondequiera que yo me encuentre, los voy a representar a todos ustedes con mucho orgullo y con todo mi corazón, siempre" [I am young and Puerto Rican, and also Latino, and I want you to know that wherever I go, I will represent all of you with pride and with all of my heart, always]. This parenthetical but meaningful statement about his multiple identities, about his Latinidad, and about the role of his voice as a singer for his community reveals not only Marc Anthony's honest commitment to his listening community and fans but also his conscious act of differentiating himself from Juan Gabriel as not Mexican, thus reinscribing the song as a Puerto Rican performative event. Simultaneously, Marc Anthony retains the "Latino" term as a signifier of the mutuality and relationality of their musical labor and of the long MexiRican sonic and musical exchanges documented earlier. I also observed a major difference in el Marc's performances of the song. While he does clearly imitate the melodramatic and excessive facial movements and gestures of Juan Gabriel, the Nuyorican singer elides the feminine bodily movements that Juanga performs onstage, the "queer" style that was unique to his nonnormative spectacle and that Alejandro Madrid has so lucidly analyzed. Although still excessive in his demeanor, evident in el Marc's face contortions, his vocality, and the use of his hands and arms, Marc Anthony's 2012 performance of "Hasta Que Te Conocí" in Viña del Mar, Chile, distinguishes itself from his Mexican inspiration by reproducing the dominant and normative masculinity that Juan Gabriel queers and rewrites as otherwise. The Nuyorican singer performs extremely long fermatas and sustained notes (as we have also noted in "Preciosa"), moves his facial muscles to express pain and melancholy, gazes at the audience in intensely reflexive modes, and moves his hands and arms strongly, with intense affect and will.

Yet el Marc leaves masculinity untouched. This alignment with patriarchy is then amplified within the soneo at the end of the song, when he refers to the woman lover as "bandolera." "Tú eres muy mala / muy mala conmigo" [You are really bad / really bad to me] is an epithet that constructs women as the source of all evil. Unsurprisingly, this motif reappears in his 2022 album, *Pa'lla Voy*, with the hit "Mala," which promised to be quite popular with its danceable, fast rhythms. The term "bandolera," never uttered by Juan Gabriel, is an icon of salsa patriarchal discourse (Aparicio 1998) that feminists have targeted in various media formats.[12] By inserting this term in his improvisatory performance, el Marc resituates himself within the longer history of patriarchal and misogynistic discourses about women rather than relocating himself in the nonnormative, ambiguously gendered space inspired by Juan Gabriel's "secreto a voces." Yet these salient contradictions between the gender politics of the song, the patriarchy of the bolero ranchera, and Juan Gabriel's corporeal and vocal queering in his concerts are not as visibly performed in the body of Marc Anthony.

Comparing Juan Gabriel's 2002 performance in Viña del Mar and el Marc's own interpretation ten years later in the same venue clearly illustrates that el Marc has designed his own aesthetics to the song, a style that while excessive in his fermatas and melancholic reflexivity again leaves untouched the possibility of countering the patriarchal discourse with queer and nonnormative corporeal movements. While both performers engage their audiences in call-and-response singing, Juan Gabriel's vocal contrasts, from soft singing at the beginning of the song to very strong and loud volumes at the "carnivalesque" ending, are accompanied by queer dancing moves—the hand movements, the at times minimalist yet erotically suggestive swaying of the hips, the vibratory moves of his chest and shoulders, for instance—and an "excessive affect" that challenges the patriarchal textures of the song's lyrics. Meanwhile, el Marc reclaims his dominant masculinity by refusing to replicate Juan Gabriel's queer movements. Does this mean we should argue that el Marc does not

---

12. María Elena Cepeda, in her February 24, 2022, presentation for Latinx media studies, Northwestern University, documents the feminist rewritings of the term *loca* in US Latinx communities, as evidenced in the podcast project of Locatora Radio, a sonic political intervention founded by Mala and Diosa that rewrites the deprecatory meanings of terms such as *loca, mala,* and *bandolera* used against women and highlights the "brilliance of womxn of color" through podcasts, audionovelas, and filmmaking.

fully realize the "brownness" within Latinidad in his performances? Is it an incomplete brownness, possibly failed in the context of gender politics? Or, could we consider, despite el Marc's untouched masculinity, that this "brown commons," as Muñoz (2020) has proposed, this suffering as Latinidad, is precisely a site that acknowledges gender differences and imagines solidarity, alliances, and community among a diverse set of masculinities as performances of gender? If, "in the face of shared wounding," listeners and singers like Marc Anthony and Juan Gabriel can inspire "a process of thinking and imagining otherwise" (Muñoz 2020, chap. 1) despite and, most poignantly, *because of their gender differences,* then "Hasta Que Te Conocí" clearly constitutes a potential site for a utopian future in which multiple masculinities, as Nicole Guidotti-Hernández (2021) and many other gender scholars have proposed, can coexist.[13] As an avid feminist listener, I certainly would hope so.

An Urtext for Latin(o) America

The hemispheric transits of "Hasta Que Te Conocí," its circulation throughout Latin America in vastly diverse formats and rhythms, justifies its status as an urtext, that is, as a song that has become a source, an origin, for numerous other singers and interpreters who have performed and recorded it. The superlative resonance of this melody and song, its canonical and immense popularity throughout Latin America, is, to be sure, evidence of its power as a site for acknowledging our grief and suffering. More than forty years after its composition, "Hasta Que Te Conocí" continues to be embraced and enjoyed by numerous audiences across diverse geographical spaces in the Americas. In this light, we can frame the circulation, migrations, and translations of the song as "sonic translocations," as Mayra Santos Febres (1997, 180) has proposed in the context of salsa music or, as Kirstie Dorr (2007, 2) writes, as "sonic rearticulations" tied to place. If translocation "cuts across national boundaries to create a community of urban locations linked by transportation, communication technologies, and the international market economy" (Santos Febres 1997, 180), Juan Gabriel's melody remains alive through its easy

---

13. Nicole Guidotti-Hernández's (2021) historical analysis of multiple masculinities in the Mexican diaspora, most specifically in the writings of Ricardo Flores Magón and among the bracero workers in the United States, proposes the possibility of acknowledging "multiple masculinities" among otherwise heterosexual, cisgendered men. She writes that she found "not a single Mexican masculinity but masculinities in the plural. What we find are the various ways that the US influenced and shaped the lives of Mexican nationals within its borders. What we find is the crucial and suppressed role that intimacy, emotion and desire played in their lives" (Introduction).

access on YouTube, which now serves as a rich archive of the numerous adaptations of the song. Dorr, in examining the critical role of "place" in global circulations of Andean music, considers "what such processes reveal about the complex interplay of text and context," an important consideration for our hemispheric tracings of the song (2). Such impressive rewritings, adaptations, and translations of the song into local and regional formats remind me of the malleability of this melody and of its potential for moving listeners and dancers across Latin(o) America, thus celebrating the diversity of our geographies and local communities (21). After decades of grappling with the politics of authenticity and the authority of original texts or cultural forms, the global flows of popular music today allow us to frame these rewritings of songs as "South American musical transits," as "references to the genealogy of interconnected musical actors, aesthetics, texts, and practices" (2). Dorr's concept of "musical transits" serves as an alternative to "nation or genre as an organizational principle," and it allows me to analyze the song as sounds "that straddle the particularisms of geographic emplacement and the dynamics of cultural travel" (2). The power of musical transits is that they highlight the interconnectedness between "sonic production" and "spatial formation" (3).

For my purposes, the numerous performances and interpretations of "Hasta Que Te Conocí" available on the internet, especially in the rich archive of YouTube, illustrate, on the one hand, the versatility and flexibility of a song that has been adapted and rearranged multiple times by a wide array of musicians and singers, and, on the other, the critical role that space, publics, and musicians play in creating "musical scenes" or events. "Hasta Que Te Conocí" thus continues to hold meaning in Latin America precisely through its reiterations: as urban dance music in clubs and concerts, as instrumental solo concerts, as instrumental repertoire by youth bands in Mexico's villages and towns, as music videos of rock en español, and as feminist rewritings. Outside of Mexico and the Americas, the song has also circulated as a soundtrack to figure skating competitions, thus allowing its melody to travel to Asia and to emerging new global listening communities. In 2016, Mexican figure skater Donovan Carrillo, who became a celebrity during the 2022 Beijing Winter Olympics, selected "Hasta Que Te Conocí" for a performance in Japan in honor of his mother, who loved Juan Gabriel. That same year, Jennifer, a young Colombian woman, competed with the song in the *La Voz Teens Colombia* reality show.

While Mexican singers like Ana Gabriel reproduce the song in its most traditional version as a bolero ranchera, the transformations of this urtext into multiple versions and rhythms reveal its power to move audiences throughout the Americas. From the merengue and salsa scenes in the Dominican

Republic and Peru, to the youth bands in Mexican villages, to the electro-pop arrangements of Mexican feminist singers, the song continues to be performed, sounded, and listened to as a moment for collective healing and grieving. These heterogeneous articulations and rewritings strongly evince the melody's critical role in providing a space and time for acknowledging the colonial violence against our communities and for grappling with our ensuing suffering and sentimiento. Simultaneously, however, these performances also capture the joy of listeners and musicians alike, affective textures that are evident in specific moments and instances. The song's hemispheric presence, its sonic translocations and musical transits, illustrates the dynamic processes through which musicians, interpreters, and audiences appropriate a song and localize it, making it their own. Given the long hemispheric popularity of boleros throughout Latin America, it is not surprising to identify such numerous iterations of "Hasta Que Te Conocí." Yet, the rewritings into such diverse formats, genres, rhythms, and instrumentations reveal an exceptional resonance rooted in the geocultural, postcolonial, and precarious lives in the Global South. Tracing the song also allows us to engage in alternative modes of embodying gender and sexuality, as "multiple masculinities" and feminist rewritings and performances transform the song into a site for the contestation and reproduction of patriarchy and multiple gender enunciations.

Dominican merengue singer Roberto del Castillo's interpretation of the song can be seen in the YouTube video of his 1985 performance in Puerto Rico and heard, with Johnny Ventura's orchestra, in his 1987 album *Justo a Tiempo* (Ortiz López 1985). Sung in the style of merengue típico [traditional merengue dance] yet with a full orchestra, del Castillo's version honors and reproduces the lyrical, intimate textures of Juan Gabriel's iconic performances. Yet, his body movements are vertically rigid and masculine in their linearity. He hardly moves his brown body sideways, singing in a delicate tone at the beginning of the song, while increasing in volume and vocality after the temporal transition of "Hasta que." Del Castillo engages in merengue dancing with the two background dancers in the second half of the performance, thus accelerating the slower initial tempo of the bolero genre and reframing the song under faster Caribbean rhythms. The sounds of the güira, the metal scraper twin to the Puerto Rican güiro, of Indigenous origins, also reframes the song instrumentally, relocating it to the Caribbean islands. The brass instruments, while echoing the mariachi sonic textures of the trumpets, resituate the melody within the sonic traditions of urban Dominican merengues and urban dance music. Most significant, however, is the central role of the soneo and improvisatory lyrics, a structural pillar of salsa music and of Afro-Caribbean sonic traditions. While del Castillo refers to the woman in the song not as "bandolera" but as "mi nena," he mostly duplicates Juan Gabriel's own lyrics in this section of the song. Despite its strong, heterosexist performance, this merengue version does suggest, in nuanced ways, contestatory gender performances in the excessive body movements of the background dancers, whom del Castillo emulates and joins. The repeated moaning that we hear as sonic background reveals a more overt sexual enactment absent in Juan Gabriel's more nuanced performances, perhaps signaling the Caribbean archipelago as a site of excess and pleasure (Ortiz López 1985).

In Lima, Peru, the popular salsa singer César Vega also performs "Hasta Que Te Conocí" as a salsa arrangement. The Peruvian salsero enacts the vocal and corporeal gestures of salsa's heteronormative discursive traditions. Through linear and straight body movements, Vega elides the hip-swaying gyrations central to Afro-Caribbean dancing choreographies yet associated in Juan Gabriel's case with queerness. His loud singing, associated with the urban textures of salsa dura, marks the beginning of the second part of the song after the initial intimate tone of the bolero genre. In his 2019 show in La Casa de la Salsa in Lima, Vega and his orchestra engaged with the audience through comments that acknowledge suffering after romantic breakups, thus framing the song as a site for healing and catharsis. Right after the passionate soneo and improvisation, in which he denounces the female lover as "muy mala conmigo" [very evil toward me], echoing Juan Gabriel's original composition, Vega asks the audience to applaud if they have already forgotten the former lover—"aquellos que ya se olvidaron de su ex" ["those who have already forgotten their ex"]. This request enacts the song and its singing not just as spectacle or entertainment but as an example of the Muñozian concept of brownness and Latinidad, despite its highly heteronormative performative texture. The salsa framework within which César Vega transforms the Mexican bolero ranchera also opens the possibility for a sense of joy and pleasure, as Alejandro Madrid noted of Juan Gabriel's 1990 concert. César Vega says salsa is "sabrosura," thus translocating the Mexican song onto a Peruvian and transnational experience of "sabor" that emerged among Puerto Rican musicians both on the island and in New York. The deployment of this signifier that entangles Mexico, Peru, Puerto Rico, and New York clearly illustrates the geographies of performance that Latinidad entails. If "sabor" is defined as "a rich essence that makes our mouths water or makes our bodies want to move," the "sabor of music moves us and heals us" (Berríos-Miranda, Dudley, and Habell-Pallán 2018, 19), thus approximating "sabor" to scholarly definitions of "affect" (Papacharissi 2015).

The song's transformation from a text with lyrics, a linguistic and verbal experience, to an instrumental version, meant exclusively for listening mode rather than as a dance hit, is clearly illustrated in Argentinian pianist Raúl Di Blasio's interpretation of "Hasta Que Te Conocí." Included in his album *Piano de America: Volume 2* (Areola/BMG, 1994), Di Blasio's virtuosic version is an instrumental sonic event. In the video for the song, without the lyrics, without the vocal affective textures associated with Juan Gabriel's iconic voice, Di Blasio pairs his piano skills and talents with natural landscapes, the musicians in the symphonic orchestra that accompanies him, and the lyrical movements of a female dancer whose translucent scarf complements and dialogues with her corporeal choreography. The ethereal and lyrical texture of the instrumental version is thus created through dance, visual images, and instrumental arrangements, particularly audible in the central role of the violins. Most notably, Di Blasio pays homage to Juan Gabriel's performances by honoring the dynamic shift that I highlighted in both Juan Gabriel's and Marc Anthony's renditions, that is, the contrast from the slow beginning of the song, accompanied by the violins and the oboe or clarinets, to the change in tempo and rhythm as the song increases in volume and changes to syncopated rhythms. Di Blasio exhibits a majestic style of performing arpeggios and covering the whole keyboard, a style very much in line with Liberace and other virtuosos of the piano. Thus, the sonic experience of this version also evinces excess in its performative arm and hand gestures, rather than in the vocalizing of the lyrics. The queer aesthetics Di Blasio establishes through his virtuosic style of piano playing suggest an acknowledgment, albeit oblique, of Juan Gabriel's "secreto a voces."

In addition, the song has become a canonical instrumental piece for many youth bands in Mexico. In stark contrast to Di Blasio's excessive style, these young mestizo and Indigenous music students—mostly male—throughout Mexico perform the song in impeccable style under the direction of their band directors and conductors. Their serious and almost stiff facial expressions during their musical performances reveal the larger sense of music as rigor and discipline, an approach that is instilled early on in most music education programs. Yet, there is also a sense of pleasure in producing together, creating harmonies, counterpoints to the melody, and working as an ensemble. In one video, the percussion section of the youth band seems to disrupt the seriousness of the performance. All young men in these bands, which, curiously, constitute homosocial spaces, display their joy and pleasure in producing the rhythms that serve as a foundation and base to the song. It is these small moments of smiles and body movements that suggest the joys and pleasures of music-making. Perhaps we can consider those "details," if not as "excess," at least as ruptures in their otherwise rigorous and disciplined performative styles.

The Mexican band Maná, one of the most popular rock en español bands in Latin America, has sold more than forty million records and won Latin Grammy and Grammy Awards in their long musical careers. In homage to Juan Gabriel, their swing and rock adaptation of "Hasta Que Te Conocí" is included on their album *Exiliados en la Bahía: Lo mejor de Maná*. The music video, released on August 27, 2012, peaked at number one on the Billboard Hot Latin Songs, and the record earned a nomination for Record of the Year at the 2012 Latin Grammy Awards. The music video reproduces the original patriarchal values of the song, as it constructs the female lover as "mala" and, most interestingly, as "hechicera." Rather than in the sounds or arrangements, predictably rock rhythms, instrumentation, and arrangements, Maná deploys visual language and images to perpetuate the heteronormative ideologies of sexism and misogyny. The suffering of the male singer-subject remains, but it feels almost secondary to the threatening signs that the female figure offers the male lover. In the visual narrative, when the woman reads tarot cards to the man, two cards are highlighted: "hechicera" and "amor," thus conflating how love is a risk and women have the potential to become "tricksters" in the romantic relationship. Her assumed treachery is reiterated in the scene when she serves him a drink but refuses to drink her own, spilling it away from the camera. This brief gesture proposes the woman as a potential killer. Moreover, the woman also appears as a potential traitor, as she appears in very intimate poses with another one of the musicians, in this case, the singer. It is not coincidental, then, that the rupture and shift after "Hasta que," which we have noted in Juan Gabriel's and Marc Anthony's performances, is signaled by the first appearance of the female figure in Maná's music video. The focus on the woman as "hechicera" dominates the visual narrative that gives meaning to the sounds of the song. It feels disappointing, to say the least, that Mexican male musicians continue to reproduce these patriarchal icons and images through their productions. El Marc, as we have already seen, has also contributed to these long-held heteronormative gender constructs.

In stark contrast to these masculinist versions, the pop Mexican singer Anahí released "Hasta Que Me Conociste" as one of the singles on her 2009 album, *Delirio*. Clearly a feminist translation of the song, her version introduces the female subject and her agency by contesting the original song's misogyny. She addresses the male as her interlocutor, telling him, "Sabes muy bien . . . que me necesitas" [You very well know . . . that you need me], and denouncing the ways in which the male lover is attached to her, always returning, "Dices que soy mala / pero vuelves / Sabes muy bien / Que tú me quieres ver / Te trato mal / Te gusta, te gusta / Dime si no / Valió la pena encontrarme / Y sufrir por mí" [You call me evil / but you return to me / You well know / that you want to see me / I mistreat you / You like it, you like it / Tell me that / It was worth finding me / And suffering for me]. While the feminist singer acknowledges that she has been cruel to her lover, she also insists that he recognize his affective dependency on her. The origins of the "suffering," in Anahí's version, reside in the male need for attention and love, not necessarily in the female behavior. Again, the feminist response to Juan Gabriel's original lyrics belongs within the long tradition of feminist singers who continue to deconstruct and rewrite patriarchal ideologies in Latin America. The musical arrangements and instrumentation produce an electropop, rock, and pop texture that, like other urban dance musics, exhorts audiences to dance. The sampling of Juan Gabriel's original melody, also evident to a careful listener, produces a palimpsest of songs in dialogic relationship to each other. As a fan commented online, "Amo esta canción en ambas versiones, Juan Gabriel y Anahí" [I love this song in both versions, Juan Gabriel and Anahi], thus evincing the simultaneity of both sonic texts in Anahí's performance.

Listening to the musical transits of "Hasta Que Te Conocí" in its myriad versions documents the heterogeneous geocultural regions in Latin America that have transformed this song into a rich panoply of sonic, visual, and choreographic experiences, thus evincing the cultural agency of diverse Latin American communities. The variety of formats that have framed the song reveal its impressive resonance and popularity, thus its status as an urtext of suffering and healing. Moreover, in more oblique ways, the song also signals the gender wars that popular music has embodied and facilitated, through feminist rewritings as well as through corporeal movements and gestures in their vocality and choreographies and specific sonic traditions that strongly enact heteronormative and masculine ideologies, such as salsa and merengue.

Triangulating Gender: Juanga, Willie, and El Marc

In this light, I return to Willie Colón, who embodied the MexiRican sonic Latinidades. Most fascinatingly, Willie Colón, "el niño malo" [the bad boy] from the early years of salsa dura in New York, sang "Hasta Que Te Conocí" in 1990, three years before el Marc, and included it on his album *Color americano*. The song begins as a slow ballad, typical of the bolero latinoamericano expectations, and then shifts to salsa arrangements and rhythms. I bring attention to the foundational undercurrents of the textures of the Latin American bolero that emerge throughout the sonic performances of popular music, bridging the diverse musical genres and traditions that circulate throughout the Americas. By acknowledging the bolero as a musical tradition that enacts the affective contours of Muñoz's Latinidad, we can clearly establish these semantic and cultural leaps between salsa in New York City and boleros and bolero rancheras in Mexico and Latin America proper.

Willie Colón's Latinidad, less an identitarian marker than a social and political project enunciated through his songs and repertoire, is also clearly documented in his musical career. In 1967, when Colón cut his first album, *El malo*, music was a platform for the countercultural and political transformations happening not only among Blacks, Chicanx, and Nuyoricans in the United States but also in Cuba and Latin America. The fact that Colón's music was banned in Nicaragua in the 1970s by the dictator Somoza, and that he was arrested several times in Central and South America for his music, most specifically for singing a parody titled "El General," is clear proof of the antiestablishment and antiauthoritarian values of his songs and of the radical ideologies of the times (Rodríguez and González, n.d.). Yet Colón is also known within the salsa community as a composer and arranger who felicitously combined a wide array of rhythms and sounds from Latin America. Like Marc Anthony, whose Nuyorican identity is not compromised as he travels sonically and physically throughout Latin America, Colón arranges his repertoire as an opening to Latinidad in sounds and rhythms: "He gave New York salsa an elegant and original sound thanks to the use of new ingredients, among these, Jíbaro music, the country music of Puerto Rico. But he also incorporated Brazilian, Colombian, and Panamanian elements" (Pérez Aldave 1990, C-4, 5; my translation). This ongoing hybridity in the larger soundscapes of Latinx music, so lucidly documented by Deborah Pacini Hernández, represented not only an opportunity for creative experimentation but in the case of Willie Colón articulated the sounds of a serious political project that constructed Latinidad as a liberation from collective suffering. In his own words: "Our community needs to hear things and we [artists] need to be able to tell our stories to the Latino empire or the Latino nation. The things we suffer in the barrio are the same things that people in Colombia, Chile and Panama suffer" (Alvarez 1997).[14] Clearly, the homologies and conflations of the precarities of our communities in the US diaspora and in Latin America proper may be open to further discussion, but the statement itself reveals the vision of a salsa musician committed to sounds, songs, and performances as sites for liberation and decoloniality. Although brief, this declaration speaks to how Nuyorican musicians, in particular salseros, played a major role as storytellers in the hemispheric constructions of Latinidad, discourses that bridged Puerto

---

14. Lydia Milagros González (1990), in her review of the 1990 Canto a Mi Tierra concert in Puerto Rico, also refers to Willie Colón as "the man who integrated Brazilian, Colombian and American beats into his music."

Ricans in Spanish Harlem and the Bronx to the larger urban and marginalized cohorts throughout Latin America.

Yet, this image of Willie Colón, much more rooted in his early years, is significantly unsettled now, when in his senior years he has become a deputy sheriff in New Rochelle, New York, where he lives, and when he has made public statements in support of then President Donald Trump. This shift in his local and national political positions, inevitably accompanied by a rigid normative masculinity, has resituated him as a conservative Latino allied with the police at a time when progressive voices are calling for defunding or reimagining of the roles of the police in Black and Brown communities. Such a change in gender politics leads me to examine the multiplicity of gender in his own musical oeuvre. My reading of Willie Colón's performative masculinities is inevitably entangled with Marc Anthony's own multiple gender constructions throughout his musical career. I would argue that these two Nuyorican artists, who embody different generational experiences, have contested each other through the singing of "Hasta Que Te Conocí," a challenge mediated through the queer Mexican divo Juan Gabriel.

In his return to Chicago in 2017, after decades away, at a concert in Millennium Park attended by a generationally, racially, and culturally diverse crowd, Colón performed "Hasta Que Te Conocí" in a most linear masculine style. By this, I mean he stood behind the microphone, hardly moving, hardly dancing to the rhythms of the song. His vocality, lacking the brilliant volume and projection of Marc Anthony's, maintained the same volume throughout. It was, in my humble opinion, a rather uneventful sonic event with very few contrasts in the singing and arrangement. Yet, despite my personal disappointment, it was after that Chicago concert that I realized Colón was the first salsero to have sung Juan Gabriel's canonical song, not Marc Anthony. Briefly put, I cannot highlight el Marc as the exceptional US Latinx voice who performs "Hasta Que Te Conocí." He is one of many other hemispheric singers from the Americas who have made the song a classic sonic experience of Latinidad as suffering. This acknowledgment inspired my analysis of gender entanglements among these three singers.

I propose that Willie Colón's 1990 performance of "Hasta Que Te Conocí" needs to be listened to as a song that invites listeners to acknowledge nonbinary gender positionalities. Not only is its composer the most renowned queer singer in Mexican musical history, despite its "secreto a voces," but Colón recorded this song only a year after his own release of "El Gran Varón," the classic salsa cut that acknowledged the suffering in Black and Brown communities during the AIDS epidemic in the 1980s. Composed by Panamanian Omar Alfanno, "El Gran Varón" has been hailed by Leila Cobo (2021a) as "a legend" and an "anthem for the gay community" (79); she writes that it is "revolutionary" that "a macho salsa man would tackle such a topic" (65). As Fernando Rex (2015) writes, Colón "fue uno de los primeros en mostrar aprecio musical hacia la comunidad gay" [was one of the first to show musical appreciation to the gay community]. The story of Simón, based on Alfanno's memories of a young gay man in his school, is that of a trans Puerto Rican man who finally reconciles with his father before his untimely death from a "strange disease." As DJs "started picking that song, . . . it rose to #1 in ten countries in Latin America" (Cobo 2021a, 78). In Willie Colón's words, "it was incredible. It snowballed" (Cobo 2021a, 78). It became a collective reference in the Puerto Rican diaspora and a "chart-topping, Grammy winning single from the 1980's" (Lockwood 2000). Despite "pushback" from gay and religious communities regarding its lyrics, "El Gran Varón" has "stood the test of time, the test of politics, and the test of political correctness" (Cobo 2021a, 65). As late as 2000, eleven years after its original release, Colón still closed many of his shows and concerts with the story of Simón. As Alan Lockwood (2000) writes in a review of a Brooklyn music event, the song has had a tremendous affective impact on our communities, as it "draws tears" and has been "doing its emotional wrenching on every radio station that plays salsa." Lockwood described the emotional effects of the song on the listeners, a collective reaction that has been common across the long decades of performing the song: "When hundreds of people around you are singing it at the tops of their voices after who knows how many hundreds of previous times, it's a strong and human and hopeful plea for acceptance and reconciliation."

I highlight this period of music-making for Willie Colón to engage with the performative potentialities of telling stories and publicly acknowledging nonbinary gender subjectivities, thus enacting the suffering of mourning, both individual and collective, during the AIDS pandemic. I thus reclaim the Willie Colón of that period, during his mid-career stage, as the one who selected Juan Gabriel's song while he also sang about the need for family reconciliations amid the numerous AIDS-related deaths. Yet this acknowledgment and legitimation of queerness could be tamed by el niño malo's lingering misogyny and patriarchy. If Leila Cobo referred to him as a "macho salsa singer" (2021a, 65), as a Latina feminist, I also cannot elide the Willie Colón who harshly attacked *El Cantante*, Marc Anthony and Jennifer Lopez's film production, for its female-centric narrative framework. If my impression was that Willie Colón had performed "Hasta Que Te Conocí" in the Chicago summer concert as a way of competing with Marc Anthony, this enmity is also evident in his strong denunciation of the movie about the personal addiction struggles of Héctor Lavoe and his love story with Puchi, his late widow. Colón's derogatory comments about these "two dominant women taking center stage in a man's world" (Gurza 2007), who fueled the film's production and narrative, strongly reveals a misogynistic stance against both Jennifer Lopez, who plays Puchi Pérez in the film, and Puchi herself, who wrote a first version of the film's script and who wanted Jennifer to play her in the film. Colón's debasing statements about Puchi clearly reveal his disapproval of their relationship as he blames her for Lavoe's untimely death: "I believe that Puchi actually caused Héctor's downfall," Colón said. "I never understood why he put up with such a negative, homely, vulgar person. The biggest crime is the canonization of Puchi so that Jennifer can play her" (Gurza 2007). The evident contradictions and juxtapositions of gender ideologies and discourses throughout Colón's musical career and public statements suggest, then, that gender, as a performative enactment, is inherently multiple and always shifting, strategic, simultaneous, and contradictory in its musical and social enunciations.

Until 2022 Marc Anthony, in contrast, had not performed any songs that explicitly interpellate or hail same-sex desire or nonheteronormative subjectivities. In his 2022 album, *Pa'lla Voy*, released in early March as I first drafted this chapter, the song "Amor No Tiene Sexo" has been a positive and most welcome surprise for the many listeners and fans who have had to adapt his heteronormative repertoire to suit their own nonbinary gendered lives. "Amor No Tiene Sexo" is initially framed as a story about a friend whose same-sex desire led to social alienation and a painful relationship to his patriarchal father, echoing "El Gran Varón": "Hoy voy a contarles la historia de un amigo / Que desde niño sufrió" [Today I will tell the story of a friend / who suffered since he was a child]. The refrain reiterates the legitimacy of love without sexual categories and legitimizes desire in all its forms. The lyrics open the possibility of considering the "amigo" as gay, trans, or fluid in their sexual desires: "Dos personas que se aman con el mismo cuerpo" [Two people who love with the same body] and "Donde está el pecado de verse por fuera y ser otro adentro?" [How is it sinful to be someone outside and another one inside?]. If, as Marc Anthony has described, *Pa'lla Voy* is "his first post-pandemic album" as "one man's story of *desamor*: Falling in and out of love," now Marc Anthony's singing persona's love is also nonbinary and queer (Cobo 2022). Yet the album also includes "Mala," already considered a "great revenge track that can become an instant classic" (Cobo 2022), reminding us of the multiple subjectivities that now circulate around gender identities and sexual ideologies.

In brief, these complicated gender discourses from both Colón and Marc Anthony may be superficially understood as strategies to increase listening audiences, but ultimately they are also markers of these singers' commitments to acknowledge the social reality of our collective and individual lives at particular moments in history. Ultimately, our critical listening of "Hasta Que Te Conocí," as performed by Willie Colón, Marc Anthony, and Juan Gabriel, suggests the intertwined textures of gender and sexuality within the collective sense of suffering and grieving in Latinx communities throughout the Americas. It is essential to recognize that salsa music, which has been largely defined in mainstream discourses as celebratory, feel-good dance music, is also a genre that acknowledges our collective suffering and inspires us to heal and grieve. Thus, the entangled relationship between Juan Gabriel, Willie Colón, and Marc Anthony. If music as performance has the potential for affective communality throughout diverse audiences, singing "Hasta Que Te Conocí" will continue to reiterate the shared experiences of gender and Latinidad throughout the hemispheric Americas.

CHAPTER 3

"I Need to Know" (1999)

Singing in English and the Sonic Struggles for Americanness

On February 18, 2021, during the COVID pandemic and lockdown, Arizona Republican Representative Debbie Lesko stated: "I worked with people that are Hispanic. I mean they're very good workers. . . . We're compassionate people, but for goodness sakes, we have to take care of American citizens, or people that are here legally, first" (Sesin 2021; ellipsis in original). As reported by NBC News, this public stance illustrates the long-held problematic logic that excludes Latinx communities from membership in the United States national imaginary, inscribing them as never fully Americans. Within a discussion about the distribution of COVID vaccines in Arizona, Lesko's words serve as a painful reminder of the long history of marginalizing Mexicans and Latinx populations and imagining them outside of Americanness, as less than, unworthy of inclusion, noncitizens. This discourse, evident in US institutions from the justice system to the media, from politics to health services, has served to prevent subordinated communities from accessing resources, holding dignity, and feeling that they truly belong to the US body politic. Yet, as the NBC News article argues, the conflation of Hispanic or Latino with noncitizens is totally erroneous and misguided. In Arizona, almost "32 percent of the population is Latino" and "fewer than 4 percent of people in the state are undocumented, according to the Pew Research Center." As Stephen Nuño, a political scientist at Northern Arizona University, who counterargues Lesko, stated: "Amid a pandemic, Lesko's horrifyingly ignorant comment makes no sense from a scientific perspective—diseases do not stop spreading just because a person is undocumented." Democratic State Senator Juan Mendez, who served with Lesko when she was in the state legislature, concluded: "Unfortunately, Rep. Lesko is only a symptom of a larger epidemic of hate and ignorance." To be sure, while the Trump regime has legitimated these public articulations of racism and exclusion against Latinx and other communities of color, this discursive violence against the human rights of our communities is not new.

I begin this chapter with this example to highlight the long and continuous history of Latinx and other vulnerable communities being positioned outside of Americanness, a context that frames my analysis of "I Need to Know." Having been constructed as "perpetual foreigners" and "illegals," Latinx individuals, families, and communities have long experienced the consequences of being situated outside of the American body politic and national imaginary. In the history of US public health, rigorous health measures were imposed on the similarly constructed "un-American" and "foreign" bracero workers who entered the United States between the 1940s and 1960s to labor under contracts and whose bodies were exposed to toxic pesticides and chemicals in those infamous hygienic programs. While their bodies were racialized as not clean enough, as sources of contamination for the larger American population, they were also desirable and welcome only as cheap labor (Loza 2016; Stern 1999). These processes, both discursive and material, simultaneously dehumanize and commodify us, placing our lives at risk. Since the founding of the United States, imported enslaved people and their descendants, members of Indigenous tribes, women, colonized subjects, and immigrants and refugees from the Global South, most notably Muslims, have been denied the human and civil rights that the so-called American mainstream takes for granted: the right to vote, citizenship, an active role in American civic institutions, and a sense of worthiness and personhood.

Marc Anthony's musical repertoire constitutes a sonic archive that stands against these exclusions and racializations. Many of his songs articulate negotiations between, and a grappling with, the in-betweenness of his Puerto Rican heritage and Latinx culture and the political identity of his legal Americanness. "I Need to Know," which catapulted him into the Anglo mainstream after his 1999 performance, invites critical reflections on the long-term debate regarding Marc Anthony's—and other Latinx subjects'—worthiness to be considered fully American and his resistance and opposition to these racist exclusions. A critical analysis of the cultural politics of singing in English, Spanish, and Spanglish, and of Marc Anthony's disavowals of his imposed participation in the Latin music boom of 1999–2000 and the language around him as a crossover act, serve as a prelude to my invitation to replay "I Need to Know," relistening to it differently. Rather than a song that crosses over into the whiteness of mainstream America, I argue that this canonical song is a sonic resistance that reframes American identity as multiracial by integrating the heterogeneous sites of musical traditions that constitute so-called American music. The song, then, summons Americanness in an alternative mode: refusing assimilation, it rewrites Americanness through the sounds of multiracial music. It thus becomes a site for discursive gestures of resistance against the sonic categories and boundaries that perpetuate the racialization of our communities. In this light, "I Need to Know" belongs to a longer cultural archive of Latinx expressive arts that have resisted these structural exclusions from Americanness and that have rewritten "America" in alternative ways.[1]

Being born in New York, after all, makes Marc Anthony a full US citizen. Yet his legality has not protected him from the racializing discourses that egregiously exclude him from belonging to his own country, as the dominant narratives of the Latin music boom and crossing over perpetuate. As Nilda Flores-González (2017) lucidly argues in her study of second-generation Latinx born in the United States, Latino millennials "were reluctant to identify as Americans" given "their inability to meet its ethnoracial criteria" as "Anglo-Saxon Protestant" (154). Yet as "citizens but not Americans," their US-based Latinidad is always already entangled in the processes of racialization and criminalization that have long persisted in this country. By redefining their American identity in various ways, they resist these dominant discourses: "[they] make claims to a national identity by emphasizing their subscription to other 'American' tropes, such as freedom, opportunity, patriotism, and multiculturalism. As such, they embrace a vision of civil nationalism in order to insert themselves into the national imaginary and create a new vision of what it means to be an American" (154).

Not unlike Flores-González's racialized subjects, Marc Anthony articulates, through his music and albums during the end of the twentieth century

---

1. There is a vast archive of arts, music, and literature that engages in critiques as well as rewritings of the imperial concept of "America": from Alurista's poetry in *Floricanto en Aztlán* (1971), where he powerfully critiques the official discourse of democracy, "with liberty and justice for all"; to Edward James Olmos's book of photography and traveling exhibit entitled *Americanos*, which documents the multiple forms of labor of Latinos/as that have contributed to the making of the United States; to Boricua rapper Residente's (2022) "This Is Not America," in which he denounces "the collateral damage that the U.S. created in Latin America" (E. Rivera 2022). See also José David Saldívar's three foundational scholarly books (1991, 1997, 2012) on Latinx, Latin American, and African American literatures, which expand "America" into a hemispheric "Americanity," all of which contest the imperial gestures of a white "America." The renaming of the Gulf of Mexico as the Gulf of America in early 2025 by Trump's regime is a more recent instance of the violent erasure of the Americas in the mappings of our hemisphere.

and the beginning of the new millennium, counternarratives that expand on the limited ethnoraciality of "American" as a signifier of whiteness, while acknowledging and denouncing the racist underpinnings of this (lack of) belonging. In this chapter, I critically engage how "I Need to Know," framed as a crossover act, is much more than a mainstream song that signals assimilation. I propose relistening to the song as a cut that integrates heterogeneous musical and sonic traditions that constitute a multiracial, alternative imaginary of Americanness, like Josh Kun's proposal of popular music "as one of our most valuable sites for witnessing the performance of racial and ethnic difference against the grain of national citizenships that work to silence and erase those differences" (2005, 11). As Catherine Rottenberg writes, "if we do want to envision a more democratic notion of 'Americanness,' then we must not only trace the way it has signified in the past and the exclusions it has produced, but we also need to be able to imagine, create, and promote alternative notions of Americanness, ones that are not only more inclusive, but are also continuously open to contestation" (2008, 132).

Kun's definition of "audiotopias" comes to mind here: as "identificatory 'contact zones,' in that they are both sonic and social spaces where disparate identity-formations, cultures, and geographies historically kept and mapped separately are allowed to interact with each other as well as enter into relationships whose consequences for cultural identification are never predetermined" (2005, 23). This is, in fact, el Marc's sonic counterresponse: his singing against the white racist exclusions of his body, his voice, and his sounds as un-American by performing the sonic traditions of a richly heterogeneous America, thus reclaiming his worthiness as American while rewriting the signifier itself.

El Marc Racialized

Nilda Flores-González's conclusion to her book *Citizens but Not Americans* indicates that her analysis was fueled by the "racist social media comments" (2017, 150) triggered by the "Star Spangled Banner" and "God Bless America" being sung, in two different professional sports events, by two Latinx public figures: Sebastién de la Cruz, a young Mexican American male singer, and Marc Anthony, both deemed "unfit to perform such patriotic songs" (150). While Marc Anthony's status as a global icon in the music industry may seem a privilege, and it is, this celebrity status has not always protected him from violent forms of racialization in the United States. His mere presence still challenges white supremacy and dominant nationalism in the country of his birth.

FIGURE 3.1. Meme featuring Marc Anthony reclaiming his US citizenship.

The reaction of some baseball fans to his singing "God Bless America" in the 2013 Major League Baseball All-Star Game held in New York City revealed the dominant exclusionary ideologies that still inform national imaginaries in the United States. In blogs following the game, Marc Anthony was called "some Spanish fuck," "a spic," and a "Mexican," racialized terms of foreignness that still situate Puerto Ricans, despite our legal citizenship, outside the national boundaries of a white, imperial America. As Jennifer Rudolph (2020) discusses, those who excluded Marc Anthony from the American national imaginary did so under "the guise of supposed patriotism" while dismissing the fact that most baseball players in the United States are indeed foreign-born and recruited from abroad (52). Thus, for Rudolph, so-called American baseball needs to be understood as a site for nativism and nationalism (53).

As a result of this racist controversy, a new phrase emerged—"singing while Latino"—that adds to the multiple iterations of racial profiling, a racializing practice to which the singer subtly responds in his album *3.0* (C. Moreno 2013; see chap. 5). In brief, his global success has not shielded him from being racialized as a Diasporican. The meme shown in figure 3.1, which circulated on social media ten years ago, constructs Marc Anthony as a singer who resists the imperial meanings of the term "American."

The circulation of this meme in social media is a strong visual signifier of el Marc's resistance to his racialization as un-American. The use of Spanglish in the meme—with "gringo cabrón" uttered in Spanish—strategically plays with the fact that el Marc, like most other US-born Puerto Ricans and Latinx, is at home in both Spanish and English. The fact that the insult to Anglos is in Spanish reveals the powerful meanings that Spanish has as a language of and for our communities that is not "listened to" or "understood" by monolingual English-speaking America. The expletive insult in Spanish acquires its powerful meaning within the irony of its lack of intelligibility for monolingual Anglo speakers. It is precisely through its lack of communication that the insult becomes powerful. The fact that the author of the meme selected Marc Anthony's face as the icon of such a resistance reveals how his listeners find affinities in his songs as sites of resistance.

It is fitting, then, that "Americanness," as a critical concept and site for contestations and debates around inclusion in the US body politic, should frame my analysis in this chapter as I explore how Marc Anthony moves in and out of the white Anglo world, the Nuyorican and Diasporican world, and among the larger Latin American hemispheric audiences. Americanness, as deployed in scholarship, refers more generally to the condition of being American—and here American is used in its historically imperial meaning, as of the United States exclusively, erasing the rest of the continent. Across the disciplines, studies about the performance of Americanness in African American and Jewish American narratives (Rottenberg 2008) or the analysis of how undocumented youth activists "signify" Americanness in ways that transcend and defy the traditional criteria behind the ideal American subjectivity and behavior (Cabannis and Gardner 2020) reveal a vast semantic field for a term that is urgently imperative not as a theoretical concept but also in its material consequences, as in securing physical survival, economic stability, and family reunifications. Cabannis and Gardner identify three approaches to Americanness, including constructing "American" as (1) a subjective feeling, (2) a status that can be earned, and (3) a quality that one can demonstrate through political engagement in the United States (2020, 99). From the public performance of ideal characteristics for immigrants to be considered Americans, to the possibility that Americanness is the result of affective social relations, to a dynamic engagement with US politics, Americanness remains, most of all, an aspiration among most Latinx individuals, whether US citizens or not. In this framework, we consider how Marc Anthony resists "the desirability of fitting into hegemonic U.S. society" (Rottenberg 2008, 2) by refusing to "cite and mime the very norms that created his intelligibility [as an American] in the first place" (6).

Americanness, more specifically, signals the degrees *of worthiness* of being American in the legal arena, as is evident in the criteria that have been deployed in the justice system in trials that argue for the suspension of deportations. As Susan Bibler Coutin (2008) has examined, for the courts to approve suspensions of deportation orders for Latin American immigrants, lawyers must argue for their clients' "degrees of deservingness" to remain in the United States. The criteria that inform the judges' final decision include "years of residency in the United States, good moral character, evidence of extreme hardship to return, church membership, tax payments, family ties, and English-language skills" (61)—all behaviors that evince the "ideal immigrants who only wanted to better their lives and who thus were pursuing the American dream"; in brief, those who strived to achieve "cultural whiteness" (62). Thus, judges assess and "establish boundaries between the deserving and the undeserving" (84) by evaluating claimants based on "hegemonically defined standards" (83) and "normative notions of race, family, and progress" (84). One of the most salient questions in these court cases focuses on language use and skills. If fluency in English is considered strong evidence for acculturation and assimilation, "bilingualism and biculturalism can weaken acculturation-based hardship arguments" (66). The use of English and, by extension, "the linguistic competence of applicants' friends and relatives may therefore have been racially coded efforts to assess applicants' cultural whiteness (84). Thus, for Latin American and other immigrants from the Global South, speaking English is a way of performing Americanness that allows the state and mainstream Anglo society to read their identities as assimilable, to acknowledge their intelligibility as Americans, and, thus, to more easily embrace them as part of the national community. This conflation of speaking English in public spaces with the worthiness of being included as an American poignantly illustrates the long-held strength and power of assimilation ideologies. Yet, as Marc Anthony's complicated language performativities reveal, English does not always guarantee full access to inclusion and membership in dominant spaces, nor does it exclusively signal assimilation.

Singing in English and Musical Translanguaging

Echoing the hegemonic value of English in the US courts, the popular music industry continues to conflate singing in English with success and with the guarantees of securing a mainstream "American" following as well as a global audience, thus reproducing the aspirational tenets of crossing over. In contrast, singing in Spanish has been bracketed, domesticated, and undermined as separate niche, audience, and musical categories, in brief, as *Latin* and thus foreign music exclusively until 2020. However, the egregious conflation of Spanish and Latin music, informed by a binary-structured antiquated logic of assimilation, is now being unsettled and dismantled by the global popularity and success of Spanish, Latin American, and Caribbean pop figures such as Bad Bunny, Maluma, J Balvin, Cardi B, and Rosalía, among others. Refusing to bow to the language of US imperial politics, they are not only singing in Spanish but reaching top degrees of global reception despite their linguistic resistance. Rosalía, for instance, "became the first artist singing entirely in Spanish to be nominated for Best New Artist at the Grammys" (Wood 2019). As Mikael Wood (2019) wrote in the *Los Angeles Times,* after the 2017 hit "Despacito," this new generation of singers can achieve pop superstardom while singing in Spanish:

> English-speaking fans will no doubt remember earlier Latin-pop booms, as when Ricky Martin and Shakira broke out in the United States in the late '90s and early 2000s—and were quickly urged to adapt their sounds to American tastes. In the wake of Luis Fonsi and Daddy Yankee's 2017 hit "Despacito," though, the generation led by Balvin and Bad Bunny rarely sing or rap in English (even as they attract English-speaking stars like Beyoncé for remixes). And instead of streamlining their approach, they exult in using their music to draw geographical and historical connections.

Bad Bunny's February 2021 performance on *Saturday Night Live,* accompanied by Rosalía, easily signaled his unrivaled position in the charts and his acceptance by Anglo and more globalized listeners who may not speak or understand Spanish. As in the 2021 Grammys, global audiences today perhaps identify more with their own generational peers, with the performer's values and nonnormative stylings, clothing, hairstyle, and musical genres (pop, reggaetón, and hip-hop) than with the specific words and linguistic signifiers deployed in the songs. In addition, the bilingual and bicultural youth—"billennials," as they are called—operate "in English, Spanish, and Spanglish" and constitute important sectors of media and popular music audiences (Avilés Santiago and Báez 2019, quoted in Rivera-Rideau 2021). Bad Bunny's Spanish songs on mainstream TV stations such as NBC may not be the first instance of Spanish sounds in English-language television spaces—let us remember Desi Arnaz's strategic use of Spanish in *I Love Lucy* during the 1960s, the Spanish words in the PBS Cuban-American TV sitcom *¿Que Pasa, USA?* during the 1970s, and *Jane the Virgin* (2014–19), in which the immigrant grandmother spoke in Spanish and her granddaughter responded in English.

But the sounds of Spanish still unsettle the monolingual boundaries and ideologies that continue to circulate among the larger so-called American public. The sounds of Spanish on television stages also signal the increasingly global circulation of Spanish not only across the United States, which now stands as the second largest Spanish-speaking country in the world (after Mexico), but also throughout Latin America, Spain, and other countries in Europe. With an estimated 470 to 500 million Spanish speakers in the world, Spanish is the second most prominently spoken native language, after Mandarin.[2]

As Leila Cobo writes, "As of 2020, Latin music is the largest-growing genre of music in the world. Once considered the realm of romantic ballads and folk songs, it has blossomed to incorporate a dizzying array of subgenres, voices, nationalities, rhythms, syncopations, and styles big and small. It is sung in Spanish and in English and in both. It is inescapable" (2021a, 4). Yet this global acceptance of singing in Spanish is relatively recent, perhaps characteristic of the new millennium and the impact of streaming technologies. In contrast, in 1999, during the Latin music boom, the music industry and producers policed linguistic boundaries and did not allow non-English songs to be performed in major shows such as the Grammys. In fact, when Tommy Mottola, then chief of Sony Music, insisted that Ricky Martin perform at the 2000 Grammys ceremonies, "the Grammys were leery about having a Spanish-language performance—this was prestreaming, of course—but Mottola, who had no doubts about Martin's stardom, pushed hard to have him on the show" (177). The rest is history, as Ricky Martin's performance unleashed the Latin music boom that ushered in the new millennium.

Marc Anthony was also associated with the Latin music boom with his first performance of "I Need to Know" on *Good Morning America* on July 23, 1999. Mainstream media and entertainment journalists categorized Marc Anthony's "I Need to Know" as a crossover act, with headlines like "A Grammy Pop Nod Further Validates Columbia's Anthony as Crossover Star" (Taylor 2000) and statements like "It's good to be the king . . . of salsa. But it's taken some fancy crossover moves and an English-language hit to get America talking about Marc Anthony" (Willman 1999). Ed Morales writes, "Marc Anthony had made a record that brought the Latin sensibility fully into the contemporary world" (2003, 89). Barry Walters (1999) refers to Marc Anthony's "bid for crossover fame," while Paul Willistein (1999) notes that "the media has singled out Anthony as next in line to follow in the dance steps of Hispanic pop sensation Ricky Martin," although he does question the narratives that frame Marc

---

2. See "Countries with the Most Spanish Speakers in the World, 2019," https://www.statista.com/statistics/991020/number-native-spanish-speakers-country-worldwide. See also Wikipedia, s.v. "Spanish language," https://en.wikipedia.org/wiki/I_Need_to_Know_(Marc_Anthony_song).

Anthony as a crossover act. Finally, Herón Márquez (2001), in his chapter dedicated to Marc Anthony, discusses the process of discovery—the "Columbus Effect"—that has framed Marc Anthony for mainstream audiences.[3] He quotes the *Washington Post*: "Anthony can sell out arenas on several continents, pack Madison Square Garden and make history with the way his albums fly up Billboard's Latin music charts—but that all barely got noticed by the somewhat insular American mainstream. He's been a salsa singer who records primarily in Spanish, and in this country, in music as in other art forms, you use English if you want to make a serious dent in the culture. Industry insiders and smitten critics have been waiting for the rest of America to discover him" (Span 1999, C-1, quoted in Márquez 2001, 79).

Yet Marc Anthony has refuted this crossover label. He has stated that he sings in English and Spanish because of his biculturalism, not because of his crossing over. In his words:

> That whole "Latin crossover" thing. I don't understand it. I'm just as American as the next guy. I'm bicultural yes, and I thank God for that. But what am I crossing over to? I was born and raised here. It is solely because I am bicultural that this tag has been put on me. It's like, you know, a Latin guy trying to come into this other world. What are they talking about? This [mainstream pop] world is as much mine as it is yours. Latin crossover would be if I took *Contra la corriente* and the world accepted it on mainstream pop charts. I sing English pop music as an American. And I'll keep singing salsa in Spanish as a Puerto Rican. That's not crossover. . . . That's biculturalism.[4] (Valdés-Rodríguez 1999, 1)

Having been born in Spanish Harlem in 1968 and spoken English as his dominant language growing up, Marc Anthony did not cross over from Spanish, as a subordinated local language, to English. In fact, he began singing in English in New York City's local clubs, recording house and freestyle dance music in the 1980s, and then shifting to salsa in Spanish by 1993 with his album *Otra Nota*.

Here I contest the binary logics that undergird perceptions of English and Spanish as separate languages and linguistic communities. A detailed analysis

---

3. The term "Columbus Effect" was coined by Wilson Valentín-Escobar in 2000 and also deployed by María Elena Cepeda in her 2001 article about the Latin music boom and the imperial logics of crossing over.

4. Herón Márquez also redefines the social meanings of Marc Anthony's singing in English as self-expression rather than as assimilation or crossing over: Marc Anthony "believed they [his fans] would understand that singing in English was just another means for Anthony to express himself artistically, not an indication that he was abandoning them" (2001, 80).

of el Marc's recordings and performances reveal that, as a bicultural person of color, he has sung, recorded, and performed in English, Spanish, and Spanglish throughout his career. In fact, not only has he inhabited all three linguistic worlds, but he has consistently code-switched between these linguistic spaces within and across his albums and throughout his larger repertoire. If his first recording of house and freestyle cuts, 1991's *When the Night Is Over*, was in English, his 1993 album *Otra Nota* marked his entry into salsa songs in Spanish. After two more Spanish-language recordings, *Todo a Su Tiempo* (1995) and *Contra la Corriente* (1997), his 1999 album *Marc Anthony* featured all English songs. Immediately following was *Libre* (2001), which marked a return not only to songs in Spanish but a hemispheric framework of Latin American sonic traditions, rhythms, and instruments that reinscribed el Marc, beyond his Nuyoricanness, as a Latin American singer of and from the Americas. This is one of the counternarratives that el Marc deploys to assert his expanded and hemispheric Americanity. As Ed Morales writes: "The resounding success of 2001's Spanish-language *Libre*, in which his salsa became increasingly sophisticated, incorporating influences like Colombian vallenato and Peruvian charango, indicated that his strength and fan base was largest in the world of the Latin beat" (2003, 89).

By claiming his Americanness through the sonic traditions of Latin America proper—the use of the cuatro, the charango, the Andean flutes, the requinto guitars, the accordion sounds in the vallenato, as well as the quintessential bolero, born in Cuba—Marc Anthony repositions himself away from the narratives of crossover, assimilation, and whiteness that domesticated him in 1999 and 2000. On *Libre* he offers his listeners a rich array of musical traditions from Latin America recognized by the multiple award nominations it received and its high standing in the charts.[5]

The traditional linguistic crossover shift from Spanish to English is perhaps more clearly evinced in el Marc's 2002 *Mended*, his second English album, which was described as "for mass consumption."[6] Let us note, however, that the two bonus tracks on *Mended* are Spanish songs, "Me Haces Falta" and "Tragedia." Various examples of linguistic shifts throughout and within certain albums clearly reveal el Marc's insistence on unsettling the music industry's hegemonic monolingual labels and boundaries. This is clearly exemplified in the unexpected inclusion of "Make It with You" on *Otra Nota*, which I discuss below, and the fact that "I Need to Know" was also recorded in Spanish, as

---

5. *Libre* was nominated for the 2002 Latin Grammy for Best Salsa Album and the 2003 Grammy for Best Salsa Album, and it reached third chart-topper in the Billboard Top Latin Albums chart. It remained at number one for fourteen consecutive weeks. See Wikipedia, s.v. "*Libre* (Marc Anthony album)," https://en.wikipedia.org/wiki/Libre_(Marc_Anthony_album).

6. Wikipedia, s.v. "*Mended*," https://en.wikipedia.org/wiki/Mended.

"Dímelo," and won the 2000 Latin Grammy Award for Song of the Year and peaked at number one on the Billboard Hot Latin Songs chart in the United States. His Spanish and Spanglish versions of "You Sang to Me" (coauthored by Marc Anthony and Cory Rooney and released in 2000) evince the multilingual spaces and cultural simultaneity that characterize el Marc's decision-making in his musical albums. Since 2002, all other recordings and compilations have been entirely in Spanish, where el Marc has found his "voice" as an interpreter of salsa love songs. Thus, the years associated with the Latin music boom and crossing over for Latinx singers such as Marc Anthony constitute the time period in which he most alternated among English, Spanish, and Spanglish, a linguistic fact that reveals his negotiations with Americanness.

In his public interviews and statements on stage, el Marc has ludically and ironically posed as a languageless or alingual performer who does not truly belong to either English or Spanish. Hailing dominant ideologies that subordinate racial minorities by dispossessing them of their heritage languages, Marc Anthony highlights the problematic colonial underpinnings of the linguistic expectations and binaries established by the music industry, journalists, entertainment media, and such. For instance, after many concerts and Spanish song recordings, Marc Anthony would comment: "Como dice Celia, my English is not very good-looking." Why would a second-generation New York–born Puerto Rican American singer deny his English-dominant proficiency by quoting Cuban exile singer Celia Cruz? Is he perhaps attempting to resituate himself within the imaginary of Spanish-speaking Latin American audiences and of Latinx immigrants in the United States? Why would he disavow his English-speaking childhood and youth, his identity as a New Yorker that clearly frames his video for "Vivir Mi Vida" with the opening aerial shots of Manhattan? Like Celia Cruz, who was one of his mentors, Marc Anthony's listening audiences are not only "American," as in the United States, but of the Americas, as *Libre* and his sold-out concerts in Viña del Mar and elsewhere in South America have evinced. El Marc's musical migrations—of sounds, melodies, rhythms, places, and listening audiences—also reframe and unsettle the articulations between place, languages, and social identities and subjectivities in the hemispheric Americas, as José David Saldívar suggests with his concept of "trans-American politics of location" (2012, 31).

At the same time, Marc Anthony has also confessed in public interviews that he didn't grow up speaking Spanish fluently. He said: "My Spanish was horrible. In some of my early interviews, I couldn't conjugate a verb. But I plowed through it, and I taught myself. It was like seeing light for the first time. Salsa gave me a voice, and it gave me a platform and it gave me an identity. I had found my culture, and I was not letting it go" (Cobo 2021b). In describing his linguistic and cultural decolonization and the process of reclaiming his Spanish as a heritage language, Marc Anthony highlights the intense labor required in this process of linguistic recovery. He "plowed through it" as requisite work for the self-taught sense of belonging in and through Spanish, the language of his migrant parents who came to New York from Puerto Rico. In his *Una Noche* concert, broadcast on YouTube on April 18, 2021, one can still detect his linguistic anxiety while speaking in Spanish, as he repeatedly resorted to English during his introductions for each song.

So, how do we make sense of Marc Anthony's public comments regarding his "not so good-looking" English as well as his "horrible" Spanish? Clearly, these public confessions uncover the hegemonic ideologies of both Anglo American and Spanish imperial presence in the Americas. As heir to both US and Puerto Rican, Caribbean, and Latin American colonial histories, Marc Anthony reminds his fans that he has been situated between English and Spanish without feeling a sense of ownership of either language. While it may be possible to interpret Marc Anthony's public comments about English and Spanish as strategies to widen his fan base, I would argue that this is also a strategy to deconstruct the imperial and colonial histories of both English and Spanish, unsettling the very traditional and hegemonic discourses that underpin linguistic ideologies and inform the conflation of national identities with monolingualism, most egregiously mobilized by the English-only movement in the United States in the late 1980s and into the 1990s. By moving in between English and Spanish, and by reminding us about his lack of sense of belonging in either, Marc Anthony is also making a meaningful intervention into the music industry's own traditional logics behind the category of Latin music as exclusively (or at least 51 percent) in Spanish. Marc Anthony's strategic decisions in his repertoire reveal important interventions that unsettle the industry's rigid monolingual frameworks. Highlighting his linguistic in-betweenness and rich heterogeneity reveals that his assumed "languagelessness" (Rosa 2019) "is converted into voice" (García and Wei 2014, 105). By producing songs across linguistic boundaries, Marc Anthony's in-betweenness "resists the asymmetries of power instilled by standard language practices" and "opens up possibilities of participation" (García and Wei 2014, 104).

Indeed, my analysis of Marc Anthony's heterogeneous linguistic practices suggests that he proposes a "translanguaging space" that allows the "multilingual user" to "integrate what we separate as different languages" and that allows for "its own transformative power" (García and Wei 2014, 23). Ofelia García and Li Wei define "translanguaging" in education and pedagogy as "the enaction of language practices that use different features that had previously moved independently constrained by different histories, but that now are experienced against each other in speakers' interactions as one new whole," rather than "bound within fixed language identities constrained by nation-states" (21). In this context, then, we can counterargue the chronological frameworks that inform traditional readings of a musical repertoire and definitions of crossover acts. I have already noted that Marc Anthony's musical performances in house, dance, and freestyle music began in English, that he later switched to singing salsa in Spanish, then re-entered the English-language musical space with "I Need to Know" in 1999, only to return to Spanish for most of his singing career since then. Yet, while this fact unsettles the unilinear narrative of crossover discourses, it also glosses over the nuanced and more complicated ways in which Spanish intervenes in his English songs and albums and vice versa, as well as the subversive modes of Spanglish that are deployed throughout.

In *Otra Nota*, for instance, considered Marc Anthony's debut album in Spanish-language salsa music, the inclusion of the English rock cut "Make It with You," a classic love song penned and first performed by Bread in the 1970s, fueled criticism that this song was "unnecessary" (Lopetegui 1993). The song indeed stands out as the only English cut on the recording, raising questions about why El Marc decided to include it in an otherwise all-Spanish salsa album. This song, in my view, allows Marc Anthony to reaffirm English as his dominant language as well as to complicate his new location as a salsa singer. He embodies both worlds and frames himself, purposefully or not, as a cultural hybrid, not only linguistically, between Spanish and English, but also musically. He asserts his bicultural performativity by rejecting musical categories altogether, as numerous other musicians do. Yet we can also ask whether by inserting this song by Bread in a salsa album, he is strategically situating himself within the assumedly British and US Anglo traditions of 1970s rock, purposefully reinserting his voice and those of so many other US Latinx rock singers and musicians into the longer history of rock 'n' roll in the United States, in which Latinx Caribbean musicians have been rendered mostly invisible. As Deborah Pacini Hernández writes, the sonic traditions, rhythms, and instrumentations behind rock 'n' roll were appropriated by mostly Chicano musicians, such as Ritchie Valens, Carlos Santana, Malo, and Azteca, not to "categorically reject rock 'n' roll and English because they were the idioms of their oppressors; rather, they sought to use these idioms to express their grievances, their resistance, and their ethnic pride" (2010, 50). While music histories tend to highlight Latino rock as a West Coast tradition performed mostly by Chicanos, it is essential as well to unearth the inter-Latino and multiracial texture of many of these bands, particularly Santana. As Marisol Berríos-Miranda, Shannon Dudley, and Michelle Habell-Pallán (2018) document in *American Sabor*, the conga player for Santana's band in its early years, Mike Carabello, was, like many other Antillean percussionists in Chicano rock bands, a third-generation Puerto Rican from San Francisco, who introduced

Santana to many of the Afro-Caribbean rhythms that informed his major hits. "Oye Como Va," in fact, illustrated the musical exchanges between the East Coast and the West Coast, as it was composed by Tito Puente and rewritten into Chicano rock by Carlos Santana.[7]

The monolingual frameworks that still structure the music industry categories elide the sonic and stylistic transculturations in "Make It with You," which concludes with an improvised soneo section in Spanish that emerges from salsa music. Marc begins and concludes the song with improvised verses in Spanish: "Yo te quiero, mi amor, yo te adoro, mi amor, Bésame, Acaríciame" [I love you, my darling, I adore you, my darling, Kiss me, Caress me]. This linguistic and improvisatory intervention, a form of tropicalized transculturation, not only legitimizes the in-betweenness, the nepantla, and the hybridity of his generational identity but also suggests that our linguistic analysis of el Marc's repertoire cannot be separated from the stylistic, sonic, and rhythmic traditions that he plays with in crossing multiple boundaries. Moreover, el Marc's music video for "Make It with You" suggests new meanings to the rock song that resituate this text within a Latinx communal framework. The visual images of him—his characteristic long hair and wire-rimmed glasses—approaching his fans at a performance, kissing women of all ages, holding a baby, and bowing to his audience expand the semantic frameworks of the song as potentially a song of love to Nuyoricans and other Latinx fans. The original song about individual desire and love is transformed, in an act of oppositional self-tropicalizing, into a Spanglish song about community, care, and mutual love. In closing, to be Nuyorican and Latinx is, for el Marc, to traverse linguistic boundaries between English, Spanish, and Spanglish; it is to reclaim English as the language of second-generation, US-born Latinx subjectivities, whose linguistic repertoires and possibilities are expanded, rather than

---

7. Deborah Pacini Hernández (2010) frames Latino rock as mostly a Chicano and West Coast phenomenon. She argues that Puerto Ricans in New York, given their coloniality, tended to reject rock 'n' roll as an assimilationist and imperialistic sonic tradition. Indeed, in New York, disco and hip-hop were much more popular among Blacks and Puerto Ricans than the electrifying rhythms of the electric guitar. Yet, as Berríos-Miranda, Dudley, and Habell-Pallán (2018) argue, unearthing the inter-Latino musicians in these bands allows us to document the musical exchanges that eventually led to these cultural and ethnic hybridities in Latino and Chicano rock. To her credit, Pacini Hernández also documents the centrality of New York Puerto Rican singers such as Tony Orlando and José Feliciano in the history of mainstream rock. Orlando's hits, such as "Candida" and "Knock Three Times" (1970) and "Tie a Yellow Ribbon 'Round the Ole Oak Tree" (1973), reveal the invisibility of these brown voices in the larger musical industry and among listeners. While we are all familiar with Feliciano, whose "Feliz Navidad," in Spanglish, became a mainstream favorite, there is very little historical documentation regarding the popularity of rock 'n' roll among New York Puerto Ricans. On the island, in contrast, rock was the preferred musical genre among upper-class blanquito adolescents and youth, a tradition that sonically structured their class and racial opposition to cocolos, the salsa-loving working-poor Afro–Puerto Rican young males. See Aparicio (1998, 69–74).

constrained, by living in between two languages. As Alisa Valdés-Rodríguez (1999) states, "The renewed drive to record in English, [according to Marc Anthony], comes not from a need for 'validation,' as some of his fans, worried that he is 'selling out,' have said, but rather from a need for self-expression."

Singing in English is, after all, Marc Anthony's birthright as a US-born Latino, as he reclaims his belonging in English, a language as Latinx as Spanish and Spanglish.[8] His polylinguistic fluidity, unsettling insertions of the other language in his albums, and self-deprecating public statements about linguistic dispossession reveal that Marc's decision-making in the process of producing music reflects, like Spanglish, "our dual worlds" and "challenges static notions of 'Latina/o identity'" (Zentella 2017, 210). I close this decolonial analysis of the simultaneities, contradictions, and nuances of singing in English with an anecdote that undermines the monolingual ideologies that frame English as only Anglo. On a 2021 Facebook post about "I Need to Know," a Mexican American male from Chicago in his early forties acknowledged that listening to the song in English transformed his musical taste by introducing him to Latino singers and interpreters who sang in Spanish. This case, not necessarily isolated, suggests that Marc Anthony's "crossover" song ironically served as a bridge and invited assimilated Latinx listeners to return to Spanish-language musical repertoires. With his wife's influence, this Mexican American man began to attend more concerts in Spanish after listening to Marc Anthony's assumedly crossover song (Aparicio 2021b).

Freestyle, Rock, R&B, and Salsa: Sounding America

"I Need to Know" became the hit single off Marc Anthony's English salsa album, *Marc Anthony* (1999). It is also the song that we all associate with the dominant narratives about Marc Anthony as a crossover act and one of the embodiments of the Latin music explosion in 1999–2000, both of which el Marc has refuted.[9] Like Becky G, who announced during the 2020 American Music Awards that "we don't have to do the crossover, because we are the crossover," Marc Anthony has, as argued in the previous section, publicly framed his singing in English as an expression of his bicultural American identity, not necessarily as his selling out to an Anglo audience. In fact, he has

---

8. Lillian Gorman (2016) also argues for the recognition of US-born Latinx singers, and their audiences, as multilingual subjects in the spaces of music-making and music reception.

9. María Elena Cepeda (2001, 76) writes, "Marc Anthony has repeatedly rejected the crossover label in both print and television interviews on the grounds that it fails to encompass the bicultural nature of U.S. Latina/o identity."

rejected the idea that *Marc Anthony* is a crossover album, since he had already recorded an English-language album, *When the Night Is Over,* in 1991. Moreover, he publicly explained that his 1999 album "had nothing to do with the purported Latin pop explosion" and that "the interest from the record companies came from the reaction to Selena's music, like, 'Whoa, there's a market out there.' They're taking artists that already have a fan base and expanding that" (Taylor 2000). Locating the origins of the Latin music boom in Selena's rising popularity after her untimely passing in 1995, Marc Anthony corrects the hegemonic and problematic dominant discourse of the boom as a logic that ultimately reifies musical categories while erasing the long history of agency and participation in musical performances for and by our communities and artists. As María Elena Cepeda lucidly argues:

> While cutting across all categories of difference, the dynamics of crossover have particularly reflected a black/white ethno-racial binary and the rigid understandings of "American" identity adhered to within the U.S. popular music industry, which has traditionally catalogued Latin(o) genres and Latina/o performers under "foreign," "ethnic," or "World" musics. Crossover, or the movement by Latina/o artists into the coveted Anglo market (wherein even veteran Latina/o performers are "discovered" by and in turn packaged as novel entities for mainstream consumption), demands considerable critical reflection. Crossover is not simply a question of assimilated Latina/o performers entering new markets because they now perform in English, reside in the United States, and record music that incorporates genres more widely associated with the Anglo/English-speaking world, such as rock or pop (D. Vargas 2012). To adhere to such logics is to ignore the realities of Latina/o musical production over time, during which hybridity has constituted the norm as opposed to the exception, and "hybrids of musical hybrids" such as bugalú, bachatón, salsatón, vallenato moderno, and crunkiao (to cite but a few examples) have been constantly surfacing under the expanding influence of globalization's time-space compression. Moreover, to question the logic of crossover is to challenge the highly gendered, raced association of rock and pop in particular with the musical production of Anglo males, a critical stance that ultimately reaffirms Latinas/os' well-documented historical contributions to global genres not typically associated with Latin(o) musical production. (2017, 144–45)

In this light, el Marc deconstructs the mainstream discourses of hegemonic Latinidad that homogenize Latin music and inform his imposed inclusion in the Latin music boom. In el Marc's own words:

"It was all BS, to be quite honest with you," he says, "a cute-coined phrase that some record executive came up with to sell records. I knew what Latin music was and 'If You Had My Love' by Jennifer Lopez is Latin music? 'She's All I Ever Had' by Ricky Martin is Latin music? My own 'You Sang to Me' is Latin music? Absolutely not. I thought it was a sham from the beginning, and I was extremely vocal about it. *For the first time, I felt like a stranger in my own country.*" (Harrington 2002a, H6; emphasis mine)

El Marc objected to everything being lumped under the "Latin music" rubric, with no effort to differentiate nationalities or musical styles among Latinx singers. These rigid categories and boundaries clearly constrain the freedom of singers and interpreters to experiment with a diverse array of musical styles, languages, and traditions. By reifying "Latin music" as only love songs or salsa songs in Spanish, the music industry robs Marc Anthony, and all Latinx singers, from experimenting with other musical genres or sonic traditions, and thus from a sense of belonging in their own country, the United States of America. When music critics like Chuck Taylor (2000), writing for *Billboard,* use words like "*infiltrated* the international mainstream consciousness" in reference to the release of Marc Anthony's (supposedly) first English-language album, *Marc Anthony,* and to his wrongly assumed crossover status, he is deeming el Marc a trespasser who does not belong, while denying the status of globality to Latinx musical voices and interpreters, as well as their right to move across musical categories. If Marc Anthony celebrated this entry into the "pop" category, this sense of pride does not preclude his feeling "like a stranger in [his] own country" or prevent him from publicly denouncing the egregious consequences of hegemonic Latinidad as well as the niches and categories that constrain him from performing his bicultural Americanity. In brief, the label "pop music," which "functions as an euphemism for 'Anglo' or 'white' music" (Cepeda 2001, 75), has been associated with el Marc since as early as 1999, when he released "I Need to Know."[10] Like renowned Latinx writer Ed Morales (2003), who describes *Marc Anthony* as "the kind of lite Latin pop that Ricky Martin and Enrique Iglesias pioneered" (89), other Latinx fans and listeners were quite disappointed when they first listened to "I Need to Know." A friend and colleague posted on Facebook in 2021: "I have

---

10. Petra Rivera-Rideau (2021) lucidly deconstructs the "Latin pop" category as a site of "Latino whiteness" that "incorporates discourses that present whiteness as more civilized, modern, and enlightened, and blackness as its allegedly more 'primitive' counterpart—the very same ideas that are infused as mestizaje in Latin America" (9). She identifies three indicators— a panethnic Latinidad, the American Dream, and respectability politics—that structure these mainstreaming and whitening discourses in the music industry. As she argues, crossing over is also racial, not just linguistic.

always really hated this song. It feels so cheesy and contrived to me. I remember when I first heard it, I was so mad that Marc was singing this cheesy song because I had been so in love with the *Contra la Corriente* album. I felt like this 'introduction' to the US mainstream includes all the faux-Latin sounds one finds in the Latin boom of the 1990s—like *Bailamos* or *Let's Get Loud,* or *La Vida Loca*" (Aparicio 2021b). Given how many Latinx listeners were disappointed at the "whitened," "lite," and "pop" sounds of "I Need to Know," in this section, I explore the possibilities of relistening to the song as a text that integrates the rich multiracial sounds and rhythms hidden behind the imagined whiteness of the United States of America.

"I Need to Know" was released on August 15, 1999, and quickly circulated within dominant Anglo spaces such as *Saturday Night Live* and as part of el Marc's repertoire during numerous tours. Seventeen years after its first performance, Marc Anthony performed the song live at the 18th Annual Latin Grammy Awards in 2016, thus signaling the song's long-term popularity and status as a classic. Its fast move up the charts (from number seventy-seven on the Billboard Hot 100 Chart the week of September 11, 1999, to number three by the week of November 27, 1999) and its certified gold status by the Recording Industry Association of America suggest that the song expanded Marc Anthony's audience into a wider mainstream audience than he had enjoyed before. By 2000, the song had been nominated for the Grammy Award for Best Male Pop Vocal Performance that year, and the Spanish version, "Dímelo," won the Latin Grammy Award for Song of the Year. Both English and Spanish versions won the American Society of Composers, Authors and Publishers (ASCAP) Award in the Pop Category in 2000.

The song blends Latin music with R&B rhythms and styles, yet its English lyrics also appeal to Anglo listeners.[11] As early as 1995, Achy Obejas reviewed a concert in Chicago that revealed the creative ways in which el Marc was fusing salsa with US urban rhythms:

> What Marc Anthony brings to salsa may seem new in its particulars, but it's absolutely authentic in its essence: a hip-hop inflection (including an electric bass played at a louder volume than one might ordinarily hear in salsa, if at all), a distinct R&B phrasing (with harmonies more akin to Boys II Men than La Sonora Ponceña) and a moratorium on nostalgia. His music is not about Latin America, but about U.S. urban centers. (1995, 14)

---

11. Barry Walters (1999) notes that "I Need to Know" "mimics generic R&B, but the arrangement, which employs traditional Latin instrumentation to ignite contemporary zig zaggy funk rhythms, is radical pop waiting to happen," while Herón Márquez (2001, 79) highlights the Latinization of the song.

Many listeners have commented that the song echoes some of the elements of el Marc's earlier freestyle cuts. Less noticed is the song's engagement with the longer history of rock 'n' roll, as the song is a Nuyorican rewriting of Tom Petty and the Heartbreakers' 1978 cut of the same title. Thus, given the sounds of rock as a subtext for Marc Anthony's "I Need to Know," and the echoes of freestyle, R&B, and salsa as well, the 1999 music video and performance of the song resituate Marc Anthony as a *quintessentially American* singer who engages dialogically with multiple musical genres and sonic traditions deemed "American." The "hidden history" of Latinx musicians, composers, and singers in American rock surfaces as we witness the brown body of el Marc singing "I Need to Know" in 1999. In this light, the song becomes a return to the past—Marc Anthony's early years of singing freestyle in New York during the 1980s and a nod to 1970s rock, given the Tom Petty subtext—and a signal to the future, as in the dominant discourses that frame Marc Anthony as a crossover during the Latin music boom of the late 1990s. Yet each marker of temporality is fraught with contradictions and complexities. The future of Latinx music was not to be defined by English songs, as the current pop reggaetoneros like Bad Bunny, J Balvin, Maluma, and others have successfully proven. And, instead of an idealizing nostalgia, the reference to Marc Anthony's freestyle singing in English may signal a counternarrative that traces a genealogy of US Latinx urban and dance musical traditions from the 1980s into the 2020s that articulated youth resistance.

El Marc himself has stated that "I Need to Know" integrates some of what he has been "doing for the past eight years, plus my influences growing up"; in sum, the song "has a little bit of everything" (Willman 1999). If el Marc "grew up with salsa inside his home and disco and R&B blasting outside" (Valdés-Rodríguez 1999), then this song, rather than a whitened or assimilated text, signals a much richer transcultural history of musical styles. Rather than a new crossover pop song that exclusively reframes him as an assimilated interpreter, newly "discovered" by white and Anglo audiences, "I Need to Know" needs to be relistened to as a text that inserts el Marc into a counterhistory of Latinx agency in US dance musics, a proposed countermemory that expands on the rigid categories that segment racial, cultural, ethnic, and linguistic communities from each other. Our counterlistening is, then, a decolonial act that contests the dominant discourses that bracket him as outside Americanness. As Dylan Robinson (2020) explains, our "responsibilities to listen differently" also require us "to examine how we have become fixated—how listening has in effect been 'fixed'—in practices of aesthetic contemplation, as a pastime or entertainment, and through its various affordances" (45). To propose "I Need to Know" as an alternative American song is a social gesture of resistance that unfixes hegemonic, whitened listening.

Reclaiming Rock

When "I Need to Know" began to circulate on commercial radio stations, a DJ in Chicagoland commented that Marc's song was not original but a copy of Tom Petty and the Heartbreakers' song of the same title.[12] This brief anecdote reveals the intertextual nature of popular music, unveiling the hidden exchanges between Latinx and Anglo musics. Most significantly, it exhorts us to reflect on the continuities, if any, between this rock song from 1978, associated mostly with white Anglo males as musicians and as listeners, and el Marc's Latinx rewriting of it. As comparable as they are, given the same repeated riff—"I need to know"—that structures their melodies, the songs are quite different and unique in terms of their arrangements and sonic and rhythmic structures. Tom Petty's song features one singing male voice, while Marc Anthony's male voice is enriched and expanded by background singers who engage in a call-and-response structure within the soneo sections, constituting numerous interlocking voices that signify, at least, sonic and rhythmic multiplicities and, at best, a space for Afro-Latinx collectivity. Tom Petty's electric guitar, which as the principal instrument in this song embodies it as a staple of rock 'n' roll sonic idiosyncrasy, is diminished in Marc Anthony's version and transformed into an ensemble with a violin, a keyboard synthesizer, and a Latino percussive ensemble that relocates the performance as an urban, modern, and multiracial cultural text. If the electric guitar serves as a symbol of whiteness and assimilation for many Puerto Ricans—who, for instance, disavowed of Ricky Martin as a "sell out" for "performing electric guitar–based music in English for the U.S. pop marketplace" (Pacini Hernández 2010, 53)[13]—it is also true that Marc Anthony has integrated this "white" instrument into many of his arrangements and performances, as in the April 18, 2021, *Una Noche* concert, when the electric guitar and guitarist played a prominent role, reminding us of the energy of rock 'n' roll shows. The four-beat measures of

---

12. I want to thank Renee Cortez from Chicago for sharing this anecdote with me in personal conversation in March 2021.

13. Pacini Hernández also states that "New York Puerto Rican musicians generally avoided the electric guitar that was so closely associated with rock 'n' roll" (2010, 51). I would agree, given the cocolo/rockero divide in Puerto Rico during the 1980s, which evinced these dichotomies and the binary class and racial meanings based on their musical tastes. Moreover, the colonial frameworks that structured the everyday lives of Puerto Ricans, both in the diaspora and on the island, may explain the decolonial disavowal or lack of identification with the electric guitar as an instrument and symbol of whiteness. Yet, there are instances that, while seemingly exceptional, do hint at the mutual exchanges between rock and salsa. John Storm Roberts (1979, 191) identifies a number of examples, such as Larry Harlow's "use of electric instruments," the use of "rock guitar" in Cortijo's 1973 *Time Machine*, Típica 73's experimentation with "reverb and other electronic gadgets on tres and bass," and the use of the "wawa pedal" in Eddie Palmieri's band.

the 1978 hit are transformed into syncopated Latinx rhythms in el Marc's version, yet Petty's song does begin the phrasing on the second half of the third beat, on the upbeat, while el Marc's phrasing does so on the second half of the first beat for the melody and on the second half of the fourth beat in the harmony. Petty's fast tempo turns into a slower, more danceable speed in el Marc's version, suggesting the moving bodies within the spaces of music clubs hailed by the music video. The opening of el Marc's "I Need to Know," which features "a synthesized violin and piano riff, which is immediately followed by a midtempo beat,"[14] does indeed integrate the sounds of contemporary R&B while incorporating Latin percussion instruments: the timbales, congas, and trumpet. If the sonic textures of the violin are traditionally associated with classical orchestral music, Mexican mariachi music, or even love songs and ballads, here the mediated sound produced by the synthesizer redefines the violin as an urban, modern instrument that fuels memories of New York Latinx freestyle music from the 1980s and early 1990s. El Marc's strategic integration of such a rich variety of musical traditions, sonic genealogies, and racial communities reveals "I Need to Know" as a profound sonoropolitical statement within the music world. The Nuyorican singer pays homage and celebrates the rich heterogeneity of his own musical upbringing through a song that has been otherwise whitened as a "crossover act."

Given this close intertextuality between the rock and Latin pop versions, "I Need to Know" is el Marc's act of musical countermemory that radically claims some presence of Nuyoricans and East Coast Latinx musicians within the longer history of American pop music and rock 'n' roll. If music histories agree on the lack of contributions of East Coast Latinx musicians and interpreters in the history of rock, el Marc requires us to at least reconsider this absence and validate the role of Nuyoricans as adolescent listeners, receptors, and listening communities who identified with the sounds of a countercultural generation. John Storm Roberts, in his canonical *The Latin Tinge* (1979), argues that Latin rock "never really got off the ground in New York." He explains that "New York Latinos were more influenced by black music than rock"—yet isn't rock derived from Black sounds and rhythms?—that the "disco scene" was "very receptive to Latinos and their music," and that "mainstream salsa had dominated" (194). Pacini Hernández (2010) argues that Chicanx musicians adopted rock 'n' roll as self-expression and that it is mostly associated as a sonic tradition of the West Coast and the Southwest—here I am thinking of Doug Sahm and Flaco Jiménez in the Texas Tornados, in

---

14. Wikipedia, s.v. "I Need to Know (Marc Anthony song)," https://en.wikipedia.org/wiki/I_Need_to_Know_(Marc_Anthony_song).

addition to Carlos Santana, Malo, and Tierra. Like Roberts, Pacini Hernández also concludes that disco and the emergence of salsa undermined the possibilities for Nuyorican musicians to engage with rock 'n' roll. Yet the short-lived boogaloo, for instance, is explained as one of the engagements of Nuyorican musicians and communities with rock and R&B rhythms. Based on rock 'n' roll's steadier 4/4 rhythms, rather than on the Cuban clave (Pacini Hernández 2010, 46), which structures salsa and other Afro-Caribbean musical genres, the New York boogaloo became the preferred musical dance style for many second-generation, US-born Latinx youth in the East Coast in the late 1960s. Most boogaloos were written either in English or in bilingual lyrics, another element that allowed the youth to identify with that style (Pacini Hernández, 2010 46).

In his 2022 album, *Pa'lla Voy*, Marc Anthony pays homage to boogaloos with the inclusion of "Gimme Some More," a cut that celebrates the New York style with translanguaging Spanglish lyrics. Marc Anthony grew up listening to boogaloos, and he was welcomed into Johnny Colón's music school in East Harlem when he was just seven years old. Colón, a Nuyorican musician and music teacher to many emerging Latinx musicians in New York City, and a musician who performed boogaloo in New York, was a mentor for el Marc when he was still too young to be officially admitted to the music school (Lapidus 2021; Ramírez Warren 2014). Returning to the "tenuous and ambivalent" presence of rock in New York (Pacini Hernández 2010, 43), the question of "whether boogaloo could or should be categorized as a variant of rock 'n' roll is certainly open to debate" (47). Yet due to the fact that Nuyorican teens "avidly embraced rock 'n' roll, especially doo-wop" (45); that by the late 1950s, "Latin music was displaced by rock" (45); and that rock itself was foundationally informed by Black sounds and syncopated rhythms, we can undoubtedly argue that el Marc also engages with rock 'n' roll as one of the many sonic traditions that he has listened to since childhood. In fact, given that Tom Petty acknowledged that "I Need to Know" was inspired by Black singer Wilson Pickett's canonical song "Land of a Thousand Dances," and in particular the riff sung by the audience in another instance of call-and-response ("Na, nananana, nananana, nananana")—evidence of the Black origins of rock 'n' roll—we can better understand el Marc's exhortation for listeners to acknowledge the song as a multiracial text structured by Black sonic and rhythmic legacies.[15] Thus, the syncopated rhythms, the sounds and textures of the trumpets and the percussion, the multiplicity of voices, the background singers, and the call-and-response structures in the song allow us listeners to situate

---

15. See Reyes and Waldman (1998).

el Marc's version as a much more complicated conjuncture of musical styles, rhythms, instrumentations, and arrangements than what the crossover narratives and definitions of "pop" both suggest and elide. If we follow the previous arguments regarding the lack of Nuyorican participation in the making of Latino rock in the United States, we must question el Marc's need to insert himself within the genealogies of rock. Yet, the rich histories of coexistence and solidarities, mutual exchanges, and musical collaborations between African Americans and Puerto Ricans both in New York and the Caribbean lead us to understand el Marc's claim to belonging to this larger musical tradition through the Black sounds and rhythms that have informed rock 'n' roll since its emergence in the 1950s.

Moreover, as Ed Morales (2003) argues, we cannot dismiss the long circulation of the habanera rhythms in early rock, as early as the doo-wop and boogie-woogie of the 1940s, to the 1956 "Louie Louie" cut, through Little Richard and Fats Domino to Elvis Presley, to the "syncopated polyrhythms to the bass guitar" in 1960s funk music (282), the contributions of Ritchie Valens in his canonical 1957 song "La Bamba," Jerry Garcia's influence on the Grateful Dead, up to the king of Latin rock, Carlos Santana. Rock has been audible for decades in the production and performance of Latinx music in the United States and vice versa. That Ray Barretto recorded with the Rolling Stones, the Bee Gees, and Bette Midler (Téllez Moreno 2017, 24) is a hidden fact that reveals the continuity, simultaneity, exchanges, and permeable boundaries among musical styles and genres that musicians experience, in addition to highlighting Latinx Caribbean musicians' contributions to rock 'n' roll.[16] By contesting the segmented music categories imposed by the music industry, el Marc showcases the rich musical exchanges that have characterized American dance music throughout the twentieth century and into the twenty-first century and inserts himself, through "I Need to Know," into the longer histories of freestyle, R&B, rock 'n' roll, and salsa.

An Homage to Freestyle

In the comments below the YouTube page for Marc Anthony's music video "I Need to Know," listeners and fans have commented that they wish Marc

---

16. *Tropical Tribute to the Beatles* (1996), a little-known recording, is another small reminder of the musical exchanges between rockeros and salseros since the 1960s. Through compelling salsa arrangements of Beatles songs, the salsa singers duly "tropicalized" the repertoire of the British rock band and underlined those hidden contributions of their syncopated rhythms and Afro-Caribbean sonic textures in rock.

Anthony was still singing freestyle, a desire that suggests that his listeners frame the song as a reiteration of early 1980s New York Latinx freestyle. Indeed, some Facebook fans (Aparicio 2021b) have commented that this song reminds them of freestyle music, including references to the beat as echoes of Stevie B and Johnny O. These comments suggest that the 1999 hit may also be a return or nod to el Marc's freestyle years and a way of pleasing his earlier fans. Defined as "a fusion of vocal styles from disco with the syncopated synthetic instrumentation of electro" (Vargas 2010, 190), Latin freestyle was sung in English and initially danced to by Latinx youth in New York City and the East Coast. Probably signaled by the synthesizer in the initial riffs of the violin and the keyboard in the song, the sonic memory of freestyle emerges throughout "I Need to Know," along with the images of multiracial bodies dancing to el Marc in the music video, which partly reproduces the visual image of freestyle dancers in warehouses and urban clubs during the 1980s and early 1990s. The central role of synthesizers in the production of electronic dance music throughout the world also frames it as a pop sound; yet that very sonic texture that mainstreams the song is also the same texture that defines "I Need to Know" as an integration of various musical styles in Puerto Rican and Latinx New York. In addition, the process of sampling through turntables creates the possibilities for a variety of musical traditions and styles to be merged and interpellated in any one song or melody, thus leading to the creation of alternative sonic genealogies and the sounds of modernity. As Madrid (2008) writes in the context of Nortec electronic music in Tijuana, "it is in the sounds and timbres of norteña and banda music, and not necessarily in the recognizable melodies or the classic recordings that such authenticity is found" (67). Moreover, Madrid also finds in the "technological manipulations" of the synthesizer an articulation "of their particular desires for a modern, cosmopolitan identity" that rearticulates "tradition and authenticity in the process" (67).

If the synthesizer produces the "emblematic beat" that positions freestyle as "a micro-genre of electronic dance music," along with Chicago house and Detroit techno, the audio hardware and sound production machine is the result of a lack of access to resources, as Vázquez (2013) argues.[17] For young, working-poor Latinx communities in New York during the 1980s, freestyle was about making a "song with scant materials" (Vázquez 2013, 111). Unable to hire a big band with multiple musicians, freestyle producers would reproduce audio bites, sounds, and phrasings as "methods of survival," an analogous practice to the politics and poetics of rascuache styles among California and

---

17. In the film *Legends of Freestyle* (Stanulis 2016), there are multiple references to the limited resources that affected freestyle singers and producers as well.

Southwest Chicanx artists. The limited nature of the circulation of freestyle—"in the informal channels of cultural economy (bootlegs, mixtapes, and used-record stores)" (Vázquez 2013, 113)—denounces the lack of commitment by the music industry to foster the local musical performances that emerged in the neighborhood clubs and local radio stations in New York City and then spread to Miami and Los Angeles (Pacini Hernández 2010, 63). Second-generation Nuyoricans and Latinx Caribbean voices, such as the Cuban American singer Nayobe, responded to the limited economic possibilities that producers and independent labels represented for the artists (Stanulis 2016; Vázquez 2013).

Additionally, freestyle itself emerged as a response to the exclusion of Nuyoricans from the circuits of hip-hop at the time. As Pacini Hernández writes: "New York Puerto Ricans' response to their marginalization from hip-hop was to reemphasize melodic vocals and romantic lyrics, aesthetic domains they could claim ownership of while at the same time maintaining their independence from the more narrowly defined realm of Latin music" (2010, 64). It was precisely within freestyle as a cultural site for engaging struggles over recognition, audibility, and power, as Pacini Hernández suggests, that Marc Anthony participated with his own vocal contributions. If the decline of freestyle in New York can be explained by radio stations' move to hip-hop exclusively (Pacini Hernández 2010, 65), "weak" productions, and limited resources overall (65), sound scholars insist that freestyle performances and recordings represent a continuity with other Afro-Caribbean styles and musical genres: "In this mechanized matrix, New York Latinos heard ancestral echoes of salsa piano lines and montuno rhythms. In the hands of producers like the Latin Rascals, Paul Robb, Omar Santana, and Andy 'Panda' Tripoli, the Pac-Man bleeps, synth stabs, and Roland TR-808 claves became a robotic jam session called freestyle" (Shapiro 2005, 273, quoted in Pacini Hernández 2010, 63).

Marc Anthony's first recorded freestyle song, "So in Love," produced by Lee Evans, now CEO of JamBox Entertainment Studios, was unfortunately never released. Yet a rare 1985 demo, "You Said You Love Me," circulates on YouTube.[18] Marc Anthony was also a backup singer to Chrissy I-eece, whose song "You Should Know by Now—Club Mix Solitario" reads almost like an inverse prelude to the title "I Need to Know." Marc Anthony's own recording, produced with Little Louie Vega, Héctor Lavoe's nephew, on *When the Night Is Over* (1991) recapitulated the Nuyorican singer's rich participation in the 1980s in freestyle in Harlem and Bronx dance clubs like the Fun House Club and the Copacabana.[19]

18. Posted by Stelios Caprini on July 15, 2018, https://youtu.be/PLddVc10W3E.
19. I want to thank Wilson Valentín-Escobar for this reference and personal memory, as Wilson attended these clubs where Marc Anthony performed during the 1980s.

As Andy Panda chronicles (Stanilus 2016), Latino freestyle in New York began in 1985 as a response to the lack of inclusion of New York Latinx voices in hip-hop, then became the preferred electronic dance music among second-generation Puerto Ricans and other Latinx in the Bronx and Spanish Harlem in particular. If the major record labels did not know "what to do with Latinos singing in English" (Panda in Stanilus 2016), local DJs like Little Louie Vega started producing music for neighborhood parties in 1980 before moving on to clubs. Once those sonic events attracted hundreds of dancing bodies, independent labels and agents began to record young singers such as Judy Torres, Lisa Lisa, Lisette Meléndez, Sa-Fire, Nayobe, George Lamond, TKA, and others. Marc Anthony's musical career began in these freestyle networks, and he later moved on to singing salsa given the unfair financial remunerations that freestyle represented. (Aaron Hanson's interview in *Legends of Freestyle* reveals Marc Anthony's struggle to get paid for his singing.) And, if freestyle saw a resurgence in major presentations in New York around 2015, it was because it had not totally died. It continues to circulate, despite the radio stations' decisions not to use airtime to promote freestyle singers and to move on to rap and hip-hop exclusively in the late 1980s and early 1990s, and despite independent labels' limited resources to promote their artists. In this light, "I Need to Know" pays homage to el Marc's early years as a singer of freestyle as well as to his early fans and listeners. Marc's contributions to freestyle also suggest that, instead of defining his songs as a continuation of salsa romántica à la Eddie Santiago, we should acknowledge the continuity of freestyle lyrics about the dramas of love, what Judy Torres has described as "songs . . . that are like really dramatic Spanish soap operas—being in love, breaking up, catching someone cheating on you, intense and passionate, slightly over dramatic" (Vargas 2010, 192), with the lyrics that el Marc would later sing in Spanish, accompanied by salsa arrangements. If, as the documentary states, freestyle was the sound of the children of salsa parents, el Marc traverses these generic and generational boundaries in his performances of "I Need to Know."

The Music Video and the Dance Floor

In his 1999 article, "Marquee Marc Anthony," Chris Willman describes the "I Need to Know" music video as "a scene straight out of L.A.'s Conga Room." Not coincidentally, the visuality of the dancing bodies in the club, whether in New York or Los Angeles, where the music video was produced, stands out as central to the production. While the video begins with a romantic moment between a woman and el Marc, the female musician playing the violin bathed under a blue light inaugurates a shift in colors that structures the rest of the video. While the love story is filmed in black and white, the club scene where Marc Anthony sings is bathed in greens and yellows, colors perhaps more associated with a kind of urban modernity seen in a city like tropicalized Los Angeles or Miami. María Elena Cepeda (in Aparicio 2021b) has observed the striking parallelisms, both "aesthetic and thematic," with Ricky Martin's video for "Livin' la Vida Loca," particularly in the "high contrast use of color, light, and shadow" as well as in the "same swinging camera angles in relationship to the performers—it's as if the video's creators sought legibility for Marc Anthony (who is being introduced to many non-Latinx listeners for the first time) vis-à-vis a 'familiar' visual discourse" (Aparicio 2021b), an analysis that frames the musical video within the discourses of the Latin music boom.

In her lucid analysis of Selena's integration of disco and freestyle, Deborah Vargas (2012) highlights the centrality of the "dance floor . . . in the staging of freestyle's visibility" (191), a space of leisure, community, and youth also evident in el Marc's music video. As Vargas describes, the dance floor serves as "a creative, physical working of space that for queer folks, working-class women of color, and youth of color remained a critical site of display within the crumbling structural realities around them, including economic downturns, displacement trends in urban areas, and, most significant, the increasing deaths owing to HIV/AIDS" (191). Highlighting freestyle as a sonic production that embraced Black and brown queer bodies on the dance floor and invited them to express their affective selves, Vargas argues that Selena "discursively summons prior generations of dancing bodies that lived in the disco and freestyle eras along with generations of Latina/os who have migrated to the United States over the decades" (193). I see a similar process of summoning these prior generations as el Marc achieves this acknowledgment through the song and video—a "generational crossroads" (Aparicio 2021b) of sorts—both temporal and spatial, regarding the politics of the dance floor and the liberatory and creative spaces that the urban clubs offered Latinx youth.

Coda: Listening in Place

During the writing of this chapter, I posted a request on Facebook exhorting friends and colleagues to share their listening and sonic experiences with this song (Aparicio 2021b). While I have integrated some into the chapter, I am compelled to conclude this analysis with an unexpected, haunting, and intimate anecdote that powerfully illustrates the spaces of critical listening that connect sounds with memories and lives. As Barry Shank (2013) has proposed, sounds are inserted "into a web of interconnected thoughts and affects." As we become "listening subjects," we "open [ourselves] up to music's effects. When engaged in musical listening, we are not trying to hear what it says, but to feel the affects that it spreads" (Shank 2013). A friend I met in the 1990s told me that she associates "I Need to Know" with the moment she realized that her marriage was over. As she was listening to Marc Anthony sing "do not leave me all alone out there," she acknowledged, during a flight to the West Coast, that her relationship to her husband was no longer tenable. Having experienced serious and critical health events that affected her spouse and her baby daughter, my friend shared with me how these very lines revealed to her that, despite her formal marriage, she was "all alone out there." My friend cannot disassociate this moment during her flight, the song, and the memory from her decision to dissolve her twenty-three-year-old relationship, a decision that profoundly transformed her life and future. She illustrates the articulation between sounds, listening, memory, the body, and place. While this is only one story, it opens the possibilities of countless other stories among Marc Anthony's listeners that have constructed social, affective, linguistic, musical, cultural, and racial meanings out of the song's performance. Thus, to define "I Need to Know" exclusively as a crossover act, as the dominant media and many Latinx and non-Latinx listeners have done, is to domesticate it, to subtract from it the possibility of rich, divergent, and multiple meanings and interpretations that all listeners produce at the moment of critical listening and that constitute the affective, social, and cultural dramas of our lives.

CHAPTER 4

"Aguanile" (2007)

Critical Listening, Mourning, and Decolonial Healing

After Hurricane María hit on September 20, 2017, Puerto Rico joined other countries in Latin America and the Global South that have collectively memorialized and mourned the thousands who have died at the hands of state violence. In Puerto Rico, 4,654 lives were lost because of the politics of colonial neglect and abandonment by the US federal government, Federal Emergency Management Agency (FEMA), and the inefficacy and corruption of the Puerto Rican government after the storm.[1] As a national community, Puerto Ricans now face the pain of acknowledging the desaparecidos among us, not only those who passed during and after the storm but those who fled in order to survive. In the light of these innumerable deaths, it is imperative to reflect critically on the process of mourning, bereavement, and grief. How do we process this mourning individually and collectively? How do we accept these deaths, clearly preventable had there been a sustained infrastructure of support and recovery?

---

1. The 4,645 deaths were reported by a 2018 Harvard University study (see Kishore et al. 2018). This estimate represents "more than 70 times the official estimate" of the Puerto Rican government of sixty-four deaths. A George Washington University study, commissioned by Governor Ricardo Rosselló, was of 2,975 deaths (Emery 2018; Milken 2018). These various estimates reveal how official history and the state erase and minimize the magnitude of these losses in colonized societies such as Puerto Rico.

While Puerto Rico continues to struggle to survive politically and economically as a debt state, in terms of food access and economic sustainability, Puerto Ricans are turning to the arts, broadly defined, for healing and grieving. For instance, young Puerto Ricans have returned to agriculture, including artisanal coffee ventures and growing fruit crops such as guavas, as a practice of healing and recovery and as structured efforts toward sustainability. The visual arts serve as a channel for healing for artists like Antonio Martorell, as in his *Es que la . . .* exhibit, as they do for performance artists like Y No Había Luz theater troupe from San Juan, whose *Circo de la Ausencia* exhibit was also installed at the National Museum of Puerto Rican Arts and Culture in Chicago. It can be seen in the dancing on the streets of Old San Juan, or in the songs being rewritten as forms of affective survival immediately after the hurricane. In addition, communal interventions such as Ritmos Resilientes by capoeira master Kojo X. Johnson, or the dancing of bomba in Afro–Puerto Rican neighborhoods, constitute important tools in soothing depression, anxiety, and despondency after the hurricane. A most poignant example is the song composed and performed by Bad Bunny, iLe, and Residente for the Paro Nacional in summer 2019, "Afilando Los Cuchillos," which has become a political anthem for the power of el pueblo in the call for a new government. The imperative for a collective acknowledgment of the lives lost in María is visible through the visual arts and through sounds, music, dance, and literature, what Carlos Rivera Santana has described as the process of "catharsis" in "posthurricane art" (2019, 179–80).[2]

My proposed listening-reading of "Aguanile" integrates music and literature as a path for grieving and mourning the deaths and trauma post-María. As Finnish cultural studies scholar Tuija Saresma argues for the need to discuss and analyze the "experiences of bereavement and the healing powers of arts and writing" (2003, 603), she shares the experience of Sirpa, a young mother who lost her baby daughter and finds solace in the song "The Most Beautiful Sea," written by Turkish writer, novelist, and screenwriter Nâzim Hikmet. Sirpa says, "The song brought comfort to my life, the song showed me the path back to life, the song helped me in my sorrow more than any words. And as death changes life, it also changed the message of that song" (Saresma 2003, 612), foregrounding the role of music and the arts in the

---

2. Rivera Santana defines "using art for social catharsis" as "an aesthetic process in which people can collectively express the complex or contradictory social, cultural and political situations that confront them" (2019, 179). By transfiguring complex realities, such as the disaster and destruction of Hurricane María, into "another intelligible form or medium," the numerous artistic expressions that emerged after the storm evinced the need for the arts to serve as healing. For Rivera Santana, the healing suggests a decolonial sensitivity to the effects of the hurricane as artists "tell the complex story of the entanglements among Hurricane María, capitalism, and colonization" (179).

requisite process of mourning and bereavement. The ocean and water specifically are also embedded in Saresma's own mourning for her younger brother, who took his life by drowning in the sea. Saresma's exploration of mourning and grief, mediated by songs and writing, allows her to explore how the arts help us remember those who have passed and mourn collectively.

These elements—water, memory, and collective mourning—are a central part of my analysis in this chapter. Approaching mourning through a sonoroliterary reading of Amina Gautier's (2014) short story "Aguanile," where sounds and written words inform each other, allows me to engage the textualizing processes of mourning and loss within the intergenerational tensions of the diasporic family of the Afro–Puerto Rican nieta [granddaughter] who narrates the story and, concomitantly, for all Boricuas after the hurricane. More specifically, I highlight the process of critical listening that the nieta engages of the Nuyorican salsa singer Héctor Lavoe's song, also titled "Aguanile," by now globalized and mainstreamed.

As defined earlier, the act of *critical listening* requires an analytical process through which the listener grapples with and acknowledges the potential meanings of the song in their social and personal world and also structurally, thus acquiring a new and empowering awareness of life and social identities. For the nieta in the story, as I will discuss, listening to "Aguanile," as performed by Lavoe and reiterated by Marc Anthony, becomes a liberatory moment for her as a Black woman in the United States diaspora. The element of water, encapsulated in the Yoruba-based title of the song (*aguan* = cleansing through water; *ile* = house), reaffirms the two simultaneous meanings of the word in African communities: "I'm home" and "healing with water."[3] Aguanile, reclaimed as an African signifier "A Wa Nilé" in Afro-Cuban poet Soleida Ríos's (2017) poetry collection, is also the title of a short story in Amina Gautier's collection *Now We Will Be Happy* (2014). More specifically, I read the short story as a textualization of the healing meanings of the song "Aguanile" in the face of the death of a loved one. I propose that reading Gautier's short story today returns "Aguanile," the globalized song, back to the sphere of family, community, and the local and national—that is, a return home. A current reading of "Aguanile" as both sonic and literary text allows us to find a language for mourning after María and, possibly, a space for relationality between the island and the diaspora, between gender subjectivities (as embodied in the nieta's difficult yet loving relationship with her abuelo), and among Puerto Ricans of diverse generational identities. I also explore the

---

3. Personal conversation with Professor Tosin Mgobi, Marquette University, October 30, 2019.

symbolic connections between the narratives about the power of the hurricane, of agua, as a potentially healing energy that has allowed Puerto Ricans to find a sense of home and sustainability, and the ensuing decolonial awareness and collective confidence that Puerto Ricans felt in their power to bring about change and eventual sovereignty immediately after Hurricane María, a power reaffirmed in el Paro Nacional, the national protest that removed Governor Ricardo Rosselló from power two years later. In the words of Christine Nieves, an organizer on the island, post-María has been "the moment when things shifted from despair to possibility" (Klein 2018, 70).

From Nuyorican Salsa to *American Idol*

The 2006 biopic *El Cantante* invites us to critically reflect on the diverse meanings that Héctor Lavoe, played by Marc Anthony, has embodied in his career, his singing repertoire, and in his personal life, for Puerto Ricans as well as mainstream US audiences. Before his passing in 1993, Lavoe was revered by his Puerto Rican community of salsa fans and listeners; after the movie, his presence in the mainstream and among non-Latinx audiences has clearly been enhanced.

Born in Ponce, Puerto Rico, Héctor Juan Pérez, renamed Lavoe in homage to his unique voice, became one of the most important salsa singers in the long history of this musical style. Considered a "cultural hero" by many fans and listeners in New York, the United States, and Latin America, Lavoe and his personal struggles with addiction, tragic events in his personal life, and his eventual battle with HIV/AIDS triggered a strong sense of empathy, hermandad and solidarity. In 1963 Lavoe moved to New York City, where he immediately began singing with local bands and eventually began his collaborations with Willie Colón with the support of late producer Al Santiago. Lavoe contributed the sounds of Puerto Rican plenas and música jíbara to the New York salsa sound, as well as a brilliant style of soneo, or improvisation, which aligned him with some of Puerto Rico's most renowned Black singers, Ismael Rivera and Cheo Feliciano. Merging the identities of the "rural jíbaro and urban Nuyorican," Lavoe and Colón "represent the translocal spaces of the Puerto Rican transnation" (Valentín-Escobar 2001, 213). In fact, *El Cantante*, which starred Marc Anthony and his then wife, Jennifer Lopez, was embraced by most Boricua audiences as a well-deserved homage to Lavoe.

Despite the collective excitement and anticipation for the film, its reception was uneven. While many viewers loved remembering and reliving the years of New York salsa in the 1970s through the story, Willie Colón and other salseros critiqued the film's failure to represent what made those years truly notable. One review in the *New York Times* wrote: "We hear it proclaimed that salsa was a revolutionary sound, a groundbreaking synthesis of Puerto Rico and New York, but the musical and historical information that would flesh out this assertion is missing" (A. Scott 2007, 2). Colón himself said, "The real story was about Héctor fighting the obstacles of a nonsupportive industry that took advantage of entertainers with his charisma and talent. Instead they did another movie about two Puerto Rican junkies" (Gurza 2007, 1).

Yet these critiques, as valid as they are as discourses of resistance against the pathologizing constructions of working-class male Puerto Rican musicians, should not overshadow the popular receptions of the film that allowed those of Lavoe's generation to reclaim the pleasures of his 1970s and 1980s performances, a collective joy that I witnessed while watching the film in a theater in Logan Square in Chicago among many Puerto Ricans, who applauded, laughed, cried, and celebrated Lavoe as their cultural hero. While the film focuses unnecessarily, as Willie Colón argues, on Lavoe's drug addiction and psychological demons, these struggles are structured into most biopics of American musicians, from Ray Charles to Johnny Cash to Elvis Presley. Most significantly, those very "demons" are also the tropes through which Lavoe becomes visible to "mainstream American music lovers" and, ironically, through which the coloniality of Puerto Ricans can be revealed. I am interested in reading Lavoe's demons alongside those of the grandfather in Gautier's story as metaphors for how colonialism and dispossession affect Puerto Rican men. Thus, *El Cantante* marks the moment that restages Lavoe as a global icon, though without totally displacing or even diminishing the social and cultural meanings that he embodied for Puerto Ricans in New York and on the island. While Lavoe's life can easily be pathologized as that of an addict, it is precisely those "demons" that facilitated such an affectively profound identification with his compatriots and listeners. Indeed, if Lavoe's own condition of abjection reminded racial minorities of their own vulnerability to be always already criminalized by US dominant society and the state, his life was "fraught with personal tragedy and suffering, elements that allowed their Latino audiences to confront their own struggles and marginalization as a result of structured social inequities" (Aparicio and Valentín-Escobar 2004, 87–88).

Marc Anthony, whose memorialization of Lavoe in the film and in his global concert tours has contributed to Lavoe's global recognition, talked to Latina entertainment journalist Leila Cobo about the human importance of Lavoe's music:

Q: Lavoe was a Latin icon, but he's certainly not well known in the mainstream. What kind of impact can you have with someone like this?

A: That's like saying, "Who was Sid Vicious and was he worthy of a movie?" No one knew and they made "Sid and Nancy." Héctor Lavoe has this intangible thing. If I were to introduce you to just his music, you would want to know the man. If I were to tell you this amazingly crazy story, you should want to hear his music. And when you have both, it's a story that needs to be told. No one can sit there and tell me his music is less important than Ray Charles' or Johnny Cash's.

Q: So you don't think this is just for Latin fans?

A: No. This is a human story. Any artist who is significant for 20 to 30 years is still viable. His music, if you released it today, would still be viable. When you have somebody like Daddy Yankee saying his only regret was he didn't get to perform with Héctor Lavoe. . . . My God, it's a whole generation removed, and it's still important. This is not small. This is not a local story. (Cobo 2007, 17)

Marc Anthony's response to the suggestion that Lavoe was too local (or ghettoized) to be worthy of a film, by connecting him to Daddy Yankee and reggaetón, strives to situate Lavoe as a foundational figure in salsa and Afro-Caribbean musical traditions. It is not surprising that generational identities and historical memories, as with Lavoe and Daddy Yankee, are also embedded in the plot of "Aguanile" the short story. Indeed, if Lavoe's death in 1993 was mourned mostly by Puerto Ricans and other Latinx in New York City and on the island, today his face appears in T-shirts and posters sold at tourist shops at the Luis Muñoz Marín International Airport in Isla Verde, San Juan, Puerto Rico (see fig. 4.1). Along with other souvenirs to bring back from the emerald, blue beaches of the Caribbean, Lavoe is now an empty signifier to many, analogous to Che Guevara's face on T-shirts sold at the Havana airport in Cuba.

Like the film, "Aguanile" the song has also been the target of multiple and at times contradictory reading-listenings. It has been likewise globalized and has shifted meanings. If for some listeners, "Aguanile" was comparable to Desi Arnaz's "Babalú" as a primitivist sonic construction of an exotic Blackness located on the African continent, Lavoe's Nuyorican style and vocals reaffirmed, for other listeners, the healing power of Santería. This meaning is reiterated visually in the scene in *El Cantante* where Lavoe visits a santera as a way of coping with his demons, constituting a site of healing that is analogous to the communal power of his other canonical songs like "Mi Gente" and "El Cantante." Vocalizing the sounds and rhythms of African origin was, indeed,

FIGURE 4.1. Héctor Lavoe souvenirs at the Luis Muñoz Marín airport in Isla Verde, San Juan, Puerto Rico. Photograph by the author.

a central practice for Afro-Caribbean and Puerto Rican musicians during the 1970s, when "Aguanile" was first performed and recorded. Inspired by the Black Arts Movement in New York City, Willie Colón and Héctor Lavoe performed this song about returning "home" through the word *aguanile*, which remits us to the Yoruba traditions in West Africa that were transported to the Caribbean archipelago. In a YouTube video of this 1972 performance, emceed by former Young Lords member Felipe Luciano, Willie Colón and Héctor Lavoe sing this song as a way of finding healing in the orishas, like Ogún and Yemayá, both indirectly referenced in the song.

This decidedly non-Western act of spiritual cleansing was one expression of the larger movement within New York salsa to honor and return to Africa, the homeland. Lavoe himself, although white-presenting, grew up in Ponce, Puerto Rico, where the plena was born and where Afro–Puerto Rican musical traditions circulated daily. Once in New York, Lavoe did not forget the Black sounds of his upbringing. Songs like "Songoro Cosongo" (*Comedia*, 1978), written by Eliseo Grenet and Nicolás Guillén, were adapted to a salsa arrangement that allowed Nuyorican youth to remember "the strength and resilience of their ancestors, who used music and dance as a form of expression and resistance" (Pierce n.d.). Songs like "Aguanile," "Quimbombo" (*El Malo,* 1967), "Che Che Colé" (*Cosa Nuestra,* 1969), and "Ghana E" (*La Gran Fuga,* 1970) constituted a repertoire that performed a return to and homage to our Blackness among Nuyoricans and Latinos.

The recuperation of Blackness as a source of pride among Nuyoricans and African Americans was also fueled by the rich musical exchanges between the salseros in New York City and their counterparts in the salsa bands emerging in the Congo, Senegal, Guinea, Côte d'Ivoire, and elsewhere in Africa. While scholars have highlighted the 1974 concert in Zaire, where the Fania All-Stars performed during the Ali-Foreman boxing match, this event tends to be framed as exceptional and unique. However, there is a longer history of African and New York salsa musical exchanges that needs to be unearthed. In 1964, the Orchestre Afro Negro, made up of Congolese university students, were recording rumbas and merengues in Belgium. In 1970, the African Khalam Orchestra from Senegal released "A Comer Lechón" to great success. In 1980, the Senegalese singer Jules Sagna recorded with his band, the Orchestra Afro-Charanga, and the Senegalese king of salsa, Laba Sosseh, recorded his album *Salsa Africana, Vol. 1.* These are but a few examples of the very rich history of African salsa music-making inspired by the Nuyorican salseros during the 1960s, 1970s, and 1980s.

Yet in Marc Anthony and J.Lo's *American Idol* performance, "Aguanile" became more neoliberal, mainstreamed, and erotically charged. While this performance was clearly resignified for a non-Latino and mainstream audience, it retained some signifiers that remit us to the longer genealogy of Afro-Caribbean sonic traditions established by Lavoe. The song is transformed from the sounds of communal healing—as in Lavoe—to a spectacle of individual and heterosexual desire, as the choreography clearly reveals. When Marc Anthony sings the elongated "A" in "Aguanile," simulating the spiritual call to the deities, J.Lo shakes her booty at the audience, thus recontextualizing the song from a communal and spiritual ritual of healing to a modern moment of sensual pleasure for all. The irony of this performance does not escape us, as the couple, despite their closing kiss that triggered a voyeuristic comment from one of the judges ("Now we know what they do at home"), announced their official separation a couple days later. While the dancers move tropicalized feathered fans to signal the spectacularization of the song, they also imitate some of the similar Santería-type movements we see in the "Aguanile" performance in *El Cantante.* Most poignantly, Sheila E.'s dynamic percussive moves on the timbales clearly connects the song, as performance, to its place in the Black Atlantic, as a diasporic articulation of its genesis in Blackness, an embodiment that counteracts the mainstream stage of *American Idol.* Not only does Sheila E.'s body reaffirm Afro-Boricua subjectivities through the percussive rhythms that hail Africa, she also becomes another central female figure who almost seems to compete with J.Lo as the protagonist in the staging of "Aguanile." The moment when Marc Anthony introduces Sheila E. and moves closer to her, almost displacing J.Lo into the secondary role of yet another backup dancer, suggests a competition and power struggle between the two female bodies, both of which ironically share the gendered disruptive role against the dominant masculinity of salsa's production history. Despite its resignification, this performance nonetheless reaffirms the long genealogy of Blackness as mediated by US mainstream television, a Blackness struggling to reclaim itself amid a mainstreamed spectacle.

More recently, "Aguanile" has been reduced to background music for an ice-skating performance by the German couple Kavita Lorenz and Joti Polizoakis during the 2018 Winter Olympics. Like most salsa music that has been globalized and resignified, "Aguanile" has become whitened, mainstreamed, and commodified. Marc Anthony has, in fact, played a major role in this shift, yet these sonic politics are complicated by the global celebration of Lavoe accompanied by a simultaneous reclaiming of Blackness that cannot be divorced from Marc Anthony's own decolonial sonic project as a Boricua interpreter.

Marc Anthony has sung "Aguanile" as the iconic opening song to many of his concerts, including the Vivir Mi Vida tour in 2014. Selecting this song as an opener suggests that Marc Anthony is fully aware of its sacred meanings as a toque de santo, a cleansing of the body through water. This meaning is well anchored in Lavoe's 1970s performance in New York that clearly remits us to the Afro-Caribbean rituals and practices of Santería and to the longer history of Lavoe's voice as reaffirming a Black aurality. Despite his white-presenting light skin, Lavoe's sounds and rhythms publicly articulated this larger genealogy of Blackness through salsa music. Whether in the Fania All-Stars concert "Live in Africa" in Zaire in 1974, or in the smaller clubs in the Bronx and in New York, Lavoe's performative Afro-Latinidad is indisputably evident, mostly in his nasal vocal stylings that reaffirmed the street sounds in New York and that remitted us to the earlier singing styles of enslaved communities in the Americas. This nasal style of singing clearly resisted a finessing or elegance usually associated with elite sonic styles.

Nuyorican rapper Fat Joe samples Lavoe's "Aguanile" in his song "Yes," with Cardi B and Anuel AA, publicly reaffirming the historical continuities between salsa dura of the 1960s and 1970s and 2000s underground reggaetón. However, this linkage also suggests that both singers participate in the egregious objectification of women's butts, which has made this cut controversial among Latinx feminist listeners.

Given this history and these complex linkages, could we still affirm that Marc Anthony's sonic reiteration of this canonical song among Caribbean Latinx audiences restructures it as a song of healing? Could we entertain the possibility that "Aguanile" as an opening song allows concertgoers to feel like one community, a collective being, adding a spiritual dimension to what otherwise is a capitalist enterprise meant to produce profit and income for the singer, its agencies, and its production company? Can it situate the concert as an event that produces community, acknowledges Blackness, and empowers Marc Anthony's listeners in their humanity? Despite the shifting meanings that "Aguanile" has experienced in its global circulations and mainstreaming, the comments of listeners and viewers in social media suggest that the sounds and rhythms do resonate with the affective textures of mourning and of nostalgia. For instance, viewers of the *American Idol* performance praised the combination of J.Lo as dancer and Marc Anthony as singer and also highlighted Sheila E.'s dynamic and brilliant drumming skills. Finally, some interpreted that performance as a eulogy to Marc and J.Lo's marriage, a relationship that had already been exposed in the tabloids as rocky. Once the separation was formally announced, fans expressed sadness and pain at their breakup. The performance, timed as it was preceding their separation, allowed listeners to mourn the joys and pleasures of having witnessed the story of this powerful Boricua couple, their family life, and the vicissitudes of their romantic relationship. This mourning of the end of Marc and Jennifer's relationship signals the larger, collective mourning that would take place after Hurricane María and that was likewise foreshadowed in Amina Gautier's short story.

On Critical Listening and Belonging

Amina Gautier's "Aguanile" is told from the point of view of the Afro–Puerto Rican nieta, a young woman who has recently bought her own house in Philadelphia but whose family resides in Brooklyn. The story highlights the intergenerational impact of family traumas informed by the politics of masculinity, the transnational lives of Puerto Rican families, and the potential for healing and reconciliation. More specifically, the nieta shares the special relationship she had with her maternal Puerto Rican abuelo, who lived on the island after having abandoned her African American grandmother for another woman and eventually moving back to Puerto Rico and starting a second family. The story is structured around the phone calls between the nieta and her grandfather, with some scenes emerging as flashbacks that reiterate the grandfather's vexed location within the nieta's nuclear family. The final phone call, which triggers the narrative itself, informs the nieta about her grandfather's passing.

After that call, the nieta remembers, through the healing power of memory, the moment when her grandfather played Héctor Lavoe's "Aguanile" to her. It is through this act of critical listening and sonic memory that the nieta, as an Afro-Latina, finds a space of belonging through the sounds and rhythms of Blackness performed within the song.

The three phone calls frame the story through voice and sounds. These conversations share the same content, since they each notify the nieta and the readers about the death of salsa musicians. The first, which opens the story, is the grandfather calling to let his nieta know about the death of Charlie Palmieri, a pioneering salsa musician from New York who performed charangas and boogaloos and who, with Lavoe, shared a strong presence in both the island of Puerto Rico and the diaspora in New York City. At the time, the nieta and her family are waiting for Hurricane Gilbert to arrive to the East Coast from Jamaica, where it had devastated the island, a reference that roots the story in 1988 and ironically foreshadows the reality of María in 2017. If hurricanes symbolize both destruction and possibility for the nieta and for Puerto Rican subjectivities, likewise "writing about the dead is always both an end to a relation and the possibility of a new beginning" (Saresma 2003, 615).

The second call refers to Héctor Lavoe's death in 1993, when the grandfather travels to New York to attend Lavoe's wake and funeral procession, a public ritual on the streets of New York that memorialized the Puerto Rican singer as both a cultural hero and a singer for and of the people (Valentín-Escobar 2001, 208). Again, these phone calls concretize the affective consequences of what critics have called "la salsa y sus muertes" [the deaths of salsa], that is, the collective demise of the foundational interpreters and musicians (J. Moreno 2015, 29; Rondón 2008, 283–308). The irony, of course, for the nieta, is that for her estranged grandfather, Lavoe's wake was much more meaningful as a ritual of mourning than his former wife's funeral, which he did not attend. Unaware that salsa music had established a sense of collective affiliation and a sense of belonging among so many Puerto Ricans of his generation, the nieta responds to her grandfather: "'I'm sorry to hear that,' I said, baffled by his ability to grieve for a stranger" (Gautier 2014, 2). While the narrator reveals her discomfort at her grandfather for grieving for salsa stars whom he never met, I would argue that her grandfather is modeling the possibility of grieving collectively. Her grandfather, who is persona non grata in her immediate family, is able to mourn for salsa musicians because this generation of salseros formed a communal space and a sense of belonging for Puerto Rican listeners, and, most poignantly, for his generation of Puerto Rican males. Thus, while masculinity allows for this constructed collectivity through the sonic spaces of salsa, it opens the possibility of collective mourning. Gautier exhorts her readers to reflect on the process of mourning. As music theorist Jairo Moreno asks, "Cómo pensar el duelo más allá de lo privado, es decir, como una posibilidad política y de colectividad?" [How do we rethink mourning beyond the private, that is, as a political and collective possibility?] (2015, 32). As Puerto Rican cultural studies scholar Jason Cortés has interrogated in his own work: "Could mourning, in effect, be categorized as a kind of resistance? Could it carry enough political value and weight to be intrinsically liberatory?" (2018, 363). If the emergence of these artistic texts for mourning in the wake of Hurricane María's deaths constitutes one more iteration of arts as resistance and healing within Latin America—the arpilleras in Chile and Argentina, protest songs in Cuba and Chile, the bossa nova in Brazil, the Abuelas de la Plaza de Mayo in Argentina, among numerous other instances—for Puerto Rico the widespread loss of life after the storm in 2017 has produced expressions of collective healing as never seen before (Rivera Santana 2019, 178–82).

The gender politics of this collective mourning emerge as we learn about the grandfather's estrangement from his former family: he was "the husband [my] grandmother had chosen not to remember, the father my mother and uncles refused to claim" (Gautier 2014, 3). As the story unfolds, we learn that the nieta was the bridge between him and the rest of her family, that she had been sent to spend a summer with him in Puerto Rico as "a peace offering" (3), and that during that visit her grandfather introduced her to salsa musicians like "Blades, Colón, Lavoe, Nieves, Palmieri, Puente," "who meant nothing to [her]" (5). The intergenerational dynamics that structure Gautier's story are central to understanding the shifting meanings of salsa music, which vary among the elders, the middle-aged, and the youth. The fact that the nieta "discovered" the iconic salsa singers through her grandfather signals the central role of elders in reclaiming the past for the present and the future and in offering a legacy to the younger generations. The wedding scene in the story, in which the groom, Chali, the grandfather's son from his second family, refuses to play Héctor Lavoe songs for the grandfather, highlights these generational gaps in sonic traditions. The grandfather thus complains to his nieta: "'Chali says he's not going to play anything by *him*.' My grandfather announced this as if it were a personal affront, something his son had done just out of spite" (10). Yet, echoing the long continuity of Afro-Caribbean rhythms and sonic traditions as a collective form of resistance, from the bomba to salsa, from salsa to reggaetón, the grandfather's act of introducing his nieta to the salsa greats is not merely an act of masculinist nostalgia but a gesture of reconciliation, a tool for decolonization and long-term resistance.

The third phone call, which serves as the closing framework for the narrative, is from one of her aunts in Puerto Rico, informing the nieta that her grandfather has passed. As the narrator remembers her grandfather in Puerto Rico, she textualizes her own memory of having listened to "Aguanile" during her visit with him. Indeed, the intersemiotic translation of the sounds, lyrics, arrangements, and performance of "Aguanile" allows the nieta to give closure to the narrative as much as she is giving closure to her own affective dilemmas with her estranged grandfather. Through her sonic memory of the song, the nieta begins to give meaning to "Aguanile" and to her own identity as an Afro–Puerto Rican woman. She finally "knew what he [the grandfather] meant. The chant of the song provided the means to chase the *demons* all away" (Gautier 2014, 15; original italics). As the lyrics, inflected with the Yoruba language and the long traditions of healing and cleansing through Santería, have long been articulated in the innumerable performances of the song, likewise Gautier's nieta also deploys the song as a language that allows her to find home with and through her grandfather. The nieta finally acknowledges the healing power of the song to exorcise her grandfather's demons, those very "demons" that also characterized Héctor Lavoe's singing and which remit us to how colonialism and dispossession affect Puerto Rican men (Aparicio and Valentín-Escobar 2004, 87–88).[4] The intergenerational tension is acknowledged, although not resolved; so too are the gender politics that allow her, as a young woman who owns her own home and refuses to marry, to forgive her grandfather's toxic masculinity, which informed his having abandoned her African American grandmother to poverty, illness, and isolation. She realizes: "He was using me to get through to them and—that night—I allowed myself to be used" (Gautier 2014, 15). Thus, she acknowledges and embraces her role as a medium that bridges her late grandfather to her mother, uncles, aunts, and siblings. She thus expresses through words the sonic memory of listening to "Aguanile":

> The song was slow to start. It began as if it were in a jungle or a forest, with the sounds of birds cawing, chirping, tittering, and screeching. Elephants trumpeted. In the distance, drums spoke and voices chanted, putting me in the mind of what I guessed African music sounded like. The song went on like this, growing without words. Then the horns kicked in, followed by a man's voice singing one lone word, stretching it to its limit, repeating it and pulling everything and more from the word he sang over and over. Without

---

4. Wilson Valentín-Escobar and I discuss how Héctor Lavoe's and La Lupe's own condition of abjection reminded racial minorities of our own vulnerabilities to be always already criminalized by US dominant society and the state. Both Lavoe's and La Lupe's lives were "fraught with personal tragedy and suffering, elements that allowed their Latino audiences to confront their own struggles and marginalization as a result of structured social inequities" (Aparicio and Valentín-Escobar 2004, 87–88).

warning, drums rolled and all the instruments seemed to come in at once. I'd never heard any kind of song like it. Beneath the familiar instruments, I heard the sounds of one I didn't know, a clanging like that of the small noisemakers sold on New Year's Eve. My grandfather identified it as the clave, the key, the rhythm, the heartbeat of all salsa. (14)

This sonic memory unfolds into critical listening, as the nieta finds home and a sense of belonging and identity in its sounds and instrumentation. She highlights how the song, "growing without words," begins as an uninterrupted instrumental crescendo, then leads to "a man's voice singing one lone word" (14), as the word "aguanile" is uttered through elongated and repeated syllables, from the initial "A" to the final "nile." The nieta's ears situate these opening sounds as "what I guessed African music sounded like," thus acknowledging her initial lack of knowledge about Black sonic and rhythmic traditions. Yet, through critical listening, she allows herself to find a sense of belonging and home in them. The nieta likewise notes her ignorance of the "clave" as "the sound of one I didn't know," yet immediately recalls her grandfather defining the "clave" as "the key, the rhythm, the heartbeat of all salsa." This is immediately followed by a reference to "the drums" that "drove the beating of my heart" and allowed her to feel that she "was moving." Thus, through this intersemiotic translation of an act of critical listening and sonic memory, the nieta is able not only to acknowledge her place in the family but to situate herself within the longer genealogies of the Black diaspora and her roots in Africa. It allows her as well to trace a longer genealogy of Afro-Puertorriqueñidad through the song's previous iterations and performances. The song itself, its sounds and the long history of Puerto Rican community-building that "Aguanile" invokes as a classic of the Nuyorican moment of salsa music, is what allows the nieta to understand the value of her grandfather: "With the music between us, I could *almost* forget that he was the man who should have been in Brooklyn with us but had abandoned us and had a whole other family who got all of his time, care, and attention" (Gautier 2014, 11). In symbolic ways, her grandfather embodies the abandonment of the diaspora and the African American identities of his first family, the nieta's mother and grandmother, and herself, whose Afro-Puerto Ricanness has been long elided and silenced within the island's mainstream constructions of cultural identity.

If, as critics have noted, Gautier's short stories emphasize the "ambiguities" of the "concept of happiness," suggested by her use of the adverb "almost," "Aguanile" the story does portray "ordinary lives in their full measure—courageous, flawed, utterly human" (Brown 2016). The inclusion of "almost" also suggests that the nieta will not totally forget the consequences of her grandfather's abandonment and, thus, the healing power of sounds, rhythms, and this song will always remain incomplete and imperfect at best. Yet her acknowledgment of the collective power of salsa music as a sonic tradition is clearly liberatory for her. As she states at the end of the short story, "When I listened to 'Aguanile' that night, I knew what he meant" (Gautier 2014, 15).

In closing, reading "Aguanile" in a reverse temporality allows me to illustrate the reconciling power of music and literature during this critical moment for Puerto Ricans, both on the island and in the diaspora, since 2019, as the mourning after Hurricane María has transformed into collective political mobilization. A critical listening of "Aguanile" allows us to acknowledge the healing power of the hurricane itself, which, like water and the powers of Yemayá, "unveiled" a new sense of confidence among Puerto Ricans on the island who have engaged in grassroots organizing as a form of survival and change, as the Paro Nacional of 2019 has illustrated. After getting organized locally, regionally, and transnationally, Puerto Ricans have recognized that they do not need to depend on either the local or the federal government for survival but on themselves and each other. As the Paro Nacional and the national protests in Puerto Rico demanding—and achieving—the resignation of Governor Ricky Rosselló suggest, most Puerto Ricans, despite party affiliations, are beginning now to acknowledge the need for decolonization in the face of the abandonment by the US federal government. Could we acknowledge that the rains and waters from María not only destroyed but also allowed Puerto Ricans to begin to heal together?

Figure 4.2 beautifully illustrates the power of water as a healing force during the Paro Nacional in 2019. As Carmen Yulín Cruz, then the mayor of San Juan, stated: "I hate to say anything positive about Maria. But what the hurricane did was force us to look at the realities of life here and how our dependency on the outside weakens our ability to ensure our people are taken care of. Maria made it evident that we need agricultural sovereignty" (Adler 2018). Sylvia de Marco, an organizer in farming projects, also stated: "After the hurricane, even people who didn't care about food started to care. It really opened people's eyes: that we have to depend on our soil, not shipping containers" (Adler 2018). This collective recognition, a sort of decolonial anagnórisis for all Puerto Ricans, is also echoed by organizer Christine Nieves: "This process of discovering the latent potential in the community has been like opening your eyes and all of a sudden seeing 'Oh wait, we're humans and there's other ways of relating to each other now that the system has stopped'" (Klein 2018, 68).

In brief, as the rich and powerful presence of music, reggaetón, dancing (like the queer perreo in front of the Cathedral in Old San Juan), and visual and performative arts such as the act of banging on cacerolas made evident

FIGURE 4.2. Paro Nacional in Puerto Rico during the summer of 2019. Photograph by Fabián Rodríguez Torres on Instagram.

during the Paro Nacional and afterward, the post-María reconstruction period has opened up the possibilities of reconciliation between the island and the diaspora, among Puerto Ricans of different generations, like the nieta and her abuelo, and among those with conflicting gender politics. The political events in July 2019, which integrated individuals from such different social and political positionalities, highlighted the potential for an alternative collectivity—a way of being puertorriqueñx—that defies traditional and mainstream notions of national belonging and that were made possible by the decolonizing and healing power of the arts. For Boricuas connected with each other, on the island and throughout the diaspora, literature, music, and the visual and performative arts allow us to reimagine the possibilities for decoloniality and collective empowerment. I hope that this critical reading of "Aguanile" contributes to the larger process of public healing, a collective experience that cannot be disconnected from our own intimate family stories of loss after the hurricane.

CHAPTER 5

"Vivir Mi Vida" (2013)

Toward a Critical Salsa Romántica and a Global South Brownness

Rethinking Salsa Romántica

During his *Cambio de Piel* tour and concert in Chicago on September 20, 2014, Marc Anthony stated that his musical repertoire was "not ballads" but "salsa." While this comment may seem contrary to his vast repertoire of love songs, it needs to be read as part of longer, contentious debates among musicians around the emergence of salsa romántica, its dominance in the musical industry, and the ensuing resistance to it by other salseros. Marc Anthony was clearly responding to earlier attacks against him by Willie Colón, who a month earlier had publicly denounced el Marc's singing as "rehashing Héctor Lavoe" and dismissed him as a "karaoke singer." Willie Colón went on to denounce the ways "balada rítmica" has replaced the "real hardcore stuff": "Where's the new stuff? A lot of what you hear on the radio just sounds like balada rítmica. I got nothing against poetry. I love a beautiful song, but where is the real hardcore stuff?" (Simián 2014).

Indeed, since the 1980s, salsa romántica and salsa erótica have replaced the oppositional communal barrio sound of the salsa dura of the late 1960s and 1970s with bolero-informed, lyrical love songs. As Chris Washburne notes, the shifts were not only in the lyrics and themes but also in the instrumentation and style, its "aesthetics":

tempos were slower, percussion and brass parts were executed in comparatively subdued fashion, and vocals were sung in a smooth, crooning style. The lyrics centered on topics of love, replacing the politically charged lyrics of Rubén Blades, Héctor Lavoe, and the like.... This new approach to salsa deemphasized images of barrio life and reduced the call for Latino unity, hence aligning itself with the sociopolitical environment of the Reagan era in the United States, in which political activism and global awareness were largely pacified. (Washburne 2008, 102)

By 2014 these shifts had become the standard sounds of salsa. Clearly, salsa romántica fit well within the neoliberal regime of a global society that privileges individualism, heteropatriarchy, and market-driven representations of love and desire. Within these internal tensions among salsa styles, Marc Anthony's Chicago concert in 2014 revealed his anxiety over being classified as exclusively a singer of ballads and love songs, a genre that has, ironically, secured his hemispheric and global standing as a celebrity (see chapter 2). The instrumentation deployed at the concert cemented a strategic highlighting of salsa dura: in contrast to many other of his concerts, there were no violins, and a strong percussion section on stage was highlighted and acknowledged throughout the evening in the instrumental improvisatory solos performed by the musicians. When Marc Anthony sang "Mi Gente" almost at the end of the concert, it was a clear homage to Lavoe's poetics and ethics of communal solidarity with Puerto Ricans and, by extension, with other Latino/a fans. In this chapter, I argue that Marc Anthony's 2013 album *3.0* and his major hit "Vivir Mi Vida" propose a new cultural politics of salsa romántica that I locate in the post-9/11 moment and that powerfully inscribes a Global South brownness structured and embodied by the political and symbolic proximity of Puerto Rican and Arab brown bodies as racialized criminal subjects. I reveal the nuanced ways that musical discourse simultaneously inhabits neoliberal individualism while it articulates a critical politics for our times. In other words, it illustrates the "possibility that salsa romántica is being ... put to use in diverse symbolic ways" (Aparicio 1998, 141).

I analyze the sonic significations of salsa romántica in *3.0* by examining the intertextuality of "Vivir Mi Vida," the hit song that opens and closes the album. As Marc Anthony himself candidly shared with his fans in the *Video Raíces*, he was introduced in an impromptu way to the Algerian raï song "C'est la Vie," composed and interpreted by Cheb Khaled. When RedOne, a Morocco-born music producer, played the song for Marc Anthony, Marc's son, Ryan, came out of his bedroom and expressed interest in it. Realizing that the song possessed a catchy rhythm and could serve as a melody for communal celebration and great dancing, Marc Anthony and Sergio George quickly arranged the salsa version in fifteen minutes, a draft that, after further finessing, eventually ended up as the first and last cut of *3.0*. Marc Anthony frames this story as taking place at a moment when he was feeling like a dinosaur in the music world, with the increasing popularity of reggaetón and the emergence of the new generation of singers like Bad Bunny, J Balvin, and Maluma. Marc Anthony's encounter with "C'est la Vie" reenergized him and fueled his interest to interpret the song as a celebration for his community.[1]

The original Algerian-French "C'est la Vie" allows listeners to interpret the otherwise celebratory dance song "Vivir Mi Vida" as a text that performs a gesture of solidarity with the Muslim and Arab world, a textualizing of a brownness rooted in the Global South. In this context, the "brownness" emerges as a signifier of solidarities across colonized and subordinated communities. Rather than settle for the dominant definitions of "brownness" as a mestizaje with aspirations for whiteness, this Global South "brownness" is grounded in political forms of resistance. In addition, the photo of a veiled Marc Anthony inside the album suggests that both sound and image constitute a nuanced response to the global symbolic violence exerted against Puerto Ricans and Arabs. To examine how salsa romántica, a subgenre that is included in many of the other songs on the album, despite its market-driven and counter-oppositional origins, enunciates anticolonial politics, I read the intertextuality of the song and the photo of the veiled Marc Anthony and propose a rereading of the discourses of love and of expressing pain in public space, through affect theory. This rethinking of salsa romántica, another instance of critical listening, allows us to reconsider the central role those other musical genres based on love, such as the bachata, boleros, and even serenatas (Johnson 2017), have assumed in the post-9/11 period.

The Global King of Salsa

Named "the King of Salsa" by the media and his fans, Marc Anthony has sold more than twelve million albums worldwide and earned a Guinness World Record as salsa recording artist (Harrington 2002b). According to Wikipedia, by the early 1990s, Marc Anthony had sold more salsa records than any other performer on the planet, solidifying his position among the most important

---

1. In his 2022 album *Pa'lla Voy*, Marc Anthony includes "Alé Alé Alé," a salsa adaptation of "Magic in the Air," which was originally written and performed by the Côte d'Ivoire musical group Magic System, suggesting that "Vivir Mi Vida" is not an exception in his repertoire.

new salsa artists to emerge in the 1990s. Since then, the Nuyorican singer's global popularity has soared even higher. His musical productions and his international tours evince and have fueled the globalization of salsa. One can hear Marc Anthony's music in Havana, Cuba, in Cali, Colombia, in Chicago, Illinois, as well as in England, Germany, Italy, and Spain, where salsa sites and dancing cultures have been well established. Jesús Trivino Alarcón (2013) framed *3.0* as a potential "boost for the Latin music market. According to Billboard, Latin music album sales declined to 4.3 million—14 percent lower than during the first half of 2012." Even then, Marc Anthony himself was not concerned about the death of salsa as a musical market; he thought the "genre is in a good place" and that "salsa is here to stay" (Trivino Alarcón 2013). The numerous awards for "Vivir Mi Vida"—including Artist of the Year, Hot Latin Song, Digital Song for the 2014 Billboard Latin Music Awards, and the 2013 Latin Grammy Awards for Album of the Year and for Best Salsa Album—evince the outstanding popularity of this song and the album. In fact, "Cautivo de Este Amor" became the theme song for the Argentinian telenovela *Lobo*. In 2022, his *Pa'lla Voy* tour took el Marc to the Netherlands, numerous cities in Spain, and the United Kingdom, and most recently, his 2024 *Historia* tour has expanded his global audibility. His global fans continue to admire his vocal dexterity and fuel his international fame through Facebook fan pages and websites.

Leila Cobo (2021a) argues that Marc Anthony's strategic decision to interpret "Vivir Mi Vida" inaugurated what she defines as "the new Latin Explosion" (225). She writes:

> For Latin music, it was the beginning of a new, previously unexplored path to globalization. With "Vivir mi vida," Marc Anthony took a track popular in another language and another hemisphere, and reimagined it to the soundtrack of Latin music, multiplying its appeal by a factor of millions. Four years later, J Balvin would do something similar with "Mi gente," only this time, all the mechanisms to measure the global success were in place. The new Latin Explosion had officially begun. (225)

The global circulation of "Vivir Mi Vida," already facilitated by its Algerian French subtext, did mark a new moment for Marc Anthony's music career. The song "single-handedly reignited interest in salsa music, bringing a new legion of fans to the genre" (Cobo 2021a, 225). In October 2013, I was visiting Havana, Cuba, for an academic conference, and I was impressed with the omnipresent soundings of "Vivir Mi Vida" throughout Old Havana, from restaurants, to radios in taxicabs, to the beaches, to the song being blasted from individual homes. It is unsurprising, then, that the hit "exploded, spending 18 weeks at No. 1 on Billboard's Hot Latin Songs chart, the first tropical single in a decade to top the tally and the longest running No. 1 tropical song in the history of the chart" (Cobo 2021a, 224). This was, indeed, a momentous peak in Marc Anthony's singing arc.

The Sonic Palimpsest

"Vivir Mi Vida" is a Latino salsa adaptation of Algerian French singer Cheb Khaled's "C'est la Vie," which celebrates life in the bodies and mouths of Algerian French diasporic subjects. While the video includes multiracial youth breakdancing, smiling, and singing, the lyrics articulate the "recuperation from a romantic disappointment" (Cobo 2021a, 224) between a North African Muslim and a Christian lover. The text grapples with religious and cultural difference in a romantic relationship, thus responding to the postcolonial conditions and history of Algerians in France as well as, more generally, to the diasporic presence of North Africans, Middle Eastern, and Arab immigrants in Western Europe. Cheb Khaled, seen in figure 5.1, is indeed a popular singer in Europe, North Africa, and globally.

Cheb (which means "young male musician") Khaled has performed raï music in Algeria and in France; like Marc Anthony, Khaled has also become a global singer whose performances and musical videos circulate internationally and speak to the multiracial youth of Europe. Marc Anthony's Spanish rewriting of Khaled's French and Arabic song is not the first Latino-Arab musical dialogue and collaboration by Khaled, who also performed "Ki Kounti" with Mexican rock singer Saúl Hernández from Caifanes. Marc Anthony's rewrite was welcomed by the Arab music industry and by Khaled's staff as a salsa song that is fueling an increasing interest in, and access to, Khaled's song ("Marc Anthony" 2013).

Raï music originated in Algeria in the 1930s as folk music and eventually became protest music among the youth. During the 1970s, some musicians and producers were killed by the state for transgressing the traditional values of Islam, as the musical style was associated with vulgarity, sexual freedom, and imperialism. Radio helped to disseminate raï music, thus facilitating its status as a national expression for Algerians. In France, it became associated with the Algerian diaspora as well as exoticized as a music of "youth subculture" (Schade-Poulsen 1999, 31). Since the 1990s, raï has become Westernized and globalized, as changes of instrumentation, song lyrics, and language (from Arabic to French) have produced larger Western listening audiences. In brief,

FIGURE 5.1. Cheb Khaled. Magharebia / Wikipedia / CC BY 2.0.

the history of raï music can be read as a site of power struggles between the Western and Arab worlds.

In "C'est la Vie," the lyrics, which celebrate life and love, switch from French to Algerian Arabic, thus indexing the bicultural and hybrid linguistic spaces created by the Algerian population in the European metropolis. It sings about the differences between a Muslim and a Christian who have fallen in love and celebrates the integration of different religions, languages, and cultures, thus disrupting the strong borders and boundaries erected by official French national imaginaries. This layering of musical texts connects the Puerto Rican communities to the global conditions of postcolonial and diasporic subjectivities. In the post-9/11 moment, this sonic palimpsest was also a clear gesture of solidarity with the Arab world. Thus, "Vivir Mi Vida" assumes an oppositional texture once we are aware of its intertextuality and its Arab subtext, which is clearly acknowledged and documented in the album credits.

Despite their similarities as celebrations of diasporic communities, there is a fissure between the individualized voice and discourse of "Vivir Mi Vida" and the collectivity and cultural memory proposed by the song's subtext. According to Cobo, Marc Anthony rewrote the original Algerian song into "an anthem of hope in the face of adversity" (2021a, 224). If the salsa song has been hailed as Marc Anthony's new chapter in his life after his divorce from Jennifer Lopez, the song as text performs the tensions between past and present, between remembrance and oblivion. While the singer insists that he needs to forget the past and enjoy the present—"y para qué llorar, pa' qué / si duele una pena, se olvida" [why cry, why / if a pain hurts, we forget it]—the intertextuality with "C'est la Vie" interrupts this trope by suggesting the centrality of cultural and collective memory for the survival of the postcolonial subject. If in "C'est la Vie" Cheb Khaled's lyrics focus on collective identities, Marc Anthony's use of the first-person possessive in his version was meant to resonate with his listeners. He "wanted people to feel it was their story when they sang it. It's their voice" (Cobo 2021a, 230). Yet this change from the collective *we* to the individual *I* remits us, contrary to Marc Anthony's intentions, to the privatization of desire, to the forces of the musical market, and to the individual ethos of neoliberalism. The love songs that follow and that constitute the whole of the album—"Flor Pálida," "La Copa Rota," "Volver a Comenzar," "Cambio de Piel," and "Hipocresía"—easily lend themselves to be listened to as love songs from a *yo* to a *tú*. The tensions with Khaled's communal lyrics undermine the absoluteness of individual desire and love, and it is essential that we acknowledge the vaivenes (back-and-forth) between the collective and the personal through both songs.

Yet Marc Anthony's specific interpellations and improvisations in the montuno sections allow listeners to anchor ourselves within a Puerto Rican collective space. When the singer shouts, "mi gente, la vida es una," this reference to his "people" establishes another intertext, that of Héctor Lavoe's "Mi Gente," which became a national hymn for Puerto Ricans in New York. Wilson Valentín-Escobar argues that Marc Anthony imitated Lavoe through what Joseph Roach has termed "restored behaviors" and memorialized the salsa singer in ways that created "trans-Boricua communal imaginations" (2001, 208). The title of Lavoe's song functions as a hailing of the audience, a sort of communal call, a collective interpellation that finds an analogous image in Marc Anthony's music video, where he performs in the streets of the Bronx amid "las caras lindas"—to use Tite Curet Alonso's song title—of his people. This brief phrasing, a political riff of sorts, produces a collective memory that brings to life Lavoe, the salsa dura of the 1970s, and the biopic *El Cantante,* in which Marc Anthony himself embodies the life and music of Lavoe. On the album, there are instances when Marc Anthony also mentions Puerto Rico and his Boricua identity, as in "Ave María, Puerto Rico, Ataca Sergio," which triggers a change in tempo and the sounds of the brass and drums, and during "Flor Pálida" (composed by Cuban guajira singer Polo Montañez), a Puerto

Rican grito that hails salsa dura and interrupts the neoliberal individual texture of the discourse of love in salsa romántica, resituating listeners onto collective and national imaginaries. Indeed, these "details," as Alexandra Vázquez (2013) proposes, not only "disturb dominant narratives" (18) but also serve as "disruptive fissures that crack many a foundational premise" (20) about salsa romántica.

The Politics of the Veil

The Puerto Rican–Arab coupling sounded in the intertextuality of "Vivir Mi Vida" finds its visual counterpart in the image of a veiled Marc Anthony inserted in the album. Well hidden in the middle pages of the liner notes, this photo takes on multiple critical meanings. At first glance, it can be dismissed as an image of a pensive and reflective singer, or a fashion statement. The veiling of his mouth is reiterated in the sunglasses that cover his eyes. While the photo (see fig. 5.2) is part of the marketing for Marc Anthony's *3.0*, it serves as a critical image of a Global South brownness.

Yet it is worth exploring how this image strikingly performs the Puerto Rican–Arab coupling, akin to the Latino-Muslim coupling that Christopher Rivera (2014) has described as "the brown threat" post-9/11. This threat justified racial profiling of, physical violence against, and policing of Latino and Arab male bodies in the United States in the name of homeland security (C. Rivera 2014, 44–64). The politics of the veil in the Western world, particularly in France with its substantial Algerian diasporic community, embodies the power struggles over national imaginaries. In fact, state efforts to ban the veil in France during the 1980s and up to 2004, when the ban was passed, suggest strong parallelisms to the simultaneous efforts to legislate English-only policies in the United States, thus criminalizing the use of Spanish in one country and the wearing of the veil in another. The veiled Marc Anthony visually indexes both ethnicities as targets of US imperialism, proposing the "interchangeability" of both male minorities as criminalized by the state (C. Rivera 2014, 45). The racial profiling of brown men (both Arab and Latino) post-9/11, according to Muneer Ahmad (2002), brings up the question not of whether "one is Muslim or Arab . . . but that one is ostensibly not American" (106).

This visual icon, then, reconnects Marc Anthony's salsa music production today to the anticolonial politics of the salsa dura in New York, best exemplified by the oppositional salsa of Willie Colón. This articulation is reaffirmed by the return to images of el barrio in the musical video of "Vivir Mi Vida." While the barrio in 2013 was constructed in the musical video as

FIGURE 5.2. Marc Anthony veiled. Album insert, *3.0* (Sony, 2013). Photograph by Alan Silfen.

pan-Latino/a—note the multiple faces, flags, and Latin American ethnicities that surround Marc Anthony's stage—the reconnection to el barrio also illustrates a longer history of Algerian and Puerto Rican solidarities and influences in social movements. The foundational decolonizing work and life of Frantz Fanon in the Puerto Rican social movements of the 1960s and 1970s comes to mind, as well as the past and current discourses targeting Puerto Rican nationalists as "terrorists." It may be too far-fetched to propose that the image of the veiled Marc Anthony indicates the singer's putative sympathies with anticolonial Puerto Rican nationalists, such as the FALN (Fuerzas Armadas de Liberación Nacional), yet it is safe to indicate that it surely troubles the pristine image of Marc Anthony as a "safe" interpreter of love ballads.[2]

---

2. Fanon's foundational role and influence on the Young Lords in New York is evinced by the showing of Pontecorvo's 1966 film *The Battle of Algiers* in their formative early years, as documented by Sonia Manzano (2012); this is one example of the decolonial solidarity between Algerians and Puerto Ricans. Later, the discursive targeting of Puerto Rican nationalists as "terrorists" in the 1970s and 1980s, and the general mainstream denouncements of these liberation movements as criminal, reemerged in 2017 in the controversy around New York's Puerto Rican Day Parade. Corporate sponsorships were revoked to denounce the naming of freed political prisoner Oscar López Rivera as grand marshal. Finally, the criminalizing of, and hate speech and violence against, Muslim Americans in the new millennium continues after 9/11 and now, at the time of writing, during the Israel-Gaza War.

I now situate Marc Anthony's veiled face as another artistic site in a wider gamut of texts that claim affinities between the Puerto Rican and North African–Arab subjectivities. Another powerful reimagining is seen in Víctor Hernández Cruz's transcultural poetic works, which connect Morocco, Puerto Rico, New York, and California, all sites of residence for the Boricua poet, who has been mostly categorized as Nuyorican. His multiple circuits across US cities, the island of Puerto Rico, most specifically the town of Aguas Buenas, where his family lives, and now Morocco, where he lives with his Moroccan wife and two children, have inspired his writing to cross linguistic borders—Spanish, English, and Arabic—and to reclaim the North African heritage among Boricuas, the Arab in us which has been rendered invisible by long decades of Western Europe's Orientalism. The poet's writings thus transform and expand the official cultural icon of Puerto Rico as the fusion of Spanish, African, and Indigenous identities that has marked us for so long. If the Arab heritage is hidden within both the Spanish and the African markers—which signal generalized European whiteness and African Blackness—Cruz's verses propose multidirectional crossings across time and space that allow the hidden Arab presence to reemerge without erasing the multiple other cultural subjectivities that constitute who we are as Puerto Rican and Caribbean communities. Victor's visit to Morocco in February 2000 was initially unplanned. In a most haphazard way, he traveled from Madrid, Spain, where he attended a conference about Latinx writers. My spouse and I recommended he travel to Tangiers in a tour, as we had done before the conference. Victor liked our suggestion and took a bus to the coast and then a ferry to Tangiers. On the bus, he met a Moroccan woman who would eventually become his wife. He went to Tangiers as a tourist, but never returned home. A year after the conference, I received a letter from Morocco, where Victor shared his decision to stay in North Africa, to marry, and to start a family there. He thanked me for recommending the trip to Tangiers. It totally changed his life and his writing. As Marisel Moreno has written about his transcultural and global poetry, "with the stroke of a pen, Hernández Cruz's verses confront head-on both the Islamophobia and the Latinophobia that has emerged because of the 'brown threat'" (2015, 314). By highlighting "the layered and multiple migrations that have shaped the worldview of this poet" (301), Moreno describes Cruz's poetic works as writing that offers us "a dynamic sense of new world belongings" (315). More recently, Sarah M. Quesada delves into a rich, sophisticated analysis of Hernández Cruz's poetry related to Egypt and defines his vision as a "South-South cosmopolitanism" (2024, 432).

I share this sense of belonging and feeling at home in Morocco, given my own North African heritage. Sometime after I visited Morocco in 2020, I

FIGURE 5.3. My grandparents Ramón Sierra Reverón and Victoria Sierra Guzmán in Granada, Spain, circa 1959. The intersection between the Arab clothing and background and the Christmas greeting in English aptly captures the multicultural palimpsests of Puerto Rican cultural identities. Rivera Sierra family collection.

discovered in my family archives a Christmas card with the photo of my two maternal grandparents, Ramón Sierra Reverón and Victoria Maria Guzmán Sierra, dressed up as Arabs in a photo studio in Granada, Spain (see fig. 5.3). They were traveling in southern Spain and, according to the family, Ramón was looking for his relatives, a fact that does not coincide with the Asturian origins documented in his birth certificate. His own father, Ramón Sierra Pérez, was born in Asturias and had migrated to Puerto Rico as a young adult. Yet my grandfather's face reminds me visually of many men I met during my visit to Morocco, echoing Cruz's words, "the peoples could exchange places / as you will see they are the same faces" (quoted in M. Moreno 2015, 311). These faces are the Arab in me, the "historical ghosts" that anti-immigrant Spain has partly refused to recognize as central to its communal identity (309), yet Puerto Ricans like my grandparents, el Marc, Cruz, and I insist on reclaiming.

Returning to the image of the veiled Marc Anthony, the racialized masculinity evoked by the photo also hails the bodies of Muslim women who cannot erase "the visible signs of their concrete difference" (Ahmed 2004, 132).

Thus, the veiled Marc Anthony could be read as a Muslim body in "drag"—both cultural-religious and gendered—through the veil that Westerns associate with the Arab female body. In *Imagining Arab Womanhood: The Cultural Mythology of Veils, Harems, and Belly Dancers in the United States,* Amira Jarmakani (2008) traces the continuity of the harem and the veil as images that have naturalized and justified US military interventions in the Middle East since the 1970s, the decade that witnessed the oil embargo. The imperial discourses that demonize Arab and Muslim subjects are political, social, and cultural constructs that have a longer history predating 9/11. Jarmakani writes: "The cultural mythology of the veil is compelling because of its citational quality—the US association of the veil with barbaric, backward, regimes and, more recently, Islamic fundamentalism, has been sedimented through media coverage of such events as the Iran hostage crisis, the 1991 Gulf War, and the U.S. invasion of Afghanistan" (143–44). As I finish revising this chapter, news images of the Israel-Gaza War and the cruel murders of over 61,000 men, women, and children in Gaza continue to haunt us. Since last year, the scarves traditional to Palestinians, the keffiyeh, are now signifiers of protest and denouncements against not only Israel military offensives but also against the US military weapons that have made these war crimes possible.

The veiled Arab woman has thus become one of the major icons of the Middle East, Islam, and Arab cultures, all of which are defined as threats to the national security of the United States and Europe. This Western collective anxiety reiterates the phobias that Orientalism had already naturalized for the European empires. The representations of veiled Arab women in Western media, journalism, advertising, and photography have grounded, through their reiteration, the dominant construction of them as repressed, secluded, and primitive, as passive victims of the putative brutality, violence, and authoritarianism of Islamic men. Clearly, this meaning, as a "mythology" and "fixed signifier" (Jarmakani 2008, 146), justifies the "notion of US military action as a project of liberation," and it furthers the imperial narrative of the "US as a benevolent force seeking to spread freedom" (146), analogous to the hegemonic construction of Latin America throughout the twentieth century that equally justified US military presence in Central America and the Caribbean and that fueled the migration of local populations into the United States.

In this context, we can argue that Marc Anthony appropriates the veil as an icon of subaltern subjectivity that simultaneously triggers and contests the dominant narratives that demonize the Arab and Muslim worlds. He produces multiple significations of political, national, and imperial import as well as of gender and sexuality. Indeed, it is through gender discourses about sexuality that national and imperial imaginaries are constructed and mediated. The veil, which is a Western signifier that we imposed on Arab cultures (*hijab* or *niqab* are the proper terms; Jarmakani 2008, 154), implies a dialectical tension between visibility and invisibility that is tied to gender, sexuality, and imperialism. The Western gaze reads the covered Arab woman's body as "a simplistic equation of being uncovered (unveiled) or revealed, with being modern and emancipated" (Jarmakani 2008, 152), thus eliding any agency on the part of Arab women to exercise control over their bodies in the public space. As Jarmakani suggests, the veiled Arab woman, as a visual icon and "fixed signifier," hides and covers not only her body but her own subjectivity, her perspectives, her agency, and her stories.

As Julia Kristeva writes, for the Algerian diaspora in France, "the muslim scarf" became a visual index of immigration politics that inscribed immigrants as a disruption of the dominant French national imaginary. If Kristeva refers to the Muslim scarf in France as a "trauma" for the French national imaginary (quoted in Ahmed 2004, 132), Ahmed furthers the relationship between the national idea and the "ideal image" of the French nation. She writes that the bodies that "cannot be recognized in the abstraction of the unmarked, cannot accrue value, and become blockages in the economy: they cannot pass as French. . . . The veil, in blocking the economy of the national ideal, is represented as a betrayal not only of the nation, but of freedom and culture itself, as the freedom to move and acquire value" (133).

Historian Joan Wallach Scott, in *The Politics of the Veil* (2007), argues for the shifting semantics of the veil contingent on the historical period. During the Algerian revolution and independence wars from France, the veil was first associated with "dangerous militancy." By 1958, the National Liberation Front was using the veil "to transport weapons and bombs past security checkpoints," a function that is visually represented in the iconic film, *The Battle of Algiers* (Scott 2007, 63). This subversive value became more generalized. As Scott argues, for Frantz Fanon, then, the veil was "a way of resisting colonial domination." It became "an instrument of subversion, the means by which the abjection of colonial subjects could be transformed into a proud and independent national and personal identity" (Scott 2007, 64). Yet Jarmakani critiques this reading because it reproduces a "cultural mythology" and because it fixes the meanings of the veil as only anticolonial, eliding the multiple meanings that it produces (2008, 157). In France, specifically, the symbolism of the veil was "overdetermined," particularly during the national debates on banning the veil, which began in the late 1980s and culminated in 2004 with the ban's legalization. In the context of school politics, the French teachers' union supported the headscarf ban since it meant securing both the nation-state and the fate of the teachers as well. Many teachers were experiencing a "loss of status and authority," and thus the headscarf became the scapegoat for these issues (Scott 2007, 114). The debates in France around the ban, uncannily similar to those in the 1980s in the United States around English-only policies, highlighted the Western and French national imaginaries that felt threatened by this piece of clothing worn mostly by young women (and, analogously, by the use of Spanish in the US). That it has become an icon of terrorism after 9/11 and in our current times of Islamic attacks in Western Europe is unsurprising.

This debate also referred to two conflicting cultural ideologies about sexuality. Covering one's head in France, a country in which heterosexuality is contingent on the visual availability of a woman's body, not only disrupts this precondition for sexuality but also castrates the French and Western male and masculine gaze. While Muslims recognize that sexuality is complicated and should be kept out from the public space (thus, the woman covers her hair, ears, and neck), in France gender equality is based on sexual gestures in public and on the visibility of women's bodies, refusing to acknowledge that sexual desire can be a problem in the public space. While supporters of the ban argued that they were challenging Muslim women's putative patriarchal oppression, Joan Scott notes that the incompatible representations of sexuality between the French and Muslim cultures reaffirmed the "inassimilability of the Muslims" in France (2007, 173).

In this light, the image of the veiled Marc Anthony suggests multiple critical meanings. It exposes the long and analogous histories of imperial expansions into Algeria and the Middle East, doubling the past interventions into Latin America and the Caribbean. It also performs a male Muslim body in drag, a gender performance that suggests the Western-Muslim debates around the meaning of the veil as worn by Arab women. (While Bedouin men wear veils in the desert to protect themselves from the heat, sun, and sand, the fact that these veiled men are also associated in the Western world with potential terrorism speaks to the fixity of the veil as an icon of racialized and criminalized otherness.) This photo, then, resignifies salsa romántica and textualizes the solidarity of brownness in the Global South by troubling the national, imperial, and gendered discourses about the body, sexuality, and religion.

Rereading Love

Returning to Chris Washburne's earlier description of salsa romántica that characterized "the lyrics centered on topics of love" as "replacing the politically charged lyrics of Rubén Blades, Héctor Lavoe, and the like" (2008, 102), in this last section I call for a rethinking of salsa romántica as a performance that moves "pain into the public domain" (Ahmed 2004, 173). Deploying affect and feminist theories, I relisten to *3.0* not as another iteration of unrequited love exclusively framed as a neoliberal discourse of individual emotion and desire but rather as a musical performance of what Sara Ahmed (2004) calls "affectionate solidarity," a term that reflects on notions of love, nation, and cultural difference.[3]

In *The Cultural Politics of Emotion,* Ahmed highlights the limitation of the notion of "multicultural love" and challenges "any assumption that love can provide the foundation for political action" (2004, 141). Instead, she argues for acknowledging that "love might come to matter as a way of describing the very affect of solidarity with others in the work that is done to create a different world" (141). This "reflective solidarity," coined by Jodi Dean, leads to the concept of an "affectionate solidarity" (quoted in Ahmed, 141). Let us trace Ahmed's arguments and discuss their implications for a relistening of love in salsa romántica.

If, as Ahmed (2004, 142n5) writes, love "has been theorized as crucial to the social bond," "as central to politics and the securing of social hierarchy," and "as necessary to the maintenance of authority"—based on the paradigm of the love of the child for the parent—then this definition would only allow us to listen to salsa romántica as a dominant discourse. These politics have easily led us, critics, to dismiss this music as un- or apolitical, as hegemonic. Patriarchal ideologies that reproduce male domination over women (as in the motifs of "celos" [jealousy], "soy dueño de ti" [I own you]), her silencing, among that of others) likewise limit our readings to a heteropatriachal one. Ahmed instead proposes that we theorize love "as an investment that creates an ideal, as the approximation of a character that then envelops the one who loves and the loved" (142). By redefining love as an emotion that produces "a collective ideal," Ahmed's proposal for a "multiculturalism" whose "imperative [is] to love difference" (133) opens the possibility of reading salsa romántica as a collective discourse. Thus, love for the nation, claimed by both the anti- and pro-immigrant sectors, allows us to understand how both arguments "rely on the structural possibility of the loss of the nation as object" (134). If multiculturalism "becomes an imperative to love difference" and "to construct a national ideal" (133), this then leads to having "others fail" (133). After 9/11,

---

3. The Latin American discourse of love, embodied in the musical genre of the bolero, has been theorized and explored by Luis Rafael Sánchez (1988) and by Iris Zavala (2000), among others. Zavala proposed that boleros are a "discurso fronterizo" [a hybrid, border discourse] and notes that as ambiguity, the bolero "expresa la política de la diferencia" [expresses the politics of difference] (13). The late Vanessa Knights (2008), in addition, proposes an allegorical interpretation of boleros, where the yearning for the absent lover—the central trope in the bolero—becomes the desire for the reconstitution of the displaced self.

multiculturalism and difference "have been viewed as a security threat" to the nation. The fear of terrorism infiltrating the nation thus produces a national ideal whereby immigrants need to assimilate, learn English, and become British (or American) in order to enjoy the rewards of "being loved in return" (134). Thus, hybridity "as a form of sociality" is contingent on "the imperative to mix with others" (134). If cultural Others would learn to mix with the rest of the nation, then "we would be as one." Yet Ahmed concludes that this "multicultural fantasy" does not necessarily constitute "a politics of love" that would solve the problems of postcolonial immigrants and diasporas in the metropolis. While she recognizes the value of love in social relations and in acknowledging our own humanity, Ahmed disagrees with the notion that "love can provide the foundation for political action" (141).

Instead, she argues for an "affectionate solidarity" that could serve as the basis for queer and feminist politics. This solidarity "grows out of intimate relationships of love and friendship" and "lets our disagreements provide the basis for connection" (Dean 1996, 17; quoted in Ahmed, 141). Thus, Ahmed favors a love that is rooted in the recognition of difference rather than in a multicultural love for a unified nation that glosses over racial, ethnic, cultural, social, and gendered difference. Given the Latino-Arab coupling evident in *3.0*, the songs of love bracketed by the intertextuality of "Vivir Mi Vida" would allow for that possibility of "affectionate solidarity" with the Arab world and with other postcolonial diasporic communities.

The public performance of pain—as in the tears, grief, and melancholia felt for the lost object of love—may also be approached as a politics for collectivity and solidarity. If feminism, "as a politics of redress, is also about the pain of others" (Ahmed 2004, 174), then it follows that to respond to pain, as collective affect, we must "speak about pain." Such "speech acts are the condition for the formation of a 'we'" (174). In this framework, when thousands of Marc Anthony's concertgoers sing his lyrics in unison, a common performance across geographical regions and diverse social identities within the listeners, the public articulation of pain can take on political and oppositional significance, not to mention trigger the potential for healing. The power of sounds, melodies, and lyrics in acknowledging pain, both individual and collective, is a common thread throughout Marc Anthony's sonic labor and repertoire.

Conclusion

As listeners, salsa fans, and Marc Anthony fans, we can choose the politics of our listening. We may prefer to listen to Marc Anthony's salsa romántica songs at the intimate, personal level; or we may think about the emotional and affective intensity between the *yo* and the *tú* as a language that articulates the negotiations among different cultural and racial others within the boundaries of any nation or in the larger, global arena. At the *Cambio de Piel* concert, the audience did not really listen but sang *with* Marc Anthony in a collective performance of affective Latinidad informed by the shared experience of racialization. Salsa romántica, in the post-9/11 moment and in our global world, can be a site from which to address the needs of a neoliberal market while simultaneously proposing critical signifiers that discursively suggest more collective, and thus politically oppositional, readings of this musical style and discourse. *3.0* exhorts us to relocate the social and global meanings of music not only in the sounds but in its intertextual palimpsests. These multilayered texts reveal the nuanced, oppositional meanings of Marc Anthony's musical project in today's racialized globalism, opening rich possibilities for reconsidering the limitations and potentialities of salsa romántica as a critical discourse of our times.

CODA

Listening as Struggle

Writing this book has been an intimate, intense journey for me as I grapple with my own lifelong limitations as a listener. I confess I am a failed listener. Despite decades of scholarship, writing, and reflecting on listening as a critical practice, despite having authored titles like *Listening to Salsa* (1998) and in particular the chapter "Listening to the Listeners," I acknowledge my own deficits as an imperfect listener. Perhaps because of my personal struggles to become a finer listener, perhaps as a compensatory aspirational gesture, I intuitively gravitated toward the act of listening as my personal metaphor and analytic for approaching sound and popular music studies. By now, listening has become an analytic in and of itself in scholarship. Alexandra Vázquez's (2013) "listening in detail," Jennifer Lynn Stoever's (2016) "the listening ear," Dylan Robinson's "hungry listening" (2020), and my own theorizing gestures at "critical listening" (Aparicio 2021a, among many others) are all concepts that have allowed us to engage the social and racial experiences of making meaning through sounds and music. However, we still struggle to define who is a good listener and what is good listening. In the process, scholars have ironically dismissed the existence of failed listeners like me.

I confess to my imperfect listening skills, to my deficient hearing, and to my distracted attention. Yet despite these deficits and perhaps because of them, I have offered readers an alternative collective way of listening to Marc Anthony's songs that grounds them within the framework of our own communal experiences of displacement and itinerancies, of our exclusions from the mainstream American imaginaries, of our Latinidad as collective and individual suffering, of our Blackness, and of our solidarities with the Algerian and North African communities. While I do not claim that Marc Anthony has been consciously intentional in framing these five songs within these social and cultural contexts, his intuitive brilliance in curating a sonic repertoire that resonates with our colonized and precarious lives cannot be denied.

At my mother's insistence, my two sisters and I each had to learn a musical instrument during our youth. In addition to Spanish dance lessons with Maria Teresa Miranda and ballet with Juan Anduze in San Juan, learning to play music was a nonnegotiable task. My oldest sister learned the guitar, I selected the piano, and my youngest sister tried the accordion. Of the three, I was the only one who continued studying music into my teenage years and into college. I managed to get admitted to Indiana University's School of Music for a bachelor's degree in music education, despite my parents' insistence that music was not an appropriate career for a woman. I was thrilled to have this opportunity.

Once in college, it didn't take me long to realize that I lacked the requisite talents to survive as a music teacher, let alone as a performer. I did well in music theory if the work was written. But when the professor played a six-note chord and asked us to write it down on the music staff, I froze, unable to identify any of those notes. All I heard was a bunch of sounds fused together, not the distinct sounds that combined into those chords. I felt so inadequate as a student among so many brilliant young musicians who were being shaped into a professional future. My classmate Flip, who played trombone, studied jazz and had the perfect pitch and musically trained ear to improvise beautifully with his instrument. In choir, I had to sing next to others who had beautiful voices. Mine, in contrast, was untrained and most of the time out of tune. I just could not hear what my classmates were able to perceive. My conducting class became a painful reminder of my listening deficiencies as I attempted to conduct my classmates to perform a piece I could not truly hear in my mind nor understand, let alone direct. Eventually, I dropped out of the music school and changed my major to comparative literature and Spanish, a decision that I never regretted and that allowed me to later reclaim music through cultural studies.

My listening deficiencies are not only musical. My spouse and my adult children still alert me to the ways they feel that I don't listen to them or remember what they said at a particular moment. I have strived to pay more attention to our conversations and diálogos, but my verbal memory is atrocious.

I remember the themes and ideas discussed but never the exact words used. I am always impressed by those around me who can recall past moments in their lives, some decades ago, and still reproduce a dialogue or a conversation. I could never do that, even in my younger years.

My sustained intellectual curiosity around listening as a critical concept, metaphor, and analytic in my own scholarly journey has long been entangled with my own struggles as a listener. When I decided to spend a decade researching salsa music, starting in the late 1980s, it was not an arbitrary decision but rather a project of returning to my training in classical piano to engage in a different musical style that was antagonistic to classical music. I had to reject the tenets I had been taught about classical music and discover, on my own, how to approach popular music with the requisite respect to the musicians who labored to offer audiences moments of joy and hope. Instead of relying on written musical notations, as classical piano demands, I had to engage with my listening ear and establish connections between and among songs without reading music.

I believe my scholarship is perhaps my way of healing from the past traumas of my life, my having to drop out of music school and acknowledge that I didn't have what it takes. As quietly as I moved from one discipline to another, I still was left with the shame of not being a good enough musician. So many times, I have felt like an intruder among those who have a keen musical ear, with or without formal training. Perhaps in another life I will be reborn into a musician with perfect pitch and listening talents that will compensate for my listening deficits now. My cultural studies approach to salsa and Latinx popular music allowed me to contribute new perspectives and produce an alternative knowledge to music history and sound studies that traditional musical studies do not address.

In closing, I return to the beginning of this book with a reference to Roberta Flack's interpretation of "Killing Me Softly with His Song." The question haunts my mind: What and who is a good listener? The singer in this song is a listener, and she is an ideal one. She is the one who sees herself in the song, a text and performance that have become a mirror to her life. She is the one who allows herself to be seduced and, most importantly, hailed by the lyrics of the song. She opens herself up and celebrates her vulnerability as she listens to the singer, a "stranger" in her life. This is, for me, what constitutes a good listener: acknowledging how sounds, music, lyrics, and rhythms can allow us to recognize our weaknesses and our frailty, our openness to be fragile and sensitive to the world around us, to life. As the singer-listener states, songs reveal "our dark despair." In this sense, this book announces my own alternative approach to good listening, a listening that allows us, as fans of Marc Anthony, to open ourselves up to the difficulties that our lives present us with, to recognize our sensibilities, and to be vulnerable together and safely. Ultimately, this is what Marc Anthony has offered us not only in the five songs that I have critically analyzed and unearthed in the previous chapters but throughout his diverse and vast musical repertoire and sonic corpus. I close with Deborah Paredez as she exhorts her readers in *American Diva* (2024, 6), "Listen again with me now."

ACKNOWLEDGMENTS

Even though I wrote most of this book after my official retirement from Northwestern University in December 2018, I owe its inspiration, conceptualization, and transdisciplinary textures to my colleagues, former PhD students, and students during my thirty-five years of teaching and scholarship. I especially want to name those intellectual interlocutors whose own writings have been central to the field of Latinx popular music and to my own writings: Wilson Valentín-Escobar, Maria Elena Cepeda, Petra Rivera-Rideau, Lorena Alvarado, Deborah Vargas, Licia Fiol-Matta, Verónica Dávila Ellis, Alejandro Madrid, and Marisol Berrios-Miranda. A special thanks to Alejandro "Chali" Hernández and Angel "Cucco" Peña for sharing information with me. A shout-out to Nora Godoy, who served as my research assistant during my residence at Marquette University in fall 2019. The generous funding and resources that accompanied the AMUW Women's Chair in Humanistic Studies at Marquette helped me to move the project ahead. My appreciation to Wilson Valentín-Escobar, María Elena Cepeda, and Petra Rivera-Rideau for reading the first drafts of two chapters. Your feedback was invaluable! To my close friends, Renee Cortez and Elizabeth Davis, for long conversations about el Marc and for their unabated enthusiasm for the book. Looking forward to many more years of listening to el Marc! To my loved ones John and Alejandro, Gaby and Brian, Braxton and Giuliana, and Camila and Anthony, for their unconditional support and to Camila for assisting me with preparing the images for the book. Finally, I express my immense gratitude to Lourdes Torres and Frederick Aldama for embracing this publication as part of their Global Latino/a Americas book series at The Ohio State University. I am much indebted to Kristen Elias Rowley, acquisitions editor at OSU Press, for her unwavering support and enthusiasm for this book and to the staff who made the book possible. Much appreciation goes to Cathy Hannabach, Rachel Fudge, and the staff at Ideas on Fire, whose acute attention to grammar, style, and organization of the content has helped me in providing readers with a clearer narrative. Cathy also prepared the index, a job that is tedious but so helpful for future readers. Finally, a shout-out to all of Marc Anthony's fans, listeners, and followers who have found hope and healing in his songs.

Some portions of chapter 5 have previously appeared in the following publications: "Marc Anthony 3.0: Toward a Critical *Salsa Romántica*," in *Rhythm and Power: Performing Salsa in Puerto Rican and Latino Communities*, edited by Derrick León Washington, Priscilla Renta, and Sydney Hutchinson, 47–58 (New York: Centro Press, 2017); "Sounding the Image and Imaging the Sound: Marc Anthony 3.0 and Critical Salsa Romántica," in *Sound, Image, and National Imaginary in the Construction of Latin/o American Identities*, edited by Pablo Vila and Héctor Fernández L'Hoeste, 207–20 (New York: Lexington Books, 2018); and "'Aguanile': Critical Listening, Mourning, and Anti-Colonial Healing," in *Critical Dialogues in Latinx Studies: A Reader*, edited by Ana Yolanda Ramos-Zayas and Mérida Rúa, 476–88 (New York: New York University Press, 2021).

REFERENCES

Abadía-Rexach, Bárbara. 2012. *Musicalizando la raza: La racialización en Puerto Rico a través de la música.* San Juan, PR: Ediciones Puerto.

Adler, Tamara. 2018. "The Young Farmers Behind Puerto Rico's Food Revolution." *Vogue,* June 20, 2018. https://www.vogue.com/article/rebuilding-puerto-rico-farms-agriculture-vogue-july-2018.

Adorno, Theodor. 1941. "On Popular Music." In *Studies in Philosophy and Social Science,* vol. 9, edited by Leo Lowenthal and Max Adorno, 24–26. New York: Institute for Social Research.

Aguilar, Rodolfo. 2020. "'Why the Heck Am I Out Here Lookin' Country?': Locating Contradictory Post-Movimiento Chicana/o/x Subjectivity in Little Joe's 'Redneck Meskin Boy' Recordings and the Emergence of an Overlapping South." *Interdisciplinary Humanities* 37 (2): 44–64.

Ahmad, Muneer. 2002. "Homeland Insecurities: Racial Violence the Day after September 11." *Social Text* 20 (3): 101–15.

Ahmed, Sara. 2004. *The Cultural Politics of Emotion.* New York: Routledge.

Alfaro, Annie. 1986. "Marco Antonio Muñiz (1986)—Entrevista programa 'Trasbatidores' con Annie Alfaro (Puerto Rico)." Posted by La Casa del Coleccionista Universal, June 20, 2019. YouTube. https://www.youtube.com/watch?v=yz41hPAL5To.

Algarín, Miguel, and Miguel Piñero. 1975. *Nuyorican Poetry: An Anthology of Puerto Rican Words and Feelings.* New York: William Morrow.

Allende-Goitía, Noel. 2014. *De "Margarita" a "El Cumbanchero": Vida musical, imaginación racial y discurso histórico en la sociedad puertorriqueña (1898–1940).* San Juan, PR: Ediciones Puerto.

Alurista. 1971. *Floricanto en Aztlán.* Los Angeles: Chicano Research Center, University of California–Los Angeles.

Alvarado, Lorena. 2012. "Corporealities of Feeling: Mexican Sentimiento and Gender Politics." PhD diss., University of California–Los Angeles.

Alvarez, Ethel. 1997. "Willie Colón, el actor." *Reforma,* December 13, 1997.

Anahí. 2009. *Mi Delirio.* EMI / Capitol Records.

Anthony, Marc. 1993. "Hasta Que Te Conocí." *Otra Nota.* RMM Records.

Anthony, Marc. 1999. "I Need to Know." *Marc Anthony.* Columbia.

Anthony, Marc. 2007. "Aguanile." *El Cantante.* Sony BMG Norte.

Anthony, Marc. 2013. "Vivir Mi Vida." *3.0.* Sony Music Latin.

Anthony, Marc. 2020. Video Raíces. Facebook. YouTube / Amazon Music. https://www.facebook.com/officialmarcanthony/videos/971284223353460/.

Anthony, Marc, and Jennifer Lopez. 2011. "Aguanile." *American Idol.* YouTube. https://music.youtube.com/watch?v=Uk-150aJJ0w.

Anzaldúa, Gloria. 1987. *Borderlands / La Frontera: The New Mestiza.* San Francisco: Kitchen Table Press.

Aparicio, Frances. 1998. *Listening to Salsa: Gender, Latin Popular Music, and Puerto Rican Cultures.* Hanover, NH: Wesleyan University Press / University Press of New England.

Aparicio, Frances. 2003. "Jennifer as Selena: Rethinking Latinidad in Media and Popular Culture." *Latino Studies,* no. 1, 90–105.

Aparicio, Frances. 2017. "Latinidades." In *Keywords for Latina/o Studies,* edited by Deborah R. Vargas, Nancy Raquel Mirabal, and Lawrence La Fountain-Stokes, 113–17. New York: New York University Press.

Aparicio, Frances. 2019. *Negotiating Latinidades: Intralatina/o Lives in Chicago.* Urbana: University of Illinois Press.

Aparicio, Frances. 2021a. "Aguanile: Critical Listening, Mourning, and Decolonial Healing." In *Critical Dialogues in Latinx Studies,* edited by Ana Yolanda Ramos-Zayas and Mérida R. Rúa, 476–88. New York: New York University Press.

Aparicio, Frances. 2021b. "Many of you know I'm writing a book about Marc Anthony's songs as sites for critical reflections on Puerto Rican colonialism, race, hybridity, identity, and global solidarities, among many other topics." Facebook, April 12, 2021. https://www.facebook.com/frances.aparicio/posts/pfbid0wGYh8XDiicNDw6kRepPcaHgU7BwnXtoB6Rd8C4q6xGTmyxPQ4wFdi4KLjguKA2evl.

Aparicio, Frances, and Cándida Jáquez, with María Elena Cepeda. 2003. *Musical Migrations: Transnationalism and Cultural Hybridity in Latin/o America.* New York: Palgrave MacMillan.

Aparicio, Frances, and Wilson Valentín-Escobar. 2004. "Memorializing La Lupe and Lavoe: Singing Transnationalism, Vulgarity and Gender." *Centro Journal* 16 (2): 78–101.

Ayala, César J. 2020. "Puerto Rico: Un Pueblo Diaspórico." UCLA.edu, June 2020. https://www.sscnet.ucla.edu/soc/faculty/ayala/prdiaspora/index.html.

Banco Popular de Puerto Rico. 1998. *Romance del Cumbanchero: La música de Rafael Hernández.* Video. BPPR-CS-98-002-4.

Baym, Nancy R. 2018. *Playing to the Crowd: Musicians, Audiences, and the Intimate Work of Connection.* New York: New York University Press.

Berríos-Miranda, Marisol, and Shannon Dudley. 2008. "El Gran Combo, Cortijo, and the Musical Geography of Cangrejos/Santurce, Puerto Rico." *Caribbean Studies* 36 (2): 121–51.

Berríos-Miranda, Marisol, Shannon Dudley, and Michelle Habell-Pallán, eds. 2018. *American Sabor: Latinos and Latinas in US Popular Music.* Seattle: University of Washington Press.

Bhutto, Fatima. 2022. "Songs of Exile." In *This Woman's Work: Essays on Music,* edited by Sinéad Gleeson and Kim Gordon, 19–29. New York: Hachette.

Blanco, Tomás. 1935. "Elogio de la plena." *Revista del Ateneo Puertorriqueño* 1 (1): 97–106. Reprinted in *Revista del Instituto de Cultura Puertorriqueña*, no. 22 (July–September 1979): 39–42.

Brown, Julia. 2016. "Interview with Amina Gautier." *Mosaic Magazine,* May 5, 2016. https://mosaicmagazine.org/amina-gautier-interview/#.XNBoXvZFw2w.

Cabannis, Emily R., and Jeffrey A. Gardner. 2020. "Signifying 'Americanness': Narrative Collective Identification Work in the Undocumented Youth Movement." *Humanity and Society* 45 (1): 99–124.

Cacho, Lisa. 2012. *Social Death: Racialized Rightlessness and the Criminalization of the Unprotected.* New York: New York University Press.

Cano-Moreno, Jorge, and Joshua Del Río. 2010. "Marc Anthony: The King of Salsa." UrbanLatino.com, September 30, 2010 (site discontinued).

Caramanica, John. 2008. "Latin Music, Intimate and Grand, Holds Court." *New York Times,* August 23, 2008, B7.

Casillas, Dolores Inés. 2014. *Sounds of Belonging! U.S. Spanish-Language Radio and Public Advocacy.* New York: New York University Press.

Cepeda, María Elena. 2001. "'Columbus Effect(s)': Chronology and Crossover in the Latin(o) Music 'Boom.'" *Discourse* 23 (1): 63–81.

Cepeda, María Elena. 2010. *Musical ImagiNation: U.S. Colombian Identity and the Latin Music Boom.* New York: New York University Press.

Cepeda, María Elena. 2017. "Music." In *Keywords for Latina/o Studies,* edited by Deborah R. Vargas, Nancy Raquel Mirabal, and Lawrence La Fountain-Stokes, 144–47. New York: New York University Press.

Cepeda, María Elena. 2022. "Locatora Radio." Latinx Digital Media Studies Virtual Seminar Series, School of Communication, Northwestern University, February 24, 2022.

Chambers-Letson, Joshua. 2020. Introduction to *The Sense of Brown* by José Esteban Muñoz. Durham, NC: Duke University Press.

Chávez, Alex E. 2017. *Sounds of Crossing: Music, Migration, and the Aural Poetics of Huapango Arribeño.* Durham, NC: Duke University Press.

Cheb Khaled. 2012. "C'est la Vie." Posted by Universal Music France, August 30, 2012. YouTube. https://www.youtube.com/watch?v=H7rhMqTQ4WI&t=9s.

Cheb Khaled and Saúl Hernández. 1996. "Ki Kounti." https://www.youtube.com/watch?v=Hide4VHbvGY.

Cobo, Leila. 2007. "Q&A: Marc Anthony Lives and Breathes Salsa." Reuters, August 9, 2007. https://www.reuters.com/article/lifestyle/qa-marc-anthony-lives-and-breathes-salsa-idUSN20352737.

Cobo, Leila. 2014. "Marc Anthony's Big Move: Inside His Salsa Return and Future Plans." *Billboard,* April 21, 2014. https://www.youtube.com/watch?v=X2d9Jx7kY34.

Cobo, Leila. 2021a. *Decoding "Despacito": An Oral History of Latin Music.* New York: Vintage Books.

Cobo, Leila. 2021b. "Marc Anthony's 30-Year Odyssey: 'When Did My Life Become This Interesting?'" *Billboard,* January 19, 2021.

Cobo, Leila. 2022. "Marc Anthony's Pa'lla Voy: Five Essential Tracks from His New Album." *Billboard,* March 4, 2022. https://www.billboard.com/music/latin/marc-anthony-pa-lla-voy-album-5-essential-tracks-1235039747/.

Collado Schwarz, Ángel. 2008. "El Borinquen de Rafael Hernández." *La Voz del Centro* podcast, episode 304, October 20. https://creators.spotify.com/pod/show/vozdelcentro/episodes/304-El-Borinquen-de-Rafael-Hernndez-en6af2/a-a4oa1r5.

Colón, Willie. 1989. "El Gran Varón." *Altos Secretos.* WAC Productions.

Colón, Willie. 1990. "Hasta Que Te Conocí." *Color Americano.* Sony.

Correa-Luna, Juan F. 2020. "James Reese Europe, Rafael Hernández Marín y los 'Harlem Hellfighters.'" *80 Grados,* July 31, 2020.

Cortés, Jason. 2018. "Necromedia, Haunting and Public Mourning in the Puerto Rican Debt State: The Case of 'Los Muertos.'" *Journal of Latin American Cultural Studies* 27 (3): 357–69.

Cotto-Thorner, Guillermo. (1951) 2019. *Manhattan Tropics / Trópico en Manhattan.* Edited by J. Bret Maney and Cristina Pérez Jiménez. Translated by J. Bret Maney. Houston, TX: Arte Público Press.

Coutin, Susan Bibler. 2008. "Suspension of Deportation Hearings and Measures of 'Americanness.'" *Journal of Latin American Anthropology* 8 (2): 58–94.

Cuadrado, J. Luis Al. 2014. "Soy de un Pueblo Alegre." Posted by Soy de Solaga, September 12. YouTube. https://www.youtube.com/user/lhasheyichjej/.

Curet Alonso, Tite. n.d. "Caras lindas." SalsaClasica.com. https://salsaclasica.com/titecuretalonso/lyrics/0/984.

Daughtry, J. Martin. 2013. "Acoustic Palimpsests and the Politics of Listening." *Music and Politics* 7, no. 1 (Winter). http://dx.doi.org/10.3998/mp.9460447.0007.101.

Dávila, Arlene. 1997. *Sponsored Identities: Cultural Politics in Puerto Rico.* Philadelphia: Temple University Press.

Dávila Ellis, Verónica. 2020. "Uttering Sonic Dominicanidad: Women and Queer Performers of Música Urbana." PhD diss., Northwestern University.

Dean, Jodi. 1996. *Solidarity of Strangers: Feminism after Identity Politics.* Berkeley: University of California Press.

Díaz Ayala, Cristóbal. 2009. *San Juan–New York: Discografía de la música Puertorriqueña, 1900–1942.* Río Piedras, PR: Publicaciones Gaviota.

Dorr, Kirstie. 2007. "Mapping El Condor Pasa: Sonic Translocations in the Global Era." *Journal of Latin American Cultural Studies* 16 (1): 11–25.

Dorr, Kirstie. 2018. *On Site, In Sound: Performance Geographies in América Latina.* Durham, NC: Duke University Press.

Duany, Jorge. 2002. *The Puerto Rican Nation on the Move: Identities on the Island and in the United States.* Chapel Hill: University of North Carolina Press.

Duany, Jorge. 2020. "'May God Take Me to Orlando': The Puerto Rican Exodus to Florida Before and After Hurricane Maria." In *Caribbean Migrations: The Legacies of Colonialism,* edited by Anke Birkenmaier, 40–56. New Brunswick, NJ: Rutgers University Press.

El Hamel, Chouki. 2013. *Black Morocco: A History of Slavery, Race, and Islam.* New York: Cambridge University Press.

Emery, David. 2018. "What Was the Actual Death Toll from Hurricane María in Puerto Rico?" *Snopes,* June 4, 2018. https://www.snopes.com/news/2018/06/04/death-toll-hurricane-maria-puerto-rico.

Espinoza Agurto, Andrés. 2022. *Salsa Consciente: Politics, Poetics, and Latinidad in the Meta-Barrio.* East Lansing: Michigan State University Press.

Fernández, María Teresa "Mariposa." n.d. "Ode to the Diasporican." Genius.com, accessed February 12, 2025. https://genius.com/Mariposa-maria-teresa-fernandez-ode-to-the-diasporican-pa-mi-gente-annotated.

Ferré, Rosario. 1991. "On Destiny, Language, and Translation; or, Ophelia Adrift in the C. & O. Canal." In *The Youngest Doll.* Lincoln: University of Nebraska Press.

Findlay, Eileen J. 2012. "Slipping and Sliding: The Many Meanings of Race in Life Histories of New York Puerto Rican Return Migrants in San Juan." *Centro Journal* 24 (1): 20–43.

Fiol-Matta, Licia. 2017. *The Great Woman Singer: Gender and Voice in Puerto Rican Music*. Durham, NC: Duke University Press.

Flores-González, Nilda. 2017. *Citizens but Not Americans: Race and Belonging Among Latino Millennials*. New York: New York University Press.

Florido, Adrian. 2019. "For Those Missing Puerto Rico, a Song About Dreaming of Home." American Archives Series. *National Public Radio*, June 20, 2019.

Furedi, Frank. 2010. "Celebrity Culture." *Society*, no. 47, 493–97.

Gabriel, Juan. 1986. "Hasta Que Te Conocí." *Pensamientos*. RCA Ariola.

Gabriel, Juan. 1987. "Juan Gabriel 1987 Hasta Que Te Conoci Live." Posted by Dannyeivonneita, May 10, 2009. YouTube. https://www.youtube.com/watch?v=V-fpjjMeDTo.

Gabriel, Juan. 1990. "Juan Gabriel—Hasta Que Te Conocí (En Vivo [Desde el Instituto Nacional de Bellas Artes])." Posted by Juan Gabriel, July 22, 2011. YouTube. https://www.youtube.com/watch?v=ga5B04YdgH4.

Gabriel, Juan. 2002. "Juan Gabriel, Hasta Que Te Conocí, Festival de Viña del Mar 2002." Posted by FestivalDeVinaChile, October 17, 2012. YouTube. https://www.youtube.com/watch?v=odcT7AHEERw.

García, David F. 2006. *Arsenio Rodríguez and the Transnational Flows of Latin Popular Music*. Philadelphia: Temple University Press.

García, Ofelia, and Li Wei. 2014. *Translanguaging: Language, Bilingualism and Education*. New York: Palgrave Macmillan.

Gautier, Amina. 2014. *Now We Will Be Happy*. Lincoln: University of Nebraska Press.

Glasser, Ruth. 1995. *My Music Is My Flag: Puerto Rican Musicians and Their New York Communities, 1917–1940*. Berkeley: University of California Press.

González, Lydia Milagros. 1990. "Colón Sings to Our Land—A Concert That Made History." *Horn of Justice Blog*, October 18, 1990. https://williecolonnews.blogspot.com/1990.

González, Martha. 2020. *Chican@ Artivistas: Music, Community and Transborder Tactics in East Los Angeles*. Austin: University of Texas Press.

González, Rigoberto. 2017. "Juan Gabriel Died One Year Ago: LGBTQ Latino Writers Reflect on His Impact." NBC News, August 28, 2017. https://www.nbcnews.com/news/latino/juan-gabriel-died-one-year-ago-lgbtq-latino-writers-reflect-n795181.

Gorman, Lillian. 2016. "Bachata as a U.S. Latina/o Home: Hybrid Musical and Linguistic Latinidades in Mexican Chicago." Presentation at Annual Meeting of the American Studies Association, Denver, CO, November 2016.

Guidotti-Hernández, Nicole. 2021. *Archiving Mexican Masculinities in Diaspora*. Durham, NC: Duke University Press. Kindle.

Gurza, Agustín. 2007. "Friendly Fire over Salsa Movie." *Los Angeles Times*, August 4, 2007. https://www.latimes.com/archives/la-xpm-2007-aug-04-et-culture4-story.html.

Halperin, Laura. 2015. *Intersections of Harm: Narratives of Latina Deviance and Defiance*. New Brunswick, NJ: Rutgers University Press.

Harrington, Richard. 2002a. "A Slow Road to Salsa." *Washington Post*, August 16, 2002, H6.

Harrington, Richard. 2002b. "The Salsa King." *South Florida Sun Sentinel*, September 12, 2002.

Hernández Cruz, Víctor. 2011. *In the Shadow of Al-Andalus*. Minneapolis, MN: Coffee House Press.

Hernández Romero, Marissel. 2020. "Cultura de cancelación en Puerto Rico: Quién la ejerce? A quién realmente afecta?" *Claridad,* August 3, 2020. https://www.claridadpuertorico.com/cultura-de-cancelacion-en-puerto-rico-quien-la-ejerce-a-quien-realmente-afecta.

Ichaso, León, director. 2007. *El Cantante.* 35 mm. Nuyorican Productions and R-Caro Productions.

Iyer, Vijay. 2004. "Exploding the Narrative in Jazz Improvisation." In *Uptown Conversation: The New Jazz Studies,* edited by Robert G. O'Meally, Brent Hayes Edwards, and Farah Jasmine Griffin, 393–403. New York: Columbia University Press.

Jarmakani, Amira. 2008. *Imagining Arab Womanhood: The Cultural Mythology of Veils, Harems, and Belly Dancers in the U.S.* New York: Palgrave Macmillan.

Jeffries, David. n.d. "Exiliados en la Bahía: Lo mejor de Maná (Sencilla). Review." *Allmusic,* accessed November 8, 2024. https://www.allmusic.com/album/exiliados-en-la-bahia-lo-mejor-de-mana-sencilla-mw0002408329#review.

Jiménez-Román, Miriam. 2001. "Yo soy Nuyorican: Así es, vengo de allá." *Diálogo* 5 (1): article 4.

Johnson, Gaye Theresa. 2013. *Spaces of Conflict, Sounds of Solidarity: Music, Race, and Spatial Entitlement in Los Angeles.* Berkeley: University of California Press.

Johnson, Gaye Theresa. 2017. "Afro Roots / Latinx Routes: The Sonic Realms of Freedom." Paper presented at Soundscapes of Latinidad: Race, Citizenship and Belonging Symposium. Evanston, IL, Northwestern University Latina and Latino Studies Program, May 12, 2017.

Khesti, Roshanak. 2015. *Modernity's Ear: Listening to Race and Gender in World Music.* New York: New York University Press.

Kishore, Nishant, Domingo Marqués, et al. 2018. "Mortality in Puerto Rico After Hurricane María." *New England Journal of Medicine,* no. 379, 162–70.

Klein, Naomi. 2018. *The Battle for Paradise: Puerto Rico Takes on the Disaster Capitalists.* Chicago: Haymarket Books.

Knights, Vanessa. 2008. "Nostalgia and the Negotiation of Dislocated Identities: Puerto Rican Boleros in New York and Nuyorican Poetry." In *Postnational Musical Identities,* edited by Ignacio Corona and Alejandro L. Madrid, 81–96. Lanham, MD: Lexington Books.

Kugel, Seth. 2002. "Latino Cultural Wars." *New York Times,* February 24, 2002, section 14, page 1.

Kun, Josh. 2005. *Audiotopia: Music, Race, and America.* Berkeley: University of California Press.

LaBelle, Brandon. 2020. *Sonic Agency: Sound and Emergent Forms of Resistance.* Cambridge, MA: MIT Press / Goldsmith Press.

La Fountain-Stokes, Lawrence. 2009. *Queer Ricans: Cultures and Sexualities in the Diaspora.* Minneapolis: University of Minnesota Press.

Lapidus, Benjamin. 2021. *New York and the International Sound of Latin Music 1940–1990.* Jackson: University Press of Mississippi.

Laviera, Tato. 2003. "Nuyorican." In *AmeRícan.* Houston, TX: Arte Público Press.

Lavoe, Héctor. 1972. "Aguanile." Posted June 27, 2016, by Tumbao Tropical. YouTube, 6:13. https://www.youtube.com/watch?v=pz65oEkJFKc.

Leigh, Heather. 2022. Introduction to *This Woman's Work: Essays on Music,* edited by Sinéad Gleeson and Kim Gordon, 1–7. New York: Hachette.

Lockwood, Alan. 2000. "El Malo at Mid-Career: Willie Colón Plays Celebrate Brooklyn!" *Brooklyn Rail* (October–November 2000). https://brooklynrail.org/2000/10/music/el-malo-at-mid-career-willie-colon-plays-celebrate-brooklyn.

Lopetegui, Enrique. 1993. "Latin Pulse: Salsa Converts and Veterans Flavor Sassy Beat with Meaning." *Los Angeles Times,* July 11, 1993.

Lopetegui, Enrique. 1996. "Marc Anthony's Putting a Real Kick in His Salsa." *Los Angeles Times,* May 1, 1996.

Loza, Mireya. 2016. *Defiant Braceros: How Migrant Workers Fought for Racial, Sexual, and Political Freedom.* Chapel Hill: University of North Carolina Press.

Luciano, Felipe. 2024. *Flesh and Spirit: Confessions of a Young Lord.* New York: Fordham University Press.

Madrid, Alejandro L. 2008. *Nor-Tec Rifa! Electronic Dance Music from Tijuana to the World.* Oxford: Oxford University Press.

Madrid, Alejandro L. 2018. "Secreto a Voces: Excess, Performance, and *Jotería* in Juan Gabriel's Vocality." *GLQ: A Journal of Lesbian and Gay Studies* 24 (1): 85–111.

Madrid, Alejandro, and Robin D. Moore. 2013. *Danzón: CircumCaribbean Dialogues in Music and Dance.* New York: Oxford University Press.

Maná. 2012. *Exiliados en la Bahía: Lo mejor de Maná.* YouTube, https://www.youtube.com/watch?v=vyC8dy8qST8.

Manzano, Sonia. 2012. *The Revolution of Evelyn Serrano.* New York: Scholastic Press.

"Marc Anthony 'Vivir mi Vida' Breathes New Life into Cheb Khaled." 2013. http://hotarabicmusic.blogspot.com/2013/09/marcanthony-vivir-mi-vida-breathes-new.html (site discontinued).

Márquez, Herón. 2001. "Marc Anthony." In *Latin Sensations,* 65–84. Minneapolis, MN: Lerner Company Publications.

Martínez, Elena. 2015. "The Greatest Jibarito Afro Boricua Rafael Hernández." *Centro Voices,* February 4, 2015. https://centropr.hunter.cuny.edu/centrovoices/arts-culture/greatest-jibarito-afro-boricua-rafael-hern%C3%A1ndez (site discontinued).

McDonnell, Terence E., Christopher A. Bail, and Iddo Tavory. 2017. "A Theory of Resonance." *Sociological Theory* 35 (1): 1–14.

McLane, Daisann. 1996. "Salsa for the High-Tops Generation." *New York Times,* August 11, 1996.

Milken Institute School of Public Health. 2018. *Ascertainment of the Estimated Excess Mortality from Hurricane María in Puerto Rico.* In collaboration with the University of Puerto Rico Graduate School of Public Health. Washington, DC: George Washington University.

Miranda, Lin-Manuel. 2024. "'He Is Our Sinatra': Lin-Manuel Miranda on Why Marc Anthony—and His New Album, *Muévense*—Are So Important." *Variety,* April 24, 2024.

Morales, Ed. 2003. *The Latin Beat: The Rhythms and Roots of Latin Music from Bossa Nova to Salsa and Beyond.* Cambridge, MA: Da Capo Press.

Moreno, Carolina. 2013. "Marc Anthony Addresses 'God Bless America' Performance's Racist Remarks After MLB All-Star Game." *Huffington Post,* July 19, 2013. https://www.huffpost.com/entry/marc-anthony-god-bless-america_n_3618420.

Moreno, Jairo. 2015. "La Salsa y sus muertes." In *Cocinando suave: Ensayos de salsa en Puerto Rico,* edited by César Colón-Montijo, 29–38. Caracas, Venezuela: Fundación Editorial el Perro y la Rana.

Moreno, Marisel. 2015. "'Swimming in Olive Oil': North Africa and the Hispanic Caribbean in the Poetry of Víctor Hernández Cruz." *Hispanic Review* 83 (3): 299–316.

Moreno, Rita. 2013. *Rita Moreno: A Memoir.* New York: Penguin Books.

Muñiz, Marco Antonio. 2024. *Por Amor.* Chandler, AZ: Editorial Misión.

Muñoz, José Esteban. 2020. *The Sense of Brown.* Edited by Joshua Chambers-Letson and Tavia Nyong'o. Durham, NC: Duke University Press. Kindle.

Naficy, Hamid, ed. 1999. *Home, Exile, Homeland: Film, Media, and the Politics of Place*. New York: Routledge.

Naficy, Hamid. 2001. *An Accented Cinema: Exilic and Diasporic Filmmaking*. Princeton, NJ: Princeton University Press.

Negrón, Marisol. 2024. *Made in NuyoRico*. Durham, NC: Duke University Press.

Obejas, Achy. 1995. "Marc Anthony's Music Captures Beat of U.S. Cities. Performer Rejects Salsa's Typical Macho Posturing." *Chicago Tribune*, August 15, p. 14.

Ortiz López, Carlos Rubén. 1985. "Johnny Ventura/Roberto Del Castillo—'Hasta Que Te Conocí' (Puerto Rico—1985)." Posted by La Casa del Coleccionista Universal, March 13, 2018. YouTube. https://www.youtube.com/watch?v=oqs8rEplPyY.

Pacini Hernández, Deborah. 1995. *A Social History of a Dominican Popular Music*. Philadelphia: Temple University Press.

Pacini Hernández, Deborah. 2010. *Oye Como Va! Hybridity and Identity in Latino Popular Music*. Philadelphia: Temple University Press.

Papacharissi, Zizi. 2015. *Affective Publics: Sentiment, Technology, and Politics*. Oxford: Oxford University Press.

Paredez, Deborah. 2024. *American Diva: Extraordinary, Unruly, Fabulous*. New York: W. W. Norton.

Parks, Malcolm R. 1981. "Ideology in Interpersonal Communication: Off the Couch and Into the World." In *Communication Yearbook 5*, edited by M. Burgoon, 79–107. New Brunswick, NJ: Transaction.

Pedreira, Antonio S. 1942. *Insularismo*. San Juan: Biblioteca de Autores Puertorriqueños.

Pérez Aldave, Agustín. 1990. "Willie Colón: From the Salsa of El Barrio to the Pan American Sound." *Diario Página Libre*, May 27, 1990, C4–C5.

Pérez Rosario, Vanessa. 2014. "Affirming an Afro-Latin@ Identity: An Interview with Poet María Teresa (Mariposa) Fernández." *Latino Studies* 12 (3): 468–75.

Picó, Fernando. 1994. "Los Mexicanos en Puerto Rico." *Claridad*, November 18–24, 1994, 19.

Pierce, Kendra. n.d. "The Meaning Behind the Song: Songoro Cosongo by Héctor Lavoe." *BeatCrave*, accessed June 4, 2024. https://beatcrave.com/w2/the-meaning-behind-the-song-songoro-cosongo-by-hector-lavoe.

Pontecorvo, Gillo, director. (1966) 2004. *The Battle of Algiers*. Rizzoli / Rialto Pictures. Criterion DVD.

Puga, Ana Elena, and Víctor M. Espinosa. 2020. *Performances of Suffering in Latin American Migration: Heroes, Martyrs and Saints*. New York: Palgrave Macmillan.

Quesada, Sarah M. 2024. "Latinx Cosmopolitanism in the Global South: Victor Hernández Cruz and the Nostalgia of Egypt." *Comparative Literature* 76 (4): 429–50.

Quiñonez, John. 2011. "The King of Salsa: Interview with Marc Anthony." *ABC Nightline*, September 25, 2011.

Ramírez Warren, Matthew, director. 2014. *We Like It Like That: The Story of Latin Boogaloo*. Documentary. POV.

Residente. 2022. "Residente—This Is Not America (Official Video) ft. Ibeyi." Posted by Residente, March 17. YouTube. https://www.youtube.com/watch?v=GK87AKIPyZY&t=55s.

Rex, Fernando. 2015. "Sin Clóset: Todos Somos Simón El Gran Varón." *El Gráfico*, July 29, 2015, https://www.elgrafico.mx/especiales/29-07-2015/sin-closet-todos-somos-simon-el-gran-varon.

Reyes, David, and Tom Waldman. 1998. *Land of a Thousand Dances: Chicano Rock 'n' Roll from Southern California*. Albuquerque: University of New Mexico Press.

Ríos, Soleida. 2017. *A Wa Nilé*. Havana, Cuba: Editorial Letras Cubanas.

Rivera, Christopher. 2014. "The Brown Threat: Post-9/11 Conflations of Latina/os and Middle Eastern Muslims in the U.S. American Imagination." *Latino Studies* 12 (1): 44–64.

Rivera, Enrique. 2022. "Puerto Rican Rapper Residente Is Challenging the Definition of America." *NPR*, August 31, 2022, https://www.npr.org/2022/08/31/1120330450/puerto-rican-rapper-residente-is-challenging-the-definition-of-america.

Rivera-Rideau, Petra R. 2015. *Remixing Reggaetón: The Cultural Politics of Race in Puerto Rico*. Durham, NC: Duke University Press.

Rivera-Rideau, Petra R. 2021. "Race, Latinidad, and Latin Pop: CNCO and Reggaetón in the Mainstream." In *The Oxford Handbook of Global Popular Music*, edited by Simone Krüger Bridge and Britta Sweers, 1–22. Online edition. https://doi.org/10.1093/oxfordhb/9780190081379.001.0001.

Rivera Santana, Carlos. 2019. "Si no pudiera hacer arte, me iba: The Aesthetics of Disaster as Catharsis in Contemporary Puerto Rican Art." In *Aftershocks of Disaster: Puerto Rico Before and After the Storm*, edited by Yarimar Bonilla and Marisol Lebrón, 178–90. Chicago: Haymarket Books.

Rivera-Servera, Ramón. 2012. *Performing Queer Latinidad: Dance, Sexuality, Politics*. Ann Arbor: University of Michigan Press.

Roberts, John Storm. 1979. *The Latin Tinge: The Impact of Latin American Music on the United States*. Oxford: Oxford University Press.

Robinson, Dylan. 2020. *Hungry Listening: Resonant Theory for Indigenous Sound Studies*. Minneapolis: University of Minnesota Press.

Rocher, Sofia. 2016. "Most Year-End Best-Selling Albums in the Tropical Albums Chart by a Solo Artist." Guinness World Records, Feb. 9. https://www.guinnessworldrecords.com/news/2016/2/guinness-world-records-honors-marc-anthony-with-tropical-album-charts-title-416078.

Rodríguez, Roberto, and Patricia Gonzales. 1999. "Viva la música: The Willie Colón Story." *Latino Link*. http://www.latinolink.com/opinion/spec0608.html (site discontinued).

Rodríguez, Víctor M. 1997. "Una lucha común: 1848–1998: Boricuas y mexicanos." *Claridad*, November 28–December 4, 1997, 34.

Rondón, César Miguel. 2008. *The Book of Salsa: A Chronicle of Urban Music from the Caribbean to New York City*. Translated by Frances R. Aparicio, with Jackie White. Chapel Hill: University of North Carolina Press.

Rosa, Jonathan. 2019. *Looking Like a Language, Sounding Like a Race: Raciolinguistic Ideologies and the Learning of Latinidad*. Oxford: Oxford University Press.

Rosen, Jody. 2013. "Marc Anthony Returns with a New Salsa Album (and Some Socks)." *New York Magazine*, July 22, 2013. http://www.vulture.com/2013/07/marc-anthony-on-his-new-album-and-clothing-line.html.

Rottenberg, Catherine. 2008. *Performing Americanness: Race, Class, and Gender in Modern African-American and Jewish-American Literature*. Lebanon, NH: Dartmouth College Press.

RTL Today. 2021. "$7.25 an Hour: Puerto Rico Welcomes Mexican Workers as Locals Opt for Pandemic Aid." April 4, 2021. https://today.rtl.lu/news/science-and-environment/a/1700072.html.

Rúa, Mérida. 2005. "Latinidades." In *Oxford Encyclopedia of Latinos and Latinas in the United States*, vol. 2, edited by Suzanne Oboler and Deena J. González, 505–7. Oxford: Oxford University Press.

Rudolph, Jennifer Domino. 2020. *Baseball as Mediated Latinidad: Race, Masculinity, Nationalism, and Performances of Identity*. Columbus: The Ohio State University Press.

Ruiz, Sandra. 2019. *Ricanness: Enduring Time in Anticolonial Performance*. New York: New York University Press.

Ruiz Vega, Omar. 2020. "New York, Puerto Rico and Cuba's Latin Music Scenes and the Emergence of Salsa Music: A Comparative Analysis." *Centro Journal* 32 (2): 4–52.

Salazar, Max. 2002. *Mambo Kingdom: Latin Music in New York*. New York: Schirmer.

Saldívar, José. 1991. *The Dialectics of Our America: Genealogy, Cultural Critique, and Literary History*. Durham, NC: Duke University Press.

Saldívar, José. 1997. *Border Matters: Remapping American Cultural Studies*. Berkeley: University of California Press.

Saldívar, José. 2012. *Trans-Americanity: Sub-Altern Modernity, Global Coloniality, and the Cultures of Greater Mexico*. Durham, NC: Duke University Press.

Sanabria, Bobby. 2021. "Reimagining West Side Story: A Critical Discussion of the Remake." Panel sponsored by Centro de Estudios Puertorriqueños, City University of New York, December 13, 2021 (virtual).

Sánchez, Luis Rafael. 1988. *La importancia de llamarse Daniel Santos*. Hanover, NH: Ediciones del Norte.

Sánchez-González, Lisa. 2001. *Boricua Literature: A Literary History of the Puerto Rican Diaspora*. New York City: New York University Press.

Sanneh, Kelefa. 2005. "Latin Singers Who Offer Three Varieties of Heartthrob." *New York Times*, September 12, 2005. https://www.nytimes.com/2005/09/12/arts/music/latin-singers-who-offer-3-varieties-of-heartthrob.html.

Santos Febres, Mayra. 1997. "Salsa as Translocation." In *Everynight Life: Culture and Dance in Latin/o America*, edited by Celeste Fraser Delgado and José Esteban Muñoz, 175–88. Durham, NC: Duke University Press.

Saresma, Tuija. 2003. "'Art as a Way to Life': Bereavement and the Healing Power of Arts and Writing." *Qualitative Inquiry* 9 (4): 603–20.

Scarano, Francisco A. 1996. "The Jíbaro Masquerade and the Subaltern Politics of Creole Identity Formation in Puerto Rico, 1745–1823." *American Historical Review* 101 (5): 1398–431.

Schade-Poulsen, Marc. 1999. *The Social Significance of Rai: Men and Popular Music in Algeria*. Austin: University of Texas Press.

Scott, A. O. 2007. "Where the Salsa Throbs, a Singer's Soul Is Revealed." *New York Times*, August 3.

Scott, Joan Wallach. 2007. *The Politics of the Veil*. Princeton, NJ: Princeton University Press.

Serrano, Basilio. 2007. "Puerto Rican Musicians of the Harlem Renaissance." *Centro Journal* 19 (2): 95–119.

Sesin, Carmen. 2021. "'Reeks of Racism': Latinos Blast Ariz. Republican Who Said Vaccinate Americans Before Hispanics." NBC News, February 18, 2021. https://www.nbcnews.com/news/latino/reeks-racism-latinos-blast-az-republican-who-said-americans-be-n1258190.

Shank, Barry. 2013. "On Popular Music Studies." *Sounding Out*, Sonic Borders Virtual Panel, February 6, 2013.

Shapiro, Peter. 2005. *Turn the Beat Around: The Secret History of Disco*. New York: Faber and Faber.

Simián, José Manuel. 2014. "Willie Colón Bringing Salsa Back to Its Old School Roots." *New York Daily News,* August 14, 2014. http://www.nydailynews.com/entertainment/music/willie-colon-bringing-salsa-back-old-school-roots-article-1.1903402.

Small, Christopher. 1998. *Musicking: The Meanings of Performing and Listening*. Middletown, CT: Wesleyan University Press.

Span, Paula. 1999. "Hotter than Salsa." *Washington Post,* October 5, 1999, C1.

Stanulis, Steve, director. 2016. *Legends of Freestyle*. Documentary. New York: Stanulis Films.

Stern, Alexandra Minna. 1999. "Buildings, Boundaries, and Blood: Medicalization and Nation-Building on the U.S.-Mexico Border, 1910–1930." *Hispanic American Historical Review* 79 (1): 41–81.

Stoever, Jennifer Lynn. 2016. *The Sonic Color Line: Race and the Cultural Politics of Listening*. New York: New York University Press.

Talavera, Enrique. 2021. *Metamórfosis musical de Puerto Rico: Del 1959 al presente*. San Juan, PR: Quique Talavera.

Taylor, Chuck. 2000. "A Grammy Pop Nod Further Validates Columbia's Anthony as Crossover Star." *Billboard* 112, no. 7 (February 12).

Teague, Anna Monroe. 2015. "Charting Rhythmic Energy in Nuyorican Salsa Music." Master's thesis, University of Texas, Austin.

Téllez Moreno, Robert. 2017. *Ray Barretto: Fuerza Gigante*. Monee, IL: Unos y Otros Ediciones.

Trivino Alarcón, Jesús. 2013. "Kingdom Come." *Latina Magazine* 17 (10): 109–14.

Trivino Alarcón, Jesús. 2020. "The Healer: Willie Colón @ 70." *Tidal,* April 27, 2020. https://tidal.com/magazine/article/willie-colon-70/1-72127.

Tuck, Eve, and K. Wayne Yang. 2012. "Decolonization Is Not a Metaphor." *Decolonization: Indigeneity, Education and Society* 1 (1): 1–40.

Turino, Thomas. 2008. *Music as Social Life: The Politics of Participation*. Chicago: University of Chicago Press.

Univision. 2016. "Juan Gabriel y su gran influencia en la carrera de Marc Anthony." August 28, 2016. https://www.univision.com/musica/juan-gabriel-y-su-gran-influencia-en-la-carrera-de-marc-anthony.

Valdés-Rodríguez, Alicia. 1999. "Best of Both Worlds." *Los Angeles Times,* September 19, 1999.

Valentín-Escobar, Wilson. 2000. "Marketing Memory / Marketing Authenticity in Buena Vista Social Club Recordings." Latin American Studies Association Congress, Hyatt Regency Hotel, Miami, Florida, March 16, 2000.

Valentín-Escobar, Wilson. 2001. "'Nothing Connects Us All but Imagined Sounds': Performing Trans-Boricua Memories, Identities and Nationalisms Through the Death of Héctor Lavoe." In *Mambo Montage,* edited by Agustín Laó-Montes and Arlene Dávila, 207–34. New York: Columbia University Press.

Vargas, Deborah R. 2010. "Can You Feel the Beat? Freestyle's Systems of Living, Loving, and Recording." *Social Text* 28, no. 1: 107–24.

Vargas, Deborah R. 2012. *Dissonant Divas in Chicana Music: The Limits of La Onda*. Minneapolis: University of Minnesota Press.

Vázquez, Alexandra T. 2013. *Listening in Detail: Performances of Cuban Music*. Durham, NC: Duke University Press.

Vega, César. 2019. "La Casa de la Salsa Performance." Posted by Pal Bailador on YouTube, November 8, 2019. https://music.youtube.watch?v=C9Vt1xjWvVo.

Walters, Barry. 1999. "Music Single Review: I Need to Know." *Entertainment Weekly,* September 3, 1999.

Washburne, Christopher. 2008. *Sounding Salsa: Performing Latin Music in New York City.* Philadelphia: Temple University Press.

Weil, Simone. (1947) 1999. *Gravity and Grace.* London: Routledge Classics.

Willistein, Paul. 1999. "The Crossover Life of Proud Hispanic Native New Yorker Marc Anthony." *Allentown Morning Call,* October 12, 1999.

Willman, Chris. 1999. "Marquee Marc Anthony." *Entertainment Weekly,* October 8, 1999.

Wood, Mikael. 2019. "Review: J Balvin and Bad Bunny Are a Latin-Pop Dream Team on 'Oasis.'" *Los Angeles Times,* July 1, 2019. https://www.latimes.com/entertainment/music/la-et-ms-j-balvin-bad-bunny-oasis-20190701-story.html.

Zavala, Iris M. 2000. *Bolero: Historia de un amor.* Madrid: Celeste Ediciones, S.A.

Zentella, Ana Celia. 2017. "Spanglish." In *Keywords for Latina/o Studies,* edited by Deborah R. Vargas, Nancy Raquel Mirabal, and Lawrence La Fountain-Stokes, 209–12. New York: New York University Press.

INDEX

Abadía-Rexach, Bárbara, 48
abjection, 31, 34–35, 41, 49, 75, 124, 132n4, 148
Abuelas de la Plaza de Mayo, 131
Aceves Mejía, Miguel, 64
Act 22 (2012), 32
affectionate solidarity, 24, 150–51
Afghanistan, 147
Africa, 11, 22, 44–46, 122, 125, 127–28, 132–33; North, 7, 10–11, 23–24, 140, 145, 154; West, 126
African American music, 38, 68, 114. See also Black music
African Americans, 50–51, 93n1, 96, 127, 129, 132–33
African Khalam Orchestra: "A Comer Lechón," 127
Afro-Antillean poetry, 44
Afro-Boricuas, 20, 23, 53, 127–28. See also Afro–Puerto Ricans
Afro-Caribbean music, 4n4, 17, 56, 81–82, 105, 113, 114n16, 116, 125–28, 131
Afro-Caribbean people, 34, 49
Afro-Cuban music, 17, 25, 67

Afro-Latinidad, 128
Afro-Latinx people, 7n6, 111, 130
Afro-Nuyoricans, 50–51
Afro–Puerto Ricans, 13, 22–23, 30, 37, 45–48, 53, 68, 105n7, 121–22, 126, 129, 132–33. See also Afro-Boricuas
Afro-Puertorriqueñidad, 133
"Aguanile," 5, 7, 10, 22–23, 120–35
Ahmad, Muneer, 143
Ahmed, Sara, 24, 148, 150–51
AIDS, 22n11, 87–88, 118, 123
"Alé Alé Alé," 138n1
Alfanno, Omar, 87–88
Alfaro, Annie, 69
Algeria, 6, 137–38, 144, 149, 154; diaspora, 143, 148
Algerian independence movement, 23, 148
Algerian music, 3, 7, 9, 24, 138; raï, 3, 14, 137, 140–41
Algerian Revolution, 148
Allende-Goitía, Noel, 37n15, 45–48
Althusser, Louis, 15
Alurista, 93n1

INDEX

Alvarado, Lorena, 71–72, 75n11, 76
American Dream, 4, 97, 108n10
American Idol, 23, 127–29
"American music," 14, 93, 124
American Music Awards, 106
American Sabor, 14, 104
American Society of Composers, Authors and Publishers (ASCAP), 109
Americanness, 22, 91–119
"Amor No Tiene Sexo," 89
Anahí: "Hasta Que Me Conociste," 84–85
Andean flute, 101
Andean music, 80
Anduze, Juan, 154
anticolonialism, 6–7, 7n6, 18, 43, 55–59, 138, 143–44, 148
Antillean music, 46, 104
Antilles, 104
Anuel AA, 128
Anzaldúa, Gloria, 75
Arab world, 138, 147–48, 151
Arabic language, 145
Arabs, 11, 137; Arab-Boricua interactions, 23–24, 138–49, 151
Arce, Margot, 47–48
Argentina, 83, 131, 139
Arizona, 91
Arjona Siaca, Erasto, 45–46
Arnaz, Desi, 98; "Babalú," 125
arpilleras, 131
assimilation, 22, 48, 93–94, 97–98, 100n4, 101, 105n7, 106–7, 110–11, 151
audiotopias, 94
autohistory, 4
Ayala, César, 31–33
Azteca, 104

bachata, 4n4, 14, 64, 67, 107, 138
Bad Bunny, 2, 4, 17, 98, 110, 138; "Afilando Los Cuchillos," 121; "El Apagón," 25
ballads, 13, 15, 67, 69, 71, 74n9, 85, 99, 112; in Marc Anthony's repertoire, 3, 7–8, 17, 24, 60, 62–66, 136–37, 144

Banco Popular de Puerto Rico: *Romance del Cumbanchero*, 20, 41–43, 52, 54
Banda Municipal de Aguadilla, 37n15
banda music, 115
bandolera, term, 78, 82
Barretto, Ray, 114
Battle of Algiers, The, 144n2, 148
Bauzá, Mario, 25
Baym, Nancy K., 11–12, 18–19
Beatles, 114n16
Becky G, 106
Bedouins, 149
Bee Gees, 114
Belgium, 127
Benítez, Lucecita, 18, 66
bereavement, 120–22
Berríos-Miranda, Marisol, 49, 104, 105n7
Beyoncé, 5n5, 98
Bhutto, Fatima, 26
biculturalism, 97–98, 100–101, 104, 106, 108, 141
Biden, Joe, 59
bilingualism, 97–98, 113. *See also* multilingualism
Billboard (magazine), 4, 63n2, 108
Billboard charts, 67, 84, 100, 101n5, 102, 109, 139–40
billennials, 98
Black Arts Movement, 50, 126
Black Atlantic, 127
Black diaspora, 49, 133
Black Lives Matter, 53
Black music, 112–14. *See also* African American music
Blackness, 40, 145, 154; and "Aguanile," 10, 22–23, 122, 125–30, 133; Caribbean, 7, 47n25, 49; and crossover category, 107, 108n10; and decoloniality, 17n10; and "I Need to Know," 22; and mestizaje, 7n6, 44, 108n10; and Nuyoricans, 7, 20, 30, 43–51, 126–27; and "Preciosa," 20, 35, 43–52; Puerto Rican, 20, 30, 43–53; and racialization, 7n6, 37–38, 47n25, 51; and rock music, 22, 105n7, 112–14; and salsa, 7, 49, 52–53, 86–87, 123, 126–30

Blades, Rubén, 131, 137, 149; "Siembra," 15
Blanco, Tomás, 44–45
blues, 1, 10, 13
boleros, 3, 15, 36–37, 42, 46, 57, 62, 64, 66, 69, 73, 81, 85, 136, 138; bolero rancheras, 65, 74, 78, 80, 82, 86; love in, 150n3; in Marc Anthony's repertoire, 20, 30, 49, 51–52, 55, 101
bomba, 4n4, 17, 47n25, 121, 131
boogaloo, 22, 50, 107, 113, 130
boogie-woogie, 114
Boricuas, 5, 24, 25, 28, 31, 33–34, 63, 66, 69, 93n1, 142; Afro-, 13, 20, 22–23, 30, 37, 45–48, 53, 68, 105n7, 121–22, 126, 127–28, 129, 132–33; and "Aguanile," 7, 122–23, 128–29, 135; and Blackness, 20, 30, 52; and "Preciosa," 35, 55; and salsa dura, 52; and "Vivir Mi Vida," 11–12, 145. *See also* Diasporicans; Nuyoricans
bossa nova, 131
Boys II Men, 109
Brazil, 86, 131
Bread: "Make It with You," 104
brown commons, 79
"brown threat," 23, 143, 145
brownness, 17n10, 118; and affect, 7n6, 21, 71–72; Global South, 6–7, 23–24, 136–52; and "Hasta Que Te Conocí," 70–72, 75–76, 79, 82, 87; and "I Need to Know," 22, 110; and rock music, 22, 105n7, 110; and "Vivir Mi Vida," 136–52

Cabannis, Emily R., 96
Caifanes, 140
California, 31, 115, 145; Los Angeles, 58, 61, 116–18; San Francisco, 104
calypso, 4n4, 17
"Cambio de Piel," 142
Cambio de Piel tour (2014), 136, 152
Canales, Blanca, 28
capitalism, 5, 11, 15–16, 18, 41, 73, 121n2, 129; racial, 12, 29
capoeira, 121
Carabello, Mike, 104
Cárdenas, Henry, 5
Cardi B, 98, 128

Caribbean, 17, 26, 29, 66, 68, 81–82, 98, 103–5, 113–16, 125–31, 145, 149; and Blackness, 7, 47n25, 49; circum-, 40, 49, 63, 64n3; translocal, 34. *See also* Afro-Caribbean music
Carnival Internacional, 66
Carrillo, Donovan, 80
Cash, Johnny, 124–25
Casillas, Dolores Inés, 1n1, 14
Catholicism, 9–10, 73
"Cautivo de Este Amor," 139
celebrity, 2, 4–5, 8, 12, 17, 19, 69, 80, 94, 137
Cepeda, María Elena, 78n12, 100n3, 106n9, 107, 118
"C'est la Vie," 14, 23, 137–38, 140–42. *See also* "Vivir Mi Vida"
Chalí Hernández, Alejandro, 26, 35–36, 40, 44n23
Chambers-Letson, Joshua, 75
charango, 101, 130
Charles, Ray, 124–25
Chávez, Alex W., 29n6
Chayanne, 54
Chicago (band): "Color My World," 10
Chicano Movement, 69
Chicano rock, 66, 104–5, 105n7. *See also* Latino rock; rock en español
Chicanxs, 9, 66, 69, 86, 104, 116. *See also* Mexican Americans
Chile, 21, 71, 86, 131; Viña del Mar, 21, 55, 74n10, 75, 77, 78, 102
circum-Caribbean, 40, 49, 63, 64n3
citizenship, 7, 22, 27n4, 91–96
civil rights, 50, 69, 92
Civil Rights Movements, 69
classical music, 2, 37, 40, 45, 112, 155
classism, 34
clave, 56–57, 113, 116, 133
Club Caribe, 67–68
Cobo, Leila, 4, 87–88, 99, 124, 139, 141
cocolo/rockero divide, 105n7, 111n13
Colo, Papo, 55
Colombia, 80, 139; Colombian music, 14, 67, 86, 101
Colón, Johnny, 113

Colón, Willie, 34, 63, 131; "Aguanile," 126; collaboration with Héctor Lavoe, 28, 123, 126; on *El Cantante*, 88–89, 123–24, 136; "El Gran Varón," 22n11, 87–89; *El malo*, 86; "Hasta Que Te Conocí," 21–22, 85, 87–88, 90; in Mexico City, 66; and salsa dura, 7, 85–87, 136, 143; "Siembra," 15

colonialism/imperialism, 17, 29, 40, 53, 55, 72, 75, 132; in "Americanness," 93n1, 95–96; and brownness, 76; and Diasporican identity, 29, 34; language politics of, 102–3; and "Preciosa," 18, 21, 26–27, 42–43, 60; and raï music, 140; and rock music, 10, 105n7, 111n13; and salsa, 15; Spanish, 57, 103; US, 26–27, 32, 34, 36, 38n18, 42, 56, 60, 98, 120, 124, 143, 147; and veiled woman trope, 147–49. *See also* decolonialism

Columbus Effect, 100

conciencia, 9

concientización, 15–16

congas, 52, 104, 112, 117

Congo, 127

Conservatorio Nacional de Música, 40

Contra la Corriente (album, 1997), 100–101, 109

"Contra la Corriente" (song), 6

Copacabana, 116

Coronado, Jorge, 7n6

Correa-Luna, Juan F., 37, 38n16, 38n18

Cortés, Jason, 131

Cortez, Renee, 111n12

Cortijo, Rafael, 40, 49; *Time Machine* (1973), 111n13

Côte d'Ivoire, 127, 138n1

Cotto-Thorner, Guillermo, 39

counterlistening, 110

Coutin, Susan Bibler, 97

COVID-19 pandemic, 31, 34, 75, 91; post-pandemic albums, 89

Creoles, 35n10, 45, 48

criminalization, 51, 93, 124, 132n4, 143, 144n2

critical listening, 3, 5n5, 11, 62–63, 90, 118–19, 138, 153; and decoloniality, 43, 120–35; definition, 1; as methodology, 14–24

crossover category, 7, 10, 22, 93, 95–114, 119

Cruz, Celia, 66, 102

Cuarteto Victoria, 38

Cuba, 27, 37–38, 40, 63, 86, 101, 131; Havana, 66, 68, 125, 139

Cuban Americans, 98, 116

Cuban music, 36, 64, 66, 113, 131; Afro-Cuban music, 17, 25, 67

Cuban Revolution, 68

Cubans, 19–20, 40, 50n27, 102, 122, 142

cultural studies, 11n8, 121, 131, 154–55

cumbia, 14, 67

Curet Alonso, Tite, 15, 142

Daddy Yankee, 125; "Despacito," 98

dance floor, 118

dancehall music, 13

danzas, 45–46

danzón, 40n21, 46, 64, 66

Daughtry, J. Martin, 24n13

Dávila, Arlene, 41

Davis, Sammy, Jr., 68

de la Cruz, Sebastién, 94

Dean, Jodi, 150

decolonialism, 17–18, 86, 102; and "Aguanile," 120–35; and "I Need to Know," 106, 110; and "Preciosa," 21, 30, 43, 57; and rock music, 111n13

del Castillo, Roberto, 81–82

Democratic Party (US), 59, 92

Desde un Principio (2000), 4n3

Detroit techno, 115

Di Blasio, Raúl, 83

Diasporicans, 22, 95–96; and "Preciosa," 9, 13, 18, 20–21, 25–60. *See also* Nuyoricans

Díaz Ayala, Cristóbal, 36

"Dímelo," 102, 109

disco, 105n7, 110, 112–13, 115, 118

displacement, 8–9, 44n24, 75–76, 150n3, 154; and decoloniality, 17n10; and "Preciosa," 13, 18, 20, 26–36, 40–43, 52–53, 57–60

Dominican music, 14, 21, 67, 80–81

doo-wop, 113–14

Dorr, Kirstie, 79–80

Downs, Lila, 72

Duany, Jorge, 28, 32

Dudley, Shannon, 49, 104

East Coast (US), 31, 105, 112–13, 115, 130
El Cantante, 7, 10, 13, 22, 88–89, 123–25, 127, 142
El Gran Combo de Puerto Rico, 49, 53
El Hamel, Chouki, 7n6
electric guitar, 105n7, 111n13
enduring time, 56
English language, 4, 33, 39n20, 65, 92, 145, 146 fig. 5.3, 151; English-only policies, 103, 143, 149; and "I Need to Know," 22, 91–119
eroticism, 19, 58, 78, 127. *See also* sexuality
Espinosa, Víctor M., 75
Espinosa Agurto, Andrés, 15–16
Estrada, Noel: "En Mi Viejo San Juan," 25–26
ethnomusicology, 27, 40
Eurocentrism, 45, 48
Europe, 8, 11, 23–24, 37–38, 40, 44, 48, 99, 140–41, 145, 147, 149
Europe, James Reese, 37–38
Evans, Lee, 116

Facebook, 11, 19, 106, 108, 115, 118, 139
Fania All-Stars, 29; *Live in Africa* concert (1974), 127–28
Fania Records, 7, 13, 15
Fanon, Frantz, 23, 144, 148
Fat Joe: "Yes," 128
Fats Domino, 114
Federación de Músicos de Puerto Rico, 68
Federal Emergency Management Agency (FEMA), 120
Feliciano, Cheo, 123
Feliciano, José: "Feliz Navidad," 105n7
fermata, 55–58, 56 fig. 1.2, 78
Fernández, Alejandro, 54
Fernández, Mariposa, 31, 33
Fernández, Ruth, 45, 47, 68
Ferré, Rosario, 34
Fiol-Matta, Licia, 18, 47
Fitzgerald, Ella, 68

Flack, Roberta, 68; "Killing Me Softly with His Song," 1, 155
"Flor Pálida," 142
Flores, Pedro, 38
Flores Magón, Ricardo, 79n13
Flores-González, Nilda, 93–94
Florida, 32, 40n21, 59, 64n3; Miami, 58, 116, 118; Orlando, 21, 31, 32n9, 35
Fonsi, Luis: "Despacito," 98
France, 14, 23, 37–38, 138–41, 143; headscarf ban, 148–49
freestyle, 22, 50, 65–66, 100–101, 104, 110, 112, 114–18
Fuerzas Armadas de Liberación Nacional (FALN), 144
Fugees: "Killing Me Softly with His Song," 1
Fun House Club, 116
funk, 109n11, 114

Gabriel, Ana, 80
Gabriel, Juan, 10, 80; "Hasta Que Te Conocí," 13, 21, 60, 62–65, 70–79, 81–85, 87–88, 90
García, David, 50n27
García, Ofelia, 103
Gardner, Jeffrey A., 96
Gautier, Amina: "Aguanile," 10, 22–23, 122, 124, 129–34
Gaye, Marvin: "What's Going On?," 15
gender, 8, 10, 14, 18, 33, 48, 53, 107, 122, 128, 131–32, 135, 151; and "Hasta Que Te Conocí," 13, 21–22, 62–63, 71–73, 78–85, 88–90; and "Vivir Mi Vida," 146–49. *See also* masculinity; misogyny; patriarchy
George, Sergio, 13, 51, 138
"Gimme Some More," 113
Glasser, Ruth, 25
Global South, 12, 75, 81, 92, 97, 120; and brownness, 6–7, 23–24, 136–52
"God Bless America," 94–95
González, Lydia Milagros, 86n14
González, Martha, 5, 15
Good Morning America, 99
Gorman, Lillian, 106n8
Grammy Awards, 4, 84, 88, 98–99, 101n5, 109
Great Depression, 38

Grenet, Eliseo, 126
grief, 23, 26, 79, 81, 90, 104, 120–22, 130, 151. *See also* mourning
guajira, 142
Guatemalans, 60
Guidotti-Hernández, Nicole, 79
Guillén, Nicolás, 126
Guinea, 127
Gulf of Mexico, 93n1
Gulf War, 147

Habell-Pallán, Michelle, 104, 105n7
Halftime, 28n5
Halperin, Laura, 75
Hanson, Aaron, 117
Harlem Hellfighters, 37
Harlow, Larry, 111n13
Hasta Que Te Conocí (TV show), 65
"Hasta Que Te Conocí" (song), 5–7, 10, 13, 21, 60–90
hemispheric Americas, 3, 12, 90, 101, 102
hemispheric Latinidad, 6, 60–61
hermandad, 62, 69, 123
Hernández, Rafael, 39 fig. 1.1, 66, 69; "Danza Capricho #7," 40; "Lamento Borincano," 25, 36–39, 41; "Preciosa," 5–7, 9, 13, 17n10, 18, 20–21, 25–60, 68, 78; "Qué Chula es Puebla," 40
Hernández, Saúl, 140
Hernández, Victoria, 36
Hernández Colón, Rafael, 53
Hernández Cruz, Víctor, 10, 23, 145
heterosexuality, 79n13, 82, 127, 149
Hikmet, Nâzım: "The Most Beautiful Sea," 121
Hill, Lauryn: "Killing Me Softly with His Song," 1
hip-hop, 2–3, 13, 50, 98, 105n7, 109, 116–17
"Hipocresía," 142
Hispanophilia, 53
Historia tour (2024), 139
horizontal hierarchies, 60, 62
house music, 50, 100–101, 104, 115
house parties, 36
human rights, 92

hungry listening, 43, 153
Hurricane Gilbert, 130
Hurricane Irma, 31, 34, 36, 54, 58
Hurricane María, 31–32, 34, 36, 58; and "Aguanile," 22–23, 120–23, 129–31, 134–35; and "Preciosa," 21, 54, 56, 58

I Love Lucy, 98
"I Need to Know," 5, 7, 10, 22, 91–119
I-eece, Chrissy: "You Should Know by Now—Club Mix Solitario," 116
Iglesias, Enrique, 108; "Bailamos," 109
iLe: "Afilando Los Cuchillos," 121
Illinois: Chicago, 6, 9, 19–20, 32n9, 35, 87–88, 106, 109, 111, 115, 121, 124, 136–37, 139
in-betweenness, 29, 45, 92, 103, 105
Indiana University, 10, 154
Indigenous peoples, 17n10, 43–44, 45, 48, 81, 83, 92, 145. *See also* Taínos
Infante, Pedro, 72
interpellation, 15, 17, 62, 73, 89, 115, 142
intertextuality, 111–12, 137–38, 141–43, 151–52
intimacy, 8, 19, 66, 70, 73, 76, 79n13, 81–82, 84, 118, 135, 151–52; and celebrity, 5n5; of listening, 4, 9–12, 15, 18, 55, 153–56
Iran hostage crisis, 147
Isla, 47
Islamophobia, 145, 147–49
Israel, 67, 147
Israel-Gaza War, 144n2, 147
Iyer, Vijay, 55

J Balvin, 98, 110, 138; "Mi Gente," 139
Jamaica, 13, 130
JamBox Entertainment Studios, 116
Jane the Virgin, 98
Jarmakani, Amira, 147–48
Jayuya uprising (1950), 28
jazz, 38, 154
Jefferson Airplane, 10
Jewish Americans, 96
jíbara/jíbaro, 35n10, 38, 40, 48, 86, 123
Jim Crow, 37
Jiménez, Flaco, 112

Jiménez, Manuel "El Canario," 38–39
Jiménez-Román, Miriam, 50
Johnny O, 115
Jones Act (1920), 27
Joplin, Janis, 10
jotería, 71–73, 76. *See also* queerness

Khaled, Cheb: "C'est la Vie," 14, 23, 137–38, 140–42, 141 fig. 5.1; "Ki Kounti," 140
Khesti, Roshanak, 1n1, 14
Kitt, Eartha, 68
Knights, Vanessa, 36, 150n3
Koji X. Johnson: Ritmos Resilientes, 121
Kristeva, Julia, 148
Kugel, Seth, 59–60
Kun, Josh, 94

La Casa de la Salsa, 82
"La Copa Rota," 142
la Deuda, 31
La India, 13
La Sonora Mantancera, 66
La Sonora Ponceña, 109
La Voz Teens Colombia, 80
LaBelle, Brandon, 1n1, 13, 16, 18, 27, 29
Laboratorios Picot, 39
Lamond, George, 117
Latin Grammy Awards, 4, 84, 101n5, 102, 109, 139
Latin music boom (1990s), 7, 22, 92–93, 98–102, 107–10, 118
Latin pop, 2–3, 65, 66, 107–8, 112
Latin Rascals, 116
Latin Trap music, 4
Latinidad, 8, 93, 152, 154; Afro-, 128; and "Aguanile," 23; and "Hasta Que Te Conocí," 6, 10, 13, 21–22, 61–90; hegemonic, 86, 107–8; hemispheric, 6, 60–61; and "Preciosa," 59–60; sonic, 13, 22, 85
Latino rock, 67, 104–5, 105n7, 112, 114. *See also* Chicano rock; rock en español
Latinophobia, 145
Latinx USA, 62, 65–66
Laviera, Tato, 33, 50

Lavoe, Héctor, 29, 34, 116, 126 fig. 4.1, 131–32, 136, 149; "Aguanile," 22–23, 122, 126–28, 130; "Che Che Colé," 127; collaboration with Willie Colón, 28, 123, 126; "El Cantante," 125; *El Cantante* biopic, 7, 10, 13, 22–23, 88–89, 123–25, 127, 142; "Ghana E," 127; "Mi Gente," 125, 137, 139, 142; "Quimbombo," 127; "Songoro Cosongo," 126
Legends of Freestyle, 115n17, 117
Leigh, Heather, 5
Lesko, Debbie, 91–92
Libre (2001), 4n3, 101–2
Lincoln Project, 59
Lisa Lisa, 117
listening, critical, 3, 5n5, 11, 62–63, 90, 118–19, 138, 153; and decoloniality, 43, 120–35; definition, 1; as methodology, 14–24
listening ear, 14, 153, 155
listening in detail, 153
listening intimacies, 4, 9–12, 15, 18, 55
Listening to Salsa, 153
Little Richard, 114
Lloréns Torres, Luis, 38
Lobo, 139
Lockwood, Alan, 88
López, Israel "Cachao," 67
Lopez, Jennifer (J.Lo), 7, 28, 58, 64, 142; "Aguanile" *American Idol* performance, 23, 127–29; in *El Cantante,* 88–89, 123; "If You Had My Love," 108; "Let's Get Loud," 109; Super Bowl halftime show (2020), 28
López Rivera, Oscar, 144n2
Lorenz, Kavita, 128
Los Tres Aces, 69
"Louie Louie," 114
love songs, 6, 13, 14, 21, 54, 60, 63, 74n9, 102, 104, 108, 112, 136–37, 142. *See also* salsa: salsa romántica
Lucca, Papo, 29
Luciano, Felipe, 50, 126

Madison Square Garden, 54–55, 64, 101
Madrid, Alejandro, 21, 40n21, 63–64, 71–73, 74n10, 76–88, 115
Maestro Cares Foundation, 6

Magic System: "Magic in the Air," 138n1
Major League Baseball All-Star Game (2013), 95
"Make It with You," 101, 104
"Mala," 78, 89
Malo, 104, 113
Maluma, 98, 110, 138
mambo, 50n27, 66
Maná, 84
Manzano, Sonia, 23n12, 144n2
Marc Anthony (1999), 101, 108
mariachi music, 64, 73, 81, 112
maroon communities, 49
Márquez, Herón, 100, 109n11
Martin, Ricky, 5, 58, 98–99, 111; "Livin' la Vida Loca," 109, 118; "She's All I Ever Had," 108
Martínez, Elena, 38n17
Martorell, Antonio, 32; *Es que la . . .* , 121
masculinity, 14, 149; and "Aguanile," 10, 128–32; and "Hasta Que Te Conocí," 63, 71–79, 81, 84–85, 87; untouched, 21, 77–79
"Me Haces Falta," 101
Meléndez, Lisette, 117
Mended (2002), 101
Mendez, Juan, 92
merengue, 4n4, 21, 67, 80, 82, 85, 127; merengue típico, 81
mestizaje, 7n6, 44, 51, 108n10, 138
metrical dissonances, 56
Mexican Americans, 9, 94, 106. See also Chicanxs
Mexican film, 63n2, 64
Mexican Independence, 63
Mexican music, 9, 13–14, 60, 63–70, 63n2, 70–72, 73, 80–82, 84, 87, 112, 140
Mexican Revolution, 69
Mexicanization, 40, 67
Mexicans, 10, 13, 19–21, 40, 60–70, 73, 75–77, 79n13, 80, 91
Mexico, 21, 26, 35, 37, 40, 62–90, 99; Mexico City, 27, 39, 44–45, 58, 66, 73; Tijuana, 115
MexiRican musical exchanges, 13, 21, 40, 61–90
MexiRicans, 6, 10, 61–90

Middle East, 140, 147, 149
Midler, Bette, 114
migrant melodramas, 75
Minuenza, Gabriela, 60
Miranda, Lin Manuel, 8
Miranda, Maria Teresa, 154
misogyny, 74n9, 78, 84, 88–89. See also patriarchy
modernity's ear, 14
monolingualism, 96, 99, 101, 103, 105–6
Montañez, Polo, 142
montuno, 20, 30, 116, 142; Nuyorican, 30, 50–58
Moody Blues, 10
Moore, Robin, 40n21, 64
Morales, Ed, 99, 101, 108, 114
Moré, Benny, 66
Morel Campos, Juan, 45
Moreno, Jairo, 131
Moreno, Marisel, 23, 145
Moreno, Rita, 61–62, 70–71
Moroccans, 7n6, 23, 137
Morocco, 137, 146; Tangiers, 145
Mottola, Tommy, 99
mourning, 23, 59, 88, 120–35. See also grief
MTV, 68
multiculturalism, 24n14, 146, 146 fig. 5.3, 150–51
multilingualism, 102, 106n8. See also bilingualism
Muñiz, Felipe, 63n2, 64
Muñiz, Marco Antonio, 13, 63–64, 67, 68–69
Muñoz, José Esteban, 7n6, 21, 63, 70–71, 73, 75–76, 79, 82, 86
Muñoz Marín, Luis, 38, 40
musicking, 11, 16, 26, 28, 74
Muslim world, 138, 147
Muslims, 11, 23n12, 92, 140–49, 144n2

Naficy, Hamid, 44n24
Nancy, Jean-Luc, 18
National Liberation Front (Algeria), 148

National Museum of Puerto Rican Arts and Culture, 121
nationalism, 29n6, 93–95; cultural, 50, 71, 73; Mexican, 71; Puerto Rican, 25, 27–28, 44, 53–54, 58, 144. *See also* patriotism
nativism, 95. *See also* racism
Nayobe, 116–17
Nazario, Ednita, 41, 43, 66
NBC, 91, 98
necropolitics, 75
Negotiating Latinidad, 10n7, 60
Negrete, Jorge, 72
Negrón, Marisol, 2n2, 53
neoliberalism, 4, 7, 29, 41, 43, 127, 137, 142–43, 150, 152
nepantla, 75, 105
New York City, 60, 95; Bronx, 4, 34, 50n27, 51, 64, 87, 116–17, 128, 142; Brooklyn, 88, 129, 133; East Harlem, 113; Harlem, 116; Marc Anthony in, 8, 22, 35, 42, 54–55, 64, 93, 100, 102–3, 110, 115, 117; music cultures in, 7, 13, 20, 25, 27–29, 36, 38, 50, 52, 56–57, 64, 82, 85–86, 100, 110, 111n13, 112–17, 123–30, 143; Puerto Ricans in, 9, 13, 20–41, 50, 52, 59, 63n2, 64, 82, 105n7, 114, 130, 142, 144n2, 145; Spanish Harlem, 50, 87, 100, 117. *See also* Nuyoricans
Nicaragua, 86
Nieves, Christine, 123, 134
9/11, 152; racist Islamophobia after, 23, 143, 144n2, 147, 149, 150–51; and "Vivir Mi Vida," 11, 137–38, 141, 143, 147
Nortec electronic music, 115
norteña music, 73, 115
North Africa, 7, 10–11, 23–24, 140, 145, 154
North African heritage, 10–11, 145
North Carolina, 37–38
Northern Arizona University, 91
nostalgia, 18, 26, 36, 42–43, 109–10, 129, 131
Nuño, Stephen, 91
Nuyorican montuno, 30, 51–55, 57–58
Nuyorican Poets Café, 33
Nuyoricans, 6, 96, 110, 122, 145; and Blackness, 7, 20, 30, 43–51, 126–27; identity of, 30–35; Marc Anthony as, 4, 7, 13, 20–21, 28, 29–30, 41–42, 49, 54, 60, 62–63, 66, 77, 86, 101, 105, 112, 116, 139; musical genealogies of, 7, 13, 28–29, 35–43, 56, 62–63, 67, 86–87, 112–16, 123–29, 133. *See also* Diasporicans

Obejas, Achy, 109
Ocasio-Cortes, Alexandria, 32
Ogún, 126
Olmos, Edward James, 93n1
Olympics: Winter 2018, 128; Winter 2022, 80
opera, 2, 55
Operation Bootstrap, 31
Orchestra Afro-Charanga, 127
Orchestre Afro Negro, 127
Orientalism, 145, 147
Orlando, Tony: "Candida," 105n7; "Knock Three Times," 105n1; "Tie a Yellow Ribbon 'Round the Ole Oak Tree," 105n1
Orquesta de Paco Tizol, 37
Orquesta Sinfónica de Oaxaca, 40
Orta, Choco, 46–49
Otra Nota (1993), 77, 100, 101, 104

Pacini Hernández, Deborah, 66n6, 67, 86, 104, 105n7, 112–13, 116
Palacio de Bellas Artes, 73, 76
Palés Matos, Luis, 44
Palestine, 147; Gaza, 144, 147
Pa'lla Voy (2022), 78, 89, 113, 138n1, 139
Palmieri, Charlie, 130
Palmieri, Eddie, 111n13
Panama, 26, 86, 87
Papacharissi, Zizi, 75
Paredez, Deborah, 156
Paro Nacional, 121, 123, 134–35
patriarchy, 72, 74, 78, 81, 84–85, 88–89, 149–50; hetero-, 137. *See also* misogyny
patriotism, 36, 44, 54, 58, 71, 93–95. *See also* nationalism
PBS, 98
Pedreira, Antonio, 44–45
Peña, Ángel "Cucco," 52
Pérez, María, 39
Pérez, Puchi, 88–89
performance studies, 11n8, 14, 34

Peru, 21, 81–82, 101
Peruvian music, 21, 82, 101
Petty, Tom: "I Need to Know," 22, 110–13
Pickett, Wilson: "Land of a Thousand Dances," 113
Picó, Fernando, 69
Pietri, Pedro, 31, 56
plena, 4n4, 4n25, 123, 126
Polizoakis, Joti, 128
"Preciosa," 5–7, 9, 13, 17n10, 18, 20–21, 25–60, 68, 78
presentational music, 57
presentational performance, 8
Presley, Elvis, 114, 124
primitivism, 45, 108n10, 125
Prohibido olvidar video (2020), 59
protest songs, 131, 140
Public Enemy: "Fight the Power," 15
Puente, Tito, 131; "Oye Como Va," 66–67, 105
Puerto Rican Day Parade (New York), 31n7, 144n2
Puerto Rican diaspora, 7, 10, 14, 62, 67, 69, 88, 122, 134–35; in New York City, 9, 13, 20–41, 50, 52, 59, 63n2, 64, 82, 105n7, 114, 130, 142, 144n2, 145; and "Preciosa," 6, 9, 25–60. *See also* Diasporicans; Nuyoricans
Puerto Rican flag, 25, 27–28, 58
Puerto Rican studies, 50
Puerto Rico Oversight, Management, and Economic Stability Act (PROMESA), 32
puertorriqueñidad, 27, 30–31, 45, 48, 52; Afro-, 133
Puga, Ana Elena, 75

¿Que Pasa, USA?, 98
queerness, 7n6, 8, 14, 22, 24n14, 53, 63, 65, 118, 134, 151; and "Hasta Que Te Conocí," 10, 13, 21, 70–78, 82–83, 87–89. *See also* jotería
Quesada, Sarah M., 145
Quetzal, 15

race, 2n2, 8, 15, 17, 72, 102, 104, 105n7, 124, 132n4, 153; and American music, 10, 14, 22, 107; and Blackness, 10, 37–38, 43–53; and crossover category, 7, 10, 22, 67, 92–97, 101, 107–12; and "Hasta Que Te Conocí," 65, 87; and "I Need to Know," 92–97, 107–15, 119; and Latinidad, 21, 62, 71; and "Preciosa," 35, 42–54, 59–60; and Puerto Rican identity, 10, 22, 34, 43–54; and sound, 14; and "Vivir Mi Vida," 23, 137, 140–43, 146–49, 151–52. *See also* racialization
racial capitalism, 12, 29
racial democracy, 50–51
racial exile, 42, 44
racial profiling, 95, 143
racialization, 50–51, 152; and Arabness, 137, 146–49; and Blackness, 7n6, 37–38, 47n25, 51; and crossover category, 7, 22, 92–97; and Mexican identity, 62; and Puerto Rican identity, 7, 22, 34, 47n25, 51–52, 60, 62, 92–97, 137
racism, 14–15, 28, 37–38, 38n18, 44, 47–48, 51, 92, 95; by Trump, 93n1; white supremacy, 50–51, 94. *See also* Islamophobia; Jim Crow; Latinophobia; nativism; white supremacy
Radio City Music Hall, 64
Rafael Cortijo y su Combo, 49
Rage Against the Machine, 15
raï music, 3, 14, 137, 140–41
rancheras, 62, 64, 71–73; bolero, 65, 74, 78, 80, 82, 86
R&B, 3, 13, 22, 50, 109–10, 112–14
rap, 93n1, 98, 117, 128. *See also* hip-hop
rascuache, 115
Recording Industry Association of America, 109
RedOne, 137
reflective solidarity, 150
reggaetón, 2, 4, 14, 98, 110, 125, 128, 131, 134, 138
relational labor, 16
Republican Party (US), 91–92
requinto guitars, 101
Residente: "Afilando Los Cuchillos," 121; "This Is Not America," 93n1
resonance, 16–17, 50, 63, 79, 81, 85; cultural, 3, 9; definition, 18
restored behaviors, 142

Revista de Artistas Mexicanos, 40
Rex, Fernando, 88
Reyes, Lucha, 72
Ricanness, 34, 133
Ríos, Soleida, 122
Rivera, Christopher, 23, 143
Rivera, Ismael, 29, 49, 123
Rivera Santana, Carlos, 121
Rivera-Rideau, Petra, 108n10
Roach, Joseph, 142
Robb, Paul, 116
Roberts, John Storm, 111n13, 112–13
Robinson, Dylan, 1n1, 43, 110, 153
Rocher, Sofia, 4n3
rock en español, 80, 84. *See also* Chicano rock; Latino rock
rock music, 3, 10, 22, 80, 84–85, 104, 107, 110–11, 113, 140; Chicano, 66–67, 104–5, 105n7; cocolo/rockero divide, 105n7, 111n13; Latino, 67, 104–5, 105n7, 112, 114. *See also* rock en español
Rodríguez, Alex, 58
Rodríguez, Arsenio, 50n27
Rolling Stones, 114
Rooney, Cory, 51, 102
Rosalía, 98
Rosselló, Ricardo, 36, 120n1, 123, 134; protests of, 134
Rottenberg, Catherine, 94
Rudolph, Jennifer, 95
Ruiz, Sandra, 34, 55–56
Ruiz Vega, Omar, 27, 36n13

Sa-Fire, 117
Sagna, Jules, 127
Sahm, Doug, 112
Sala Museo Rafael Hernández, 40
Salazar, Max, 36
Saldívar, José David, 93n1, 102
Salón 21, 66
salsa, 155; and "Aguanile," 23, 122–34; and "Hasta Que Te Conocí," 65–66, 78–82, 85, 90; in Héctor Lavoe's repertoire, 7, 28, 34, 37, 122–26; and "I Need to Know," 22, 106–10, 114; "King of Salsa," 19, 99; in Marc Anthony's repertoire, 2–7, 12–14, 17, 22–23, 42, 65–66, 99–106, 116–17; Peruvian, 21; and "Preciosa," 28–30, 37, 48–53, 56–57; relation to rock, 111n13, 112–13, 114n16; salsa consciente, 15; salsa dura, 7, 56, 85, 128, 136, 142–43; salsa erótica, 136; salsa romántica, 3, 13, 23, 117, 136–52; and "Vivir Mi Vida," 23, 136–52; in Willie Colón's repertoire, 7, 22, 28, 34, 85–88
Sanabria, Bobby, 64
Sánchez, Luis Rafael, 73, 150n3
Sánchez-González, Lisa, 33
Santa Rosa, Gilberto, 41, 43
Santana, Carlos, 10, 104, 113–14; "Oye Como Va," 66–67, 105
Santería, 125, 127–28, 132
Santiago, Al, 123
Santiago, Eddie, 4n3, 117
Santos, Romeo, 4n3
Santos Febres, Mayra, 79
Saresma, Tuija, 121–22
Saturday Night Live, 98, 109
Scott, Joan Wallach, 148–49
Section 936, 31
Selena, 107, 118
Senegal, 127
sentimiento, 62–63, 71–72, 76, 81
serenatas, 138
sexual violence, 61–62
sexuality, 33, 62, 127, 140, 147–49; and "Amor No Tiene Sexo," 89; and "Hasta Que Te Conocí," 13, 21, 63, 73, 81–82, 90; Marc Anthony's sex appeal, 4, 19, 58; racially gendered, 127–28. *See also* eroticism
Shakira, 98
Shank, Barry, 118
Sheila E., 127–29
Sierra Guzmán, Victoria, 10, 146, 146 fig. 5.3
Sierra Pérez, Ramón, 146
Sierra Reverón, Ramón, 146, 146 fig. 5.3
singer as listener, 2, 12, 42
"singing while Latino," 95
slavery, 7n6, 17, 92, 128
Slick, Grace, 10

Small, Christopher, 11, 26n2, 28, 51
"So in Love," 116
social death, 75
Somos Una Voz, 58
Somoza dictatorship, 86
son music, 51–52
"Soñando con Puerto Rico," 25
sonic labor, 8, 24, 151
sonic migrations, 20
sonic palimpsests, 24, 140–43
sonic rearticulations, 79
sonic translocations, 79, 81
Sony Music, 5, 99
Sosseh, Laba: *Salsa Africana, Vol. 1*, 127
sound territory, 43
sounds of belonging, 14
South-South cosmopolitanism, 145
Southwest (US), 63, 112, 116
Spain, 46, 48, 53, 99, 139; Granada, 146, 146 fig. 5.3; Madrid, 145; Spanish colonialism, 103
Spanglish language, 33, 92, 96, 98, 102, 104–6, 113
Spanish heritage, 11, 44, 145
Spanish language, 19, 30, 34, 61–62, 70, 92, 109, 140, 149; criminalization of, 143; and crossover category, 95–106; love ballads in, 7, 13, 66, 108; and Puerto Rican identity, 30; salsa in, 65, 104–5, 108, 117
sponsored identities, 41
Spotify, 4
"Star Spangled Banner," 94
Stevie B, 115
Stoever, Jennifer Lynn, 1n1, 14, 153
suffering, 8, 10, 13, 21, 23, 60–90, 124, 132n4, 154
Supremes, 68
syncopation, 46, 51–52, 56–57, 83, 99, 112–15

Taínos, 11, 46, 48
Talavera, Enrique "Quique," 68
Taylor, Chuck, 63n2, 108
Teague, Anna Monroe, 56
Teatro Puerto Rico, 64

Telemundo, 58
Temptations, 68
terrorism: linguistic, 75; racially gendered, 23, 144, 149, 151
Texas Tornados, 112
thinking voice, 18
Thomas, Piri, 50
3.0 (2013), 4n3, 95, 137–39, 143–44, 144 fig. 5.2, 150–52
Tierra, 113
Típica 73, 111n13
TKA, 117
Todo a Su Tiempo (1995), 101
Tom Petty and the Heartbreakers, 110
Toña la Negra, 66
Torres, Judy, 117
"Tragedia," 101
transculturation, 40, 62, 67, 105, 110, 145
translanguaging, 97–106, 113
transnationalism, 8, 14, 22, 29n6, 40, 49, 52, 64, 66n6, 82, 129, 134
Trinidadian music, 17
Trío Borinquen, 38
Tripoli, Andy "Panda," 116–17
Trivino Alarcón, Jesús, 139
Tropical Tribute to the Beatles (1996), 114n16
trova, 36
Trump, Donald, 22n11, 59, 75, 87, 92, 93n1
Tuck, Eve, 17n10
Turino, Thomas, 8, 57

Una Noche concert (2021), 103, 111
Universidad Interamericana Metropolitan Campus, 40
Univision, 58, 70
untouched masculinity, 21, 77–79
US Congress, 32
US Navy, 36

Valdés-Rodríguez, Alisa, 106
Valens, Ritchie, 104; "La Bamba," 114
Valentín-Escobar, Wilson, 57n30, 100n3, 116n19, 132n4, 142

vallenato, 101, 107
Vargas, Chavela, 72
Vargas, Deborah, 118
Vázquez, Alexandra, 19, 55, 74, 115, 143, 153
Vega, César, 82
Vega, Little Louie, 116–17
veil, politics of, 23–24, 138, 143–49, 144 fig. 5.2
Velázquez, Nydia, 32
Ventura, Johnny, 81
"Verde Luz," 25
Video Raíces, 137
Vieques, 32, 36
Viña del Mar concert (2002), 21, 74n10, 75, 78
"Vivir Mi Vida," 5–7, 10–11, 14, 19, 23–24, 102, 136–52
Vivir Mi Vida tour (2014), 128
"Volver a Comenzar," 142

Walters, Barry, 99, 109n11
Washburne, Chris, 136, 149
water, 23, 122, 128, 134
Wei, Li, 103
Weil, Simone, 72
West Coast (US), 104–5, 112, 119
West Side Story, 64
Western gaze, 148–49
When the Night Is Over (1991), 101, 107, 116

white supremacy, 50–51, 94
whiteness, 35n10, 43, 62, 70, 126, 128, 145; and "American music," 10; and brownness, 7n6; and crossover category, 93–97, 101, 107, 108–12; and mestizaje, 44, 138; and Puerto Rican identity, 22, 44–51, 53, 95–96; and rock music, 111–12
Willistein, Paul, 99
Willman, Chris, 117
Wilson, Woodrow, 27n4
Wood, Mikael, 98
World War I, 27, 38
World War II, 26

"¿Y Cómo Es Él?," 6
"Y Hubo Alguien," 6
Y No Había Luz: *Circo de la Ausencia*, 121
Yang, K. Wayne, 17n10
Yemayá, 126, 134
Yoruba people, 122, 126, 132
"You Said You Love Me," 116
"You Sang to Me," 6, 102, 108
Young Lords, 50, 126
YouTube, 9, 27, 59, 74n10, 80–81, 103, 114, 116, 126
Yulín Cruz, Carmen, 134

Zaire, 127–28
Zavala, Iris, 150n3

GLOBAL LATIN/O AMERICAS
FREDERICK LUIS ALDAMA AND LOURDES TORRES, SERIES EDITORS

This series focuses on the Latino experience in its totality as set within a global dimension. The series showcases the variety and vitality of the presence and significant influence of Latinos in the shaping of the culture, history, politics and policies, and language of the Americas—and beyond. It welcomes scholarship regarding the arts, literature, philosophy, popular culture, history, politics, law, history, and language studies, among others.

Replaying Marc Anthony: Sonic, Political, and Cultural Resonances
FRANCES R. APARICIO

Zones of Encuentro: Language and Identities in Northern New Mexico
LILLIAN GORMAN

Sanctuary: Exclusion, Violence, and Indigenous Migrants in the East Bay
CRUZ MEDINA

Everyday Dirty Work: Invisibility, Communication, and Immigrant Labor
WILFREDO ALVAREZ

Building Confianza: Empowering Latinos/as Through Transcultural Health Care Communication
DALIA MAGAÑA

Fictions of Migration: Narratives of Displacement in Peru and Bolivia
LORENA CUYA GAVILANO

Baseball as Mediated Latinidad: Race, Masculinity, Nationalism, and Performances of Identity
JENNIFER DOMINO RUDOLPH

False Documents: Inter-American Cultural History, Literature, and the Lost Decade (1975–1992)
FRANS WEISER

Public Negotiations: Gender and Journalism in Contemporary US Latina/o Literature
ARIANA E. VIGIL

Democracy on the Wall: Street Art of the Post-Dictatorship Era in Chile
GUISELA LATORRE

Gothic Geoculture: Nineteenth-Century Representations of Cuba in the Transamerican Imaginary
IVONNE M. GARCÍA

Affective Intellectuals and the Space of Catastrophe in the Americas
JUDITH SIERRA-RIVERA

Spanish Perspectives on Chicano Literature: Literary and Cultural Essays
EDITED BY JESÚS ROSALES AND VANESSA FONSECA

Sponsored Migration: The State and Puerto Rican Postwar Migration to the United States
EDGARDO MELÉNDEZ

La Verdad: An International Dialogue on Hip Hop Latinidades
EDITED BY MELISSA CASTILLO-GARSOW AND JASON NICHOLS

www.ingramcontent.com/pod-product-compliance
Lightning Source LLC
Chambersburg PA
CBHW020738230426
43665CB00009B/481